ADIRONDACK CUISINE

Also by the authors:

The Adirondack Cookbook
Armand C. VanderStigchel & Robert E. Birkel, Jr.

Chicken Wings Across America
Armand C. VanderStigchel

Also from Berkshire House Publishers:

The Adirondack Book: A Complete Guide
(Great Destinations™ Series)
Elizabeth Folwell

New England Cooking: Seasons & Celebrations
Claire Hopley

The New Red Lion Inn Cookbook
Suzi Forbes Chase

Soups & Stews for Fall and Winter Days
Liza Fosburgh

Soups & Salads for Spring and Summer Days
Liza Fosburgh

The Kripalu Cookbook: Gourmet Vegetarian Recipes
Atma Jo Ann Levitt

Apple Orchard Cookbook
Janet Christensen & Betty Bergman Levin

ADIRONDACK CUISINE

ARMAND C. VANDERSTIGCHEL
and
ROBERT E. BIRKEL, JR.

BERKSHIRE HOUSE PUBLISHERS
Lee, Massachusetts

Adirondack Cuisine
Copyright © 2002 by Berkshire House Publishers
Black-and-white photographs by credited sources.

Color photography by A. Blake Gardner, except as noted.

Edited by Constance Lee Oxley
Cover, book design, and typesetting by Jane McWhorter, Blue Sky Productions
Index by Elizabeth T. Parson

Library of Congress Cataloging-in-Publication Data

VanderStigchel, Armand C.
Adirondack cuisine / Armand C. VanderStigchel and Robert E. Birkel, Jr.
    p. cm
Includes index.
ISBN 1-58157-056-2
    1. Cookery—New York (State)—Adirondack Mountain Region. I. Birkel, Robert E.
II. Title.

TX715.V273 2002

2001043779

ISBN 1-58157-056-2

Berkshire House books are available at substantial discounts for bulk purchases by corporations and other organizations' promotions and premiums. Special personalized editions can also be produced in large quantities. For more information, contact:

Berkshire House Publishers
480 Pleasant Street, Suite 5
Lee, Massachusetts 01238
800-321-8526
E-mail: info@berkshirehouse.com
Web: www.berkshirehouse.com

Manufactured in Singapore

10 9 8 7 6 5 4 3 2 1

In memory of Robert Birkel, Sr.
A friend and father to us all.
The gatekeeper of Saratoga Springs and the Adirondacks.

AUTHOR'S NOTE

In 1995, while enjoying my first visit to Saratoga Springs, New York, I came across a charming bookstore on Main Street. In the shop window, my attention was drawn to an array of books, calendars, and posters, featuring beautiful color images of the Adirondack mountains and lakes. I was surprised that a region so beautiful was only thirty minutes away from Saratoga by automobile. I purchased maps and guidebooks and spent my final vacation days exploring the Adirondack region instead of betting on horses at the track.

My buddy Robert Birkel, whose father worked for the Saratoga Racetrack, caught the Adirondack fever and was game for my suggestion to compile a book about food in this region. As a professional chef, I was looking for ideas to publish a cookbook, but wanted to avoid clichés. Inspiration came quickly, once I became acquainted with the region's friendly folk, food purveyors, and inns. A small idea evolved into a charming publication *The Adirondack Cookbook,* featuring recipes from restaurants, inns, and home cooks in the Adirondacks. Between enormous press support and regional flair, it became an Adirondack bestseller for years to come.

Encouraged by this success, it was time to take this cooking style to a national level with the assistance of professionals believing in the cause. After years of traveling, research, and recipe experimentation with ingredients native to the region, we proudly present you with this new title, *Adirondack Cuisine.* Through our strong devotion and with the help of others, we hope to have contributed a piece of culinary history in honor of American regional cuisine.

ACKNOWLEDGMENTS

After we published our first paperback book of Adirondack recipes in 1996 and sold it successfully throughout the Adirondacks, I envisioned a day when a beautiful, color-illustrated book on Adirondack-style cooking would come into being, showcasing the wonderful cuisine and scenic beauty of the Adirondacks for folks throughout America. We turned to Berkshire House Publishers of Lee, Massachusetts, to help us in this important culinary endeavor — the first nationally distributed book on Adirondack-style cuisine. Since Berkshire House produces many titles about travel and cooking, we were delighted to have this adventurous, gutsy group of wonderful people working with us on this project

I hereby salute the entire Berkshire House staff for their vision and dedication to this book. Thank you, Publisher Jean Rousseau for keeping us on an even keel as captain; Editorial Director Philip Rich for your patience, inspiring E-mail, and guidance; Marketing Director Carol Bosco Baumann for bringing the project to Berkshire House, your kindness is appreciated; Office Managers Mary Osak and Leslie Ceanga for cheerfully greeting us after long road

trips across the region; Editor Constance Lee Oxley for editing and loving the recipes; and Designer Jane McWhorter for justified criticism and unrelenting perfection. Thumbs up to A. Blake Gardener for beautiful indoor food photography at the Friend's Lake Inn. Breakfast will never be the same at the inn!

A great thank you to all restaurants, chefs, food purveyors, bed-and-breakfasts, inns, lodges, hotels, and Adirondack friends for submitting information, recipes, and documents for this book. A very special thanks and gratitude to Greg and Sharon Taylor of the Friend's Lake Inn in Chestertown, New York, for accommodating the indoor photo shoot for two days and for providing us with Adirondack-style rooms for inspiration. Compliments to the Friend's Lake Inn kitchen crew, a group of down-to-earth, hard-working culinarians: Executive Chef Timothy Warnock, Sous Chef Kirk Gibson, and Assistant Intern Emily Hummel. Former Chef Tim Stephenson is wished good health on your road to recovery.

Applause for serve and cookware company Europaeus, Peekskill, New York, for providing plates for our photo shoot — thank you, Mr. Schwartz!

A high five to John and Lorrie Hosley of Hoss's Country Corner in Long Lake, New York, for hosting their annual Adirondack author signing on the second Tuesday of August for the promotion of Adirondack books. Behind the scenes, we must acknowledge Rob Igoe and the crew of North Country Books of Utica, New York, for distributing Adirondack titles throughout the region, even to the most remote areas.

On Long Island, we must thank my friends and colleagues at the Miller Place Inn and a special olive branch to Office Manager Cynthia Bila for keeping the manuscript on track and tailored to the publisher's specifications — great job! Further thanks to LuAnne Fitzgerald, Elly and Artie Grodsky, Buddy Marino (the Godfather), Mickey (where's my Saranac beer?), and Chefs Mike Alleva (Executive Sous), Rich Jacobs (herb man), and Marty Campbell (the factor). Also thanks to Maître d' Lisa and Brandon for the great gossip! To Mark, Jerry, and Bill at Corny Acres Farm for great produce finds for my recipes. A salute to Mike Morrisson and the crew of the "Long Island Gourmet TV Show" and Cablevision; Producer Alex Cordero (I am hungry so I am grumpy); Camera 1 Mike "the Rock" Rockfeld; "Make-up Mike" Rappold (where's the buffet?); and Nancy Nugent (you guys don't need me here . . .). Thank you to Cablevision's Peggy, Amy, and Jason for patience and support. Furthermore, to WGBB 1240 AM "The Radio Gourmet," a thank you to Joey Alcarese for inspiration and for believing and to the Fusco's and Paul "the Engineer." Thanks to Fran of *Dish D' Jour* magazine and all involved with the James Beard Foundation, a great cause to award culinary scholarships to the less fortunate. And last but not least, thanks to my co-author, business partner, and friend Robert Birkel, Jr., aka the "Sauerbraten King," for keeping me organized, road ready, and writing our first book.

Robert would like to thank Henrietta, Robinetta, Brian, Jean, and Jackie Birkel for inspiration. A special thanks to Blanca for joining him on his sauerbraten trips. Thanks to US Laboratories in Farmingdale, New York. And a special greeting to June Clow, Auntie Bertie, and Grandma Harris.

A salute to all cooks!

CONTENTS

CONTENTS

INTRODUCTION

Covering six million acres of beautiful scenery, featuring high mountain ranges, towering pines, tranquil lakes, and luscious valleys, the Adirondack State Park is a true treasure of the Northeast. As the largest State Park in the nation, it has a year-round population of 130,000 residents and attracts millions of visitors each year from all over the world, who come in search of scenic beauty, tranquility, hiking, canoeing, fishing, and many other recreational opportunities.

In the late 1800s and early 1900s, artists, adventurers, and wealthy vacationers arrived by train. They usually stayed for weeks at a time and left their mark in the architecture, furniture, painting, and great camps of the area. At the same time, the region was more industrialized than today, and logging camps, mining towns, and tanneries drew a diversity of immigrants. With the arrival of the automobile, the park began to attract more casual tourists, and the creation of the Adirondack Forest Preserve put a halt to most of the logging and reinstated the forest as wild forestlands on state property. The construction of the "Northway" (Interstate 87) in 1967 brought tourism to an all-time high, and many people found reason to start a tourist-related business or to build a second vacation home in the newly discovered "vacation wonderland." From that point on, the melting pot of cultures and the hard work of locals and regional entrepreneurs made the park grow into what it is today — a great place to visit, to enjoy, or to live.

As for the cooking, the regional cuisine did not take off until the early 1990s, when culinary graduates began working for discerning propri-etors who encouraged their chefs to create a regional style, using local ingredients. In this new millennium — as you will see in this book — Adirondack-style cooking has developed fully, following years of experimentation by the chefs and cooks throughout the North Country. In the face of increased demand for their products, artisan food purveyors have stepped up their production of cheese, fruits, vegetables, maple syrup, and game. Regional cuisine not only creates new dishes, it also establishes a recognizable culinary tradition.

While Adirondack-style cuisine is on the verge of obtaining national recognition, other Adirondack-related interests, culture, and goods have gained worldwide popularity. How can we forget the novel and motion picture *The Last of the Mohicans,* which actually took place in Lake George and Glens Falls (Cooper's Cave). In 1932 and 1980, the picturesque town of Lake Placid was the home of the Winter Olympic Games and is still hosting many sport-related national events. Adirondack architecture, a blend of the old classic camps, with a touch of oriental and rustic log cabin, is replicated in many states for vacation homes. Adirondack-style rustic furniture, including the famous Adirondack chair, has achieved nationwide appreciation from designers and consumers.

The time has come to bring the cooking style of the Adirondacks to the world of food lovers. Close your eyes and think of wild berries, mushrooms, orchard fruits, wild honey, trout, salmon, fowl, and game . . . yes, you are on the right train — All Aboard! Adirondack cuisine next stop!

ADIRONDACK CUISINE

DEFINING
ADIRONDACK CUISINE

The Adirondack region has undergone a culinary renaissance. Many visitors from dining capitals like New York City are saying that you can enjoy a great variety of well-prepared foods here, be they gourmet or simple down-home cooking. The food of the Adirondacks, with its abundance of high-quality produce and fruits, pure maple syrup, wild honey, fresh morel mushrooms, succulent native berries, various fish, game, and fowl, great wine from the neighboring Finger Lakes Region, and the exciting, authentic cooking of its restaurant chefs and home cooks alike make the Adirondacks a must for everyone serious about regional food and drink.

As good as the above sounds, it was not always this good. Throughout most of the 1900s, tasteless grub was served at pubs, stagecoach stops, and inns, with the exception of the grand hotels, where exclusive French cuisine was served to the rich and famous. As tourism made headway in the 1960s, restaurants and snack bars catered to the taste of the masses — either typical American hamburger fare or red sauce Italian. It was not until the late 1980s that America stopped being a French-cuisine copy-cat and focused on what our own farmers and purveyors regionally had to offer. The birth of American regional cuisine came slowly, fueled by the success of Paul Pruhomme's first successful cookbook on Cajun cooking, *Goodbye Coq Au Vin . . . Hello Jambalaya!*

Due to the increasing number of culinary graduates in the Northeast, where celebrated instructors emphasized the importance of regional cooking and the use of local products, many tired restaurants and inns received an infusion of gastronomic creativity when they introduced the new talent at the stoves. Along with classic standbys to hold the steady patrons, beautiful new dishes were created with regional flair, which excited restaurant critics and discerning patrons alike. Pioneers like the Friend's Lake Inn in Chestertown, the Wawbeek Resort in Tupper Lake, the Mirror Lake Inn in Lake Placid, and The Point were groundbreakers who combined these dishes with perfect dining-room settings and extensive wine lists. With forestlands offering an abundance of wild mushrooms, berries, maple syrup, fowl, and game, and with little farms along the shores of Lake Champlain producing fresh vegetables, orchard fruit, and honey, the ingredients and tools for a new regional cuisine were there for the picking!

So how would one define the character of this cooking style? For that we must consider the ingredients used by the Native Americans and pioneers centuries ago. Game and fish were protein, honey and maple syrup were sweeteners, mushrooms and wild berries were pleasant snacks. Today, we combine these basics with everyday available ingredients, like chicken, pork, or beef. Adding to this mix the strong cooking influences from New England and the ethnic traditions of people living in the park, we conclude that Adirondack cooking is a blend of down-home rustic, traditional, and gourmet — with an emphasis on hearty flavors.

Following the eating preferences of each season, both home cooks and chefs draw upon the season's bounty, especially in remote areas. In the fall, the beautiful fruits and vegetables from the farms are prepared fresh or canned and preserved for the winter to come. When the first snow falls, hearty soups and chili are prepared with easy-to-store dried beans and winter root vegetables. As spring arrives, the first fresh vegetables, berries, mushrooms, and seafood from the eastern seaboard are prepared. Freshly tapped maple syrup from winter's end and early spring is generously poured on breakfast favorites at Sunday brunch. After Memorial Day, fresh strawberries, blueberries, blackberries, and plums are skillfully used in pies and baked goods sold at general stores and farm stands. Local chefs tend to their herb gardens and negotiate for new products from the local artisan farmers. Throughout the summer, fresh-caught trout sizzles in a heavy skillet over a campfire, and fresh corn accompanies every picnic and summer celebration. Every season is a good food season in the Adirondacks!

CHAPTER 1

ADIRONDACK FALL

Many folks regard fall as the year's matinee-idol season. Distant are the hot days of summer — in their place are the cool, sunny days of autumn. The reds, yellows, and golds of the leaves adorn the hills as if laid down by an artist's brush, creating the unique spectacle that draws thousands of visitors every year.

Along winding roads throughout the Adirondack Park and by the shores of Lake Champlain, harvest fruits and vegetables sparkle on farm stands — a celebration of the season and a harbinger of the holidays to come. Cider mills and orchards cater to a steady stream of shoppers looking for homegrown produce for their kitchen tables — or perhaps just an apple to eat along the way. String-tied boxes of fresh fruit pies are carefully loaded into trunks of cars and SUVs. Displays of ghoulish pumpkins and scarecrows, seemingly impervious to the weather, greet us at every turn from wooden porches, manicured yards, and vegetable gardens, a constant reminder of Halloween.

Driving along America's most scenic highway, Interstate 87 (the Northway), we can see multicolored hot-air balloons on the horizon, gracefully rising from fields near Glen Falls. Outdoor craft shows, art exhibits, garage sales (the world's largest is in Warrensburg), apple festivals, and boisterous Oktoberfests add to the excitement of this most beautiful time of the year — Fall in the Adirondacks!

In this chapter, and those to follow, we present recipes that show a strong emphasis on the use of local ingredients. The various fruits from orchards near the Vermont border, the vegetables grown in the fertile surrounding valleys, the maple syrup, wild honey, forest mushrooms, and fish and game from the central and western portion of the Adirondack Park have been combined with some store-bought ingredients to make recipes that reflect the season and the area's regional food.

Maple BBQ Duck Confit with Wild Rice-Currant Pancakes

Start your meal with duck confit, a specialty originating from Gascony in France. It is prepared by an ancient method of processing meat (mostly duck, goose, and pork). The meat is salted and slowly cooked in its own fat. When cooked, it is placed in a stoneware crock and covered with its cooking fat. The fat acts as a seal and preservative. Refrigerated, it can last a long time. In this recipe, the process is simplified; a salted fresh duck is slowly roasted, while continuously being basted with its own fat. After cooking, the meat is removed from the bone, shredded, and marinated in a savory BBQ sauce. The savory minipancakes are not only an hors d'oeuvre or appetizer, but also are great as a side dish for a hearty meal with venison, pork, and other game. Be sure to buy real wild rice, not imitations.

One 5-pound duck, gizzards removed
Kosher salt as needed
Black pepper as needed
Vegetable oil as needed
1 recipe Confit (see below)

1 recipe Wild Rice-Currant Pancakes (see below)
Sour cream as needed
¹/₂ cup seeded finely diced cucumber for garnish
Snipped fresh chives for garnish

1. Preheat the oven to 350° F. Wash the duck inside and outside and pat dry. Season heavily with the kosher salt and black pepper (80:20 ratio).

2. Place the duck in a heavy, deep ovenproof pot or Dutch oven. Place in the oven and roast for 3 hours, continuously basting the duck with its own melted fat. Remove from the oven and let cool.

3. Once cooled, remove the meat and skin from the carcass. Keep the skin separate. In a medium skillet, heat ¹/₂" vegetable oil over high heat. Add the skin and fry until crispy.

4. In a large food processor or with a knife, shred or finely chop the duck meat and skin together. Set aside.

5. Prepare the Confit.

6. Prepare the Wild Rice-Currant Pancakes.

7. On a large serving platter, place the pancakes. Place 1 teaspoon of the confit atop each pancake. Place a dot of the sour cream atop the confit. Garnish with the cucumbers and chives. Serve immediately as an hors d'oeuvre or appetizer. Great for a party!

CONFIT

Shredded duck meat from 1 duck (see step 4. above)
1 ¹/₂ cups smoky barbecue sauce (preferably Bulls-Eye)
2 tablespoons Grade A Adirondack maple syrup
1 tablespoon white vinegar

¹/₄ cup brewed hot coffee
¹/₂ tablespoon onion powder
¹/₂ tablespoon garlic powder
2 teaspoons A-1 sauce
¹/₄ teaspoon ground cloves
¹/₂ cup seeded finely diced cucumber

1. Preheat the oven to 350º F. In a medium mixing bowl, combine the reserved shredded duck meat, barbecue sauce, syrup, vinegar, coffee, onion powder, garlic powder, A-1 sauce, cloves, and cucumbers and mix well.

2. Place the mixture in a small baking pan and cover with aluminum foil. Warm the mixture in the oven for 5 minutes. Keep warm.

WILD RICE-CURRANT PANCAKES

2 cups wild rice*
4 cups chicken stock
2 tablespoons dried black currants
Vegetable oil as needed
1 small red onion, finely minced
1 shallot, finely minced
1 celery stalk, finely minced
2 ounces shiitake mushrooms, thinly sliced
  with stems removed
Pinch salt and black pepper

2 tablespoons white vinegar
2 tablespoons granulated sugar
1 teaspoon finely chopped fresh rosemary
2 tablespoons lingonberry preserves
²/₃ cup seasoned bread crumbs
1 ¹/₂ cups all-purpose flour
²/₃ cup finely chopped scallions
2 tablespoons onion powder
³/₄ teaspoon salt
4 eggs, beaten

1. In a medium saucepan, combine the rice, stock, and currants. Bring to a simmering boil and simmer for 35 minutes, or until the rice is soft but still al dente. Drain and set aside.

2. In a medium skillet, heat ¹/₄" vegetable oil over high heat. Add the onion, shallot, celery, and mushrooms and sauté until the onion is transparent. Add the pinch salt and black pepper, vinegar, sugar, and rosemary and sauté for 2 minutes. Remove from the heat.

3. Transfer the mushroom mixture to a large mixing bowl. Add the reserved rice and mix well. Fold in the preserves, bread crumbs, flour, scallions, onion powder, ³/₄ teaspoon salt, and eggs and mix well. The mixture should be thick and pliable enough to make small walnut-sized balls.

4. In a medium skillet, heat 1" vegetable oil over high heat. Place 6 rice balls in the oil. Press down and flatten them with a fork to make 2" diameter pancakes. Brown on both sides until firm. Keep warm. Repeat the procedure with the remaining rice mixture. Makes about 50 pancakes (2" size).

* See Food Sources in the Appendix.

Scallion & Maple Mustard-Crusted Baby Lamb Chops with Pine Green Pesto

A delicious appetizer, great for special gatherings, and a sure hit served as a hot hors d'oeuvre. The beautiful green of the scallion crust and pesto, combined with the intense earthy flavors of the sage sauce infusion, make it a special Adirondack dish.

1 recipe Maple Mustard (see below)
1 rack baby lamb chops, cleaned, trimmed, and defatted
1 bunch scallions, finely diced
3 tablespoons seasoned bread crumbs
3 tablespoons melted unsalted butter
1 recipe Pine Green Pesto (see next page)

1. Prepare the Maple Mustard. With a brush, generously coat the top surface of the lamb rack with the maple mustard, but set aside 2 teaspoons.

2. Preheat the oven to 375º F. In a small mixing bowl, combine the scallions, bread crumbs, and 2 tablespoons of the melted butter and mix until compact.

3. Carefully press the bread crumb mixture onto the mustard- coated surface of the lamb rack. Place the lamb rack in a small greased baking dish. Carefully dab the crust with the remaining melted butter using a soft pastry brush.

4. Place the lamb rack in the oven and roast for about 15 minutes, or until the crust is golden brown. Set aside to settle juices.

5. Prepare the Pine Green Pesto.

6. Carefully slice the lamb rack into lamb chop sections without disturbing the crust. Place and arrange on a serving platter. Dab the chops with the pesto or serve in a dipping bowl. Serves 8.

MAPLE MUSTARD
3 tablespoons deli or Dusseldorf mustard
2 tablespoons Grade A Adirondack maple syrup
¼ teaspoon prepared grated horseradish
½ teaspoon Jack Daniel's whiskey
1 teaspoon warm honey

In a small mixing bowl, whisk all of the above ingredients until smooth.

PINE GREEN PESTO

2 tablespoons golden raisins, soaked in hot water
1 teaspoon toasted pine nuts
1 teaspoon mint jelly
1 tablespoon chopped fresh parsley
8 fresh sage leaves
2 teaspoons reserved Maple Mustard (see previous page)
¹/₂ cup virgin olive oil

1. In a blender or food processor, place all of the ingredients, except the oil, and pulse until the ingredients are fine.

2. Slowly add the oil until a green, smooth emulsion appears. Scrape the side and bottom of the blender and blend again. Use the pesto to drizzle or dip the lamb chops.

To toast pine nuts: *Preheat the oven to 300° F. In a baking pan, place the pine nuts in a single layer and toast in the oven for 6–7 minutes or until golden brown, stirring frequently. Let the pine nuts cool completely*

Westport Autumn Pumpkin Butter

Located on the northeastern end of the Adirondack State Park is Westport, a charming town amid the farming section of the North Country, which provides a "produce lifeline" to the inhabitants of the dense woodlands in the north-central section of the Park. Sugar pumpkins are purchased in the fall and processed into pumpkin butter, which is a great alternative to dairy butter – delicious on a slab of sourdough or corn bread and perfect for the winter months to come. Many of the farm stands sell this butter.

One 3-pound sugar pumpkin
1 cup apple cider
1 cup firmly packed light brown sugar
$^1/_2$ teaspoon ground allspice
$^1/_8$ teaspoon ground ginger
$^1/_8$ teaspoon vanilla extract
$^1/_2$ teaspoon spiced rum

1. Preheat the oven to 400º F. Cut the pumpkin in half and scoop out the seeds and strings. Cut each half into quarters.

2. Place the pumpkin quarters skin-side down in a baking dish. Add $^1/_2$ cup of the cider. Cover with aluminum foil and bake for 50 minutes, or until the pumpkin is tender.

3. Remove from the oven and reduce the temperature to 250º. Scrape the pumpkin flesh from the skin. Transfer the pumpkin to a food processor and puree.

4. Measure 3 cups of the puree into a heavy medium saucepan. Add the remaining cider, brown sugar, allspice, ginger, vanilla extract, and rum. Bring the mixture to a slow simmer, stirring constantly, until the sugar is dissolved.

5. Transfer the mixture to a nonstick 9" x 13" baking dish, spreading it out evenly. Place in the oven and bake for 1 hour.

6. Remove from the oven, stir well, and spoon while hot into a hot sterilized Mason jar. Fill to $^1/_4$" from the top. Wipe the rim clean with a towel dipped in hot water. Place the lid on the jar and seal tightly. Repeat with the remaining pumpkin butter. Cool and refrigerate. Shelf life is 2–3 months. Makes 2 cups.

Cremini Mushroom & Chicken Soup

Mushrooms are an often-used ingredient in Adirondack cooking, especially wild ones, treasured by mushroom foragers. For those in the big city, looking to replicate a piece of the Adirondacks, there are store-available substitutes, such as shiitake, oyster, and cremini mushrooms that have the same woodsy aroma found in the wild species. Cremini mushrooms are shaped like the popular white mushrooms, but they have a dark reddish appearance, a meatier texture, and a lightly woodsy fragrance. This recipe is for a delicious creamy soup, guaranteed to have a broad appeal.

7–8 ounces boneless chicken breasts
Olive oil as needed
1 medium onion, diced ¼"
2 celery stalks, diced ¼"
8 ounces cremini mushrooms, cleaned
½ teaspoon finely chopped fresh rosemary
1 teaspoon finely chopped fresh sage
½ teaspoon finely chopped fresh thyme
½ cup chardonnay wine
1 tablespoon granulated sugar

2 tablespoons white vinegar
2 quarts chicken stock or bouillon
4 ounces uncooked broad egg noodles
2 teaspoons onion powder
1 teaspoon garlic powder
½ teaspoon white pepper
2 cups heavy cream
Roux* as needed
2 tablespoons chopped fresh parsley
2 tablespoons chopped fresh chives

1. With a sharp knife, cut the chicken breasts into ¼" pieces. Set aside.

2. In a heavy medium saucepan, heat ¼" olive oil over high heat. Add the chicken and sauté until lightly browned. Add the onion, celery, half of the mushrooms, rosemary, sage, and thyme and sauté until the onion is transparent.

3. Add the wine, sugar, and vinegar. Bring to a simmering boil and reduce the liquid by half. Add the stock and simmer for 15 minutes to develop flavor.

4. Add the noodles, onion powder, garlic powder, and white pepper and simmer for 15 minutes, or until the noodles are just cooked. Add the cream and remaining mushrooms and simmer for 5 minutes. Add in needed roux to thicken, enough to coat the back of a soupspoon. (Do not break the noodles.)

5. If the roux is added, simmer for 3 minutes more. Remove the soup from the heat and add the parsley and chives. Serves 6–8.

* See Cooking Basics in the Appendix.

Trail Marker Pigeon Pea Autumn Chili

If you are planning an autumn hike through the majestic Adirondack Mountains, prepare this extremely nutritious chili in advance. After letting it cool, fill freezer bags and freeze them until right before your trip. By the time you are up on the trail and hungry, you can heat the bags in hot water over an open fire and get a surge of energy to continue your trek. Homebodies can top the chili with some local cheddar cheese and a spoonful of sour cream and enjoy the football play-offs.

One 16-ounce bag dried pigeon peas
Olive oil as needed
2 shallots, finely minced
2 garlic cloves, finely minced
2 pounds ground beef
1 small onion, diced 1/4"
2 celery stalks, diced 1/4"
1 red bell pepper, diced 1/2"
1 cup 1/2" diced acorn squash
1 cup 1/2" diced rutabaga
1 teaspoon finely chopped fresh rosemary
1 teaspoon finely chopped fresh thyme
1 teaspoon ground paprika
1 teaspoon ground cumin

2 teaspoons chili powder
1/2 teaspoon ground coriander
1/2 teaspoon ground red pepper
1 teaspoon celery salt
1 teaspoon dried marjoram
2 bay leaves
10 cups beef stock
Two 6-ounce cans tomato paste
1/4 cup honey
1/4 cup Grade A Adirondack maple syrup
2 tablespoons A-1 sauce
1 cup cooked corn kernels
2 cups chopped scallions
Salt as needed

1. Soak the beans overnight in 2 quarts cold water or "quick soak" by boiling the beans in 2 quarts water for 2 minutes and then setting aside for 1 hour.

2. In a heavy, deep ovenproof pot or Dutch oven, heat 1/4" olive oil over high heat. Add the shallots and garlic and lightly brown. Add the ground beef and sauté until golden brown. Drain the fat. Add the onion, celery, and bell pepper and sauté until the onion is transparent.

3. Add the squash, rutabaga, rosemary, thyme, paprika, cumin, chili powder, coriander, red pepper, celery salt, marjoram, and bay leaves. Mix and sauté for 3 minutes. Drain the soaked beans and add to the pot. Mix well.

4. Add the stock and tomato paste. Bring to a simmering boil and simmer, covered, over low heat until the beans are tender.

5. Add the honey, syrup, A-1 sauce, and corn and simmer for 10 minutes more. Add the scallions and salt if needed. If chili is too thick, add more stock as needed. Makes 6–8 large bowls.

Champlain Valley Roasted Corn & Leek Bisque

A beautiful September day calls for a road trip heading north on Route 22 through Ticonderoga, New York. It is a truly panoramic experience of rolling farmlands surrounded by high mountain peaks to the west and an occasional view of Lake Champlain to the east. Corn is a highly featured crop in this region and is delicious when roasted and used with local leeks and scallions in this unique bisque.

4 fresh ears of corn, shucked
5 tablespoons pomace olive oil
1 medium onion, finely chopped
2 large garlic cloves, finely chopped
$\frac{1}{2}$ tablespoon granulated sugar
1 whole leek stalk, well cleaned and finely chopped
1 tablespoon finely chopped fresh cilantro
1 $\frac{1}{2}$ tablespoons unsalted butter
2 tablespoons all-purpose flour
1 cup champagne
6 cups chicken stock or broth
1 tablespoon finely chopped scallions
1 teaspoon onion powder
$\frac{1}{2}$ teaspoon garlic powder
Salt and black pepper as needed

1. Preheat the oven to 450° F. With a sharp knife, scrape the corn kernels off the ears and place on a nonstick, butter-greased baking sheet. Place in the oven and roast for 15 minutes, or until the kernels are light golden brown. Remove from the oven and set aside.

2. In a large saucepan, heat the olive oil over high heat. Add the onion, garlic, and sugar and sauté until golden brown. Add half of the leeks and sauté until transparent. Mix in the cilantro and sauté for 1 minute more. Add and melt the butter. Add the flour and mix with the onion-leek mixture. Sauté and stir for 3 minutes. Add the champagne and mix well. Simmer for 3 minutes until the mixture has thickened, stirring frequently.

3. Add the stock, scallions, onion powder, garlic powder, half of the reserved roasted corn and remaining leeks and bring to a boil. Lower the heat and simmer for 5 minutes.

4. With a hand blender or food processor, puree the soup mixture. Return the pureed mixture to the saucepan. Fold in the remaining roasted corn. Add the salt and black pepper as needed.

5. Ladle the soup into a small carved pumpkin or acorn squash. A garnish could be snipped fresh chives or some panfried leek strips. Serves 4–6.

Yellow Split Pea Bisque with Smoked Apple-Chicken Sausage

Foregoing our green split peas for the winter months to come, we choose this lighter yellow split pea soup for a brisk fall evening. We're ready to savor its mellow creamy texture paired with chunks of smoky sausage and crispy fresh corn kernels from the fields of northeastern New York, along Lake Champlain.

Olive oil as needed
1 cup finely diced fatback salt pork, skin removed (about 3 ounces)
1 small onion, finely diced
2 celery stalks, finely diced
1 medium carrot, finely diced
$1/2$ tablespoon finely chopped fresh thyme
$1/2$ tablespoon finely chopped fresh sage
2 bay leaves
One 16-ounce bag dried yellow split peas
8 cups chicken stock or bouillon
3 cups water
3 cups chicken stock or bouillon
2 cups heavy cream
$1/2$ pound smoked apple-chicken sausage*, thinly sliced
1 $1/2$ cups cooked fresh corn kernels
1 tablespoon finely chopped fresh chives or scallions

1. In a large saucepan, heat $1/4$" olive oil over high heat. Add the salt pork and fry until golden brown. Add the onion, celery, carrot, thyme, sage, and bay leaves and sauté until the onion is transparent. Add the split peas and mix well.

2. Add the 8 cups stock and the water. Bring to a simmering boil and simmer for 45 minutes, or until the peas are soft and mushy.

3. With a food processor or hand blender, puree the peas until smooth. Slowly add the 3 cups stock and heavy cream and blend until smooth. The soup should have a spoon-coating, thick consistency. Set aside the soup.

4. In a medium sauté pan, heat $1/4$" olive oil over high heat. Add the sausage and sauté until golden brown. Add the corn and chives and sauté for 2 minutes.

5. Reheat the reserved soup. Add three-fourths of the corn-sausage mixture to the soup. After the soup is divided among bowls, use the remaining one-fourth of the corn-sausage mixture for garnish. Serves 6–8.

* *See Food Sources in the Appendix.*

Cranberry Lake Bean & Crawfish Salad

Deep in the heart of the Adirondacks is Cranberry Lake, a gem among nature enthusiasts and truly worth the long drive. Beans are a main staple for the locals, especially in fall and winter. The crawfish, a sweet water habitant, is a perfect accompaniment in this salad. Cranberry beans are available at most farm stands and markets in the fall, distinctive for their bright red-and-white shells.

1 ¹/₂ cups fresh cranberry beans, shelled
1 fresh sage sprig
1 fresh rosemary sprig
1 fresh thyme sprig
1 bay leaf
Salt as needed
Water as needed
3 tablespoons pomace olive oil
4 strips apple wood-smoked bacon*, coarsely chopped
2 garlic cloves, thinly sliced
1 pound cooked crawfish tails (langoustines), peeled
3 tablespoons fresh lemon juice
Black pepper as needed
1 tablespoon chopped fresh parsley
2 tablespoons chopped fresh basil
1 tablespoon extra-virgin olive oil

1. In a medium saucepan, combine the shelled beans with the sage, rosemary, thyme, bay leaf, and ³/₄ teaspoon salt. Cover with water and bring to a boil over high heat. Once boiling, immediately lower the heat and bring to a simmer. Cover and cook the beans for 15–20 minutes or until tender. Drain the beans and discard the herb sprigs and bay leaf. Set aside the beans.

2. In a large skillet, heat the olive oil over high heat. Add the bacon and fry until lightly browned. Quickly add the garlic and crawfish and toss and sauté until hot. Add the lemon juice and a dash of salt and black pepper and mix well.

3. Add the drained beans and toss with the bacon and crawfish mixture for 1 minute. Add the parsley, basil, and extra-virgin olive oil. Carefully mix so beans don't break. Add more salt and black pepper as needed. Serve warm or at room temperature. Serves 4.

* See Food Sources in the Appendix.

Venison-Cider Pot Roast

Try this unusual twist on pot roast "woodsman style," which uses lean venison meat, combined with cider as a marinade and a sauce with wild blueberries. Wild game meat is leaner than domestic cuts and should be cooked slowly in moist heat by braising, as in this recipe. Wild blueberries thrive in the Adirondack region from early June to early October. Juicy and sweet, they add a unique touch to the well-rounded sauce.

4 pounds venison top round roast, tied
2 quarts apple cider
6 whole cloves
3 bay leaves
Vegetable oil as needed
2 medium carrots, coarsely chopped
2 celery stalks, coarsely chopped
1 medium onion, coarsely chopped

2 quarts water
3 tablespoons dried currants
2 tablespoons honey
2 teaspoons red wine vinegar
1/2 cup fresh blueberries
Cornstarch and water as needed
5 tablespoons unsalted butter
Salt and black pepper as needed

1. In a plastic container, combine the venison, 1 quart of the cider, cloves, and bay leaves. Cover with plastic wrap and refrigerate in the marinade for 2 days, turning the meat every 12 hours to ensure equal marinating. Remove the meat from the marinade and pat dry.

2. Preheat the oven to 350° F. In a heavy, deep ovenproof pot or Dutch oven, heat 1/4" vegetable oil over high heat. Add the venison and brown on all sides. Add the carrots, celery, and onion and sauté until the onion is transparent.

3. Place in the oven and roast, uncovered, for 30 minutes, or until the vegetables and venison appear golden brown. Add the remaining cider and the 2 quarts water. Cover the pot with aluminum foil and braise the meat for 2 hours, or until the meat is just fork tender.

4. Remove the venison from the pot. Place on a meat platter and let rest.

5. Strain the pan juices and marinade into a small saucepan. Add the currants, honey, vinegar, and blueberries. Bring to a simmering boil and simmer over low heat for 5 minutes. Thicken with a little cornstarch mixed with water until you can lightly coat the back of a spoon. Whisk in the butter until smooth. Add the salt and black pepper if needed.

6. Remove from the heat. Slice the pot roast on a platter and cover with the blueberry sauce. Serves 4–6.

Thendara Pepper-Crusted Filet with Cognac-Merlot Sauce

Thendara, a pretty town deep in the southwestern portion of the Adirondacks, is notorious for cold weather early in the fall. A pepper- and Cognac-spiked beef is a welcome dish for one of those chilly days. Serve with Speculator Fingerling Hash Browns (see page 22).

1/4 cup cracked black pepper
1 teaspoon kosher salt
Two 8-ounce filet mignon tenderloin medallions
2 tablespoons coarse mustard
2 tablespoons vegetable oil
3 medium garlic cloves, thinly sliced
1/2 teaspoon finely chopped fresh rosemary
2 tablespoons sun-dried cranberries
1/4 cup Cognac
1/4 cup merlot wine
1/2 cup brown gravy
1/4 cup heavy cream
2 slices Brie cheese
2 fresh rosemary sprigs for garnish
1 tablespoon pumpkin seeds for garnish

1. In a flat dish, blend the cracked pepper and kosher salt. Brush the filets on one side with the mustard. Dip the mustard side of the filets into the pepper mix. Press and crust the filets until fully covered.

2. Preheat the oven to 350° F. In a medium ovenproof skillet, heat the vegetable oil over high heat. Once the oil reaches the smoking point (light haze), carefully place the filets pepper-side down into the hot oil. Sear the filets until the pepper crust appears golden brown. Carefully turn the filets with a spatula and sear the other side. Drain the excess oil from the pan and place the pan with the filets in the oven. Cook the filets to desired doneness, adding the garlic, rosemary, and cranberries.

3. Return the pan with the filets to the stove over high heat. Add the Cognac and flambé or cook down the alcohol until almost gone. Add the merlot and cook down to almost syrup. Remove the filets from the pan and keep warm.

4. Add the gravy and cream to the pan and whisk until incorporated and smooth. Place the warm filets in a baking dish, top with the Brie, and place under the broiler just to melt the cheese.

5. If serving with the hash browns, place the filets atop the hash browns and drizzle with the sauce. Garnish each plate with 1 rosemary sprig and 1/2 tablespoon pumpkin seeds. Serves 2.

Cider Mill Pork Loin Roast with Sweet Potato Hay

The best part of the fall is enjoying fresh pressed apple cider from orchards and farm stands in and around the Adirondacks. Besides being a refreshing beverage, cider is a great marinade for chicken or pork dishes. In this recipe, we combined apple cider with cranberry nectar as a marinade to achieve a spectacular flavor. Serve with Smashed Amaretto Yams (see page 21).

PORK
1 quart apple cider
1 quart cranberry nectar or cranberry juice
¹/₂ tablespoon ground cinnamon
3 pounds boneless pork loin, tied
1 medium carrot, coarsely chopped
2 celery stalks, coarsely chopped
1 small onion, coarsely chopped
2 Red Delicious apples, peeled, cored, and finely chopped
1 teaspoon dried rosemary
1 teaspoon dried thyme
Salt and black pepper as needed
2 cups water
2 teaspoons cornstarch mixed with water
1 tablespoon unsalted butter

SWEET POTATO HAY
1 sweet potato, peeled
Vegetable oil as needed
Salt and black pepper as needed

1. Prepare the pork by combining the cider, cranberry nectar, and cinnamon in a glass or plastic bowl and mix well. Immerse the pork in the marinade and cover with plastic wrap. Marinate the pork for 24 hours in the refrigerator, occasionally turning every 6 hours.

2. Preheat the oven to 350° F. Remove the pork from the marinade. Drain and pat dry. Set aside the marinade.

3. In a heavy roasting pan or Dutch oven, sprinkle out evenly, the carrot, celery, onion, and apples (the mirepoix). Season the pork with the rosemary, thyme, salt, and black pepper.

4. Place the pork in the oven and roast for 20 minutes, or until pork and mirepoix appear golden brown. Add the reserved marinade and the 2 cups water. Reduce the temperature to 325°, cover the pork with aluminum foil, and roast for 2 hours.

5. Remove the foil and roast, uncovered, for 10 minutes more to crisp the roast. Remove from the oven and let the roast stand for 20 minutes before slicing, in order to settle juices.

6. Pour the pan juices through a chinois or strainer. Press the mirepoix firmly to extend captured juices.

7. Pour the strained juices into a small saucepan and bring to a simmering boil. Add the cornstarch mixture as needed to form a spoon-coating glaze. Quickly whip in the butter until smooth. Season with more salt and black pepper if needed.

8. Prepare the sweet potato by shaving the potato into long thin strips (julienne cut) with a mandoline or kitchen grater. Place the strips into a bowl of ice water.

9. Heat the oil in a fryer or deep pan to 350º F. Remove the strips from the ice water and pat dry on a paper towel. Carefully drop the strips into the hot oil and fry until brown and crispy. Remove the strips from the oil and season with the salt and black pepper. Slice the pork, drizzle with the sauce, and top with the crispy sweet potato hay. Serves 4–6.

Watkins Glen

ARMAND C. VANDERSTIGCHEL

Farmers' Market Grilled Chicken with Pumpkin Oil-Infused Vegetable Bouquet

Throughout the North Country, farmers' markets are held once or twice a week in various town squares. Local farmers and bakers are happy to have an outlet for selling direct to the consumer. Their goods are super fresh, and many are organic. This recipe uses a string of ingredients available at most markets. Pumpkin seed oil is available at most specialty stores or can be ordered by mail. Derived from roasted pumpkin seeds, it is wonderful with salads and sautés.

CHICKEN

$^1/_2$ cup virgin olive oil
$^1/_2$ teaspoon finely chopped fresh thyme
$^1/_2$ teaspoon finely chopped fresh sage
$^1/_2$ teaspoon finely chopped fresh rosemary

$^1/_2$ teaspoon black pepper
Kosher salt as needed
Four 6-ounce boneless chicken cutlets

VEGETABLE BOUQUET

2 tablespoons pomace olive oil
1 $^1/_2$ tablespoons pumpkin seed oil*
8 baby red pearl onions, peeled
8 medium shiitake mushrooms, stems removed
$^1/_2$ cup $^1/_2$" diced yellow squash
$^1/_2$ cup $^1/_2$" diced zucchini
$^1/_2$ cup $^1/_2$" diced red bell pepper

$^1/_2$ cup whole pecans
8 seedless green grapes
$^1/_4$ cup white vinegar
3 $^1/_2$ tablespoons warm honey
$^1/_2$ teaspoon kosher salt
$^1/_2$ teaspoon black pepper
$^1/_8$ teaspoon ground allspice

1. Prepare the chicken by combining the olive oil, thyme, sage, rosemary, black pepper, and salt in a small mixing bowl and mix well. Place the chicken in a shallow dish and pour the mixture over the chicken. Cover with plastic wrap and marinate for 2 hours in the refrigerator.

2. Prepare the vegetables by heating the olive oil and half of the pumpkin oil in a medium skillet. Add the pearl onions and sauté for 3 minutes until brown. Add the mushrooms, squash, zucchini, bell pepper, pecans, and grapes and sauté for 2 minutes. Deglaze the pan with the vinegar. Add the honey, salt, black pepper, and allspice and mix well.

3. Remove the pan from the heat and stir in the remaining pumpkin oil. Set aside and keep warm.

4. Preheat the grill or barbecue to high heat. Remove the chicken from the marinade and set aside the marinade. Place the chicken on the grill and quickly grill mark both sides. Lower the grill to a low-medium heat and continue cooking the chicken until cooked through, while occasionally brushing with the marinade.

5. Transfer the grilled chicken to a plate and spoon the warm vegetable bouquet over each chicken cutlet. Serve immediately. Serves 4.

* See Food Sources in the Appendix.

Whiteface Rainbow Trout Napoleon with Idaho Flapjacks & Mustard, Cream & Tomato Concasse

The west branch of the Ausable River, bubbling over the river stones along the foot of Whiteface Mountain, is populated by the rainbow trout, a species much sought after by fly-fishing enthusiasts. Mild, white, and flaky, it is a perfect fish to panfry and incorporate in this tasty recipe. The flapjacks are part of the building blocks of the napoleon. They are delicious individually and can be served as a side dish or appetizer, especially with applesauce, lingonberries, or sour cream.

1 recipe Idaho Flapjacks (see below)
1 recipe Mustard, Cream & Tomato Concasse (see below)
1 cup all-purpose flour
3 large eggs, beaten
1 cup yellow cornmeal
$^1/_2$ teaspoon salt
$^1/_2$ teaspoon black pepper
$^1/_4$ teaspoon dried thyme
Two 6–8-ounce rainbow or Idaho farm-raised trout, skinned and boneless
Vegetable oil as needed
2 tablespoons unsalted butter
2 tablespoons chopped fresh chives for garnish
2 tablespoons finely diced plum tomatoes for garnish

1. Prepare the Idaho Flapjacks.

2. Prepare the Mustard, Cream & Tomato Concasse.

3. Set up a breading station by placing the flour, eggs, and cornmeal in separate bowls. Add the salt, black pepper, and thyme to the cornmeal and mix well.

4. Cut each fillet crosswise in half. Dredge the pieces first in the flour, then the eggs, and then press firmly into the cornmeal. Place the breaded fillets on a plate and set aside.

5. In a medium skillet, heat $^1/_2$" vegetable oil over medium heat. Once the oil is hot, carefully place the trout pieces in the oil. Fry to golden brown on both sides until the fish feels firm. Drain the oil from the pan. Add the butter and melt over low heat, making sure the butter soaks and flavors the fish without burning. Turn off the heat.

6. On each of 2 plates, place 1 flapjack. Spoon on 1 tablespoon concasse. Top with one piece of trout. Top the trout with 1 tablespoon concasse. Cover with another flapjack. Spread the flapjack with 1 tablespoon concasse. Add another piece of trout. Top the trout off with 2–3 tablespoons concasse. Sprinkle with the chives and diced tomatoes. Serve immediately. Serves 2.

IDAHO FLAPJACKS

2 Idaho potatoes, peeled
1 small onion, peeled
2 tablespoons granulated sugar
³/₄ teaspoon salt
2 large eggs, beaten
¹/₄ cup heavy cream
¹/₃ teaspoon finely chopped fresh rosemary
1 ¹/₂ teaspoons grated Parmesan cheese
1 cup high-gluten bread flour
Vegetable oil as needed

1. Using the large holes of a grater, shred the potatoes into a small bowl of water. Remove the potatoes from the water and place in a strainer. Firmly press all of the water out of the potatoes.

2. Place the potatoes in a medium mixing bowl. Using the grater with the large hole side, shred the onion into the potatoes. Add the sugar, salt, eggs, cream, rosemary, cheese, and flour. Fold the mixture together (do not whip) until smooth and mixed. The mixture should have a compact consistency, if not add more flour.

3. In a medium skillet, heat 1" vegetable oil over medium heat (do not bring to a smoking point). Place ¹/₂ cup of the potato mixture in the oil. With a spatula, form a 5" wide ¹/₂" thick pancake.

4. Cook each side for 2–3 minutes or until golden brown and firm. Remove from the oil with a spatula and place on paper towels to drain. Keep warm. Makes 4–6 flapjacks.

MUSTARD, CREAM & TOMATO CONCASSE

¹/₂ cup white wine
2 tablespoons minced shallots
³/₄ cup heavy cream
¹/₄ cup sour cream
1 teaspoon yellow mustard
2 tablespoons finely diced scallions
¹/₄ teaspoon black pepper
Pinch salt
2 tablespoons finely chopped fresh parsley
1 plum tomato, coarsely chopped

1. In a medium skillet over medium heat, reduce the wine and shallots until almost dry. Add the cream, sour cream, and mustard and whisk until smooth. Add the scallions and black pepper.

2. Reduce the cream mixture until almost thick. Add the salt, parsley, and tomato and simmer over low heat for 1 minute. Apply the concasse to the trout. Serves 2.

Smashed Amaretto Yams with Caramelized North Country Pears

How beautiful is the color orange, the official color of the fall season. We eagerly travel North Country back roads to see the harvest of orange pumpkins, squash, and sweet yams. This delicious side dish is a great complement to pork, turkey, or game, especially for the upcoming holidays!

1 $\frac{1}{2}$ pounds sweet yams, peeled and diced 1" (about 5 yams)
Juice of 2 oranges
Water as needed
2 Bartlett pears, peeled and diced $\frac{1}{2}$"
1 tablespoon granulated sugar
$\frac{1}{4}$ teaspoon ground cinnamon
4 tablespoons melted unsalted butter
$\frac{3}{4}$ teaspoon salt
$\frac{1}{4}$ teaspoon black pepper
1 $\frac{1}{2}$ tablespoons honey
4 tablespoons heavy cream
2 tablespoons Amaretto liqueur

1. In a medium saucepan, combine the yams, orange juice, and water to cover. Bring to a simmering boil and simmer for 15 minutes, or until the yams are fork tender.

2. Preheat the oven to 350º F. In a small bowl, combine the pears, sugar, cinnamon, and 1 tablespoon of the melted butter and mix well. Place the pear mixture on a small greased baking sheet and spread out evenly. Place in the oven and roast for 15 minutes or until golden brown. Remove from the oven and set aside.

3. Drain the water from the yams and add the remaining butter, salt, black pepper, honey, cream, and liqueur. With a hand masher, mash the yams until smooth.

4. With a rubber spatula, fold the roasted pears into the yam mixture. Add a pinch of salt and black pepper if necessary. Sprinkle with more cinnamon and serve. Serves 4–6.

Speculator Fingerling Hash Browns

A significant number of the people of Speculator, a small town south of Indian Lake at the crossroads of Routes 30 and 8, are active in local trades, such as timber and construction. A sturdy dish of these hash brown potatoes made from yellow fingerling potatoes, available at most North Country farm stands, will do just fine for breakfast and dinner!

2 tablespoons vegetable oil
¹/₄ cup finely diced andouille or smoked sausage
1 small onion, thinly sliced
¹/₂ cup peeled, cored, and diced Red Delicious apple
3 fresh sage leaves, finely chopped
³/₄ teaspoon finely chopped fresh rosemary
Pinch salt and black pepper
6 medium yellow fingerling potatoes, diced, cooked, and cooled
1 teaspoon brown sugar
¹/₂ teaspoon Grade A Adirondack maple syrup
2 teaspoons white vinegar
2 teaspoons unsalted butter
¹/₄ cup diced scallions

1. In a medium skillet, heat the vegetable oil over high heat. Add the sausage, onion, apple, sage, rosemary, salt, and black pepper and sauté until golden brown.

2. Add the potatoes and toss with the mixture until hot. Add the brown sugar, syrup, vinegar, and butter. Heat and toss until incorporated.

3. Once the potatoes are hot, add the scallions. Add more salt and black pepper if needed. Serve warm with eggs, or steaks (see page 15). Serves 2.

Keeseville Mountain Berry Orchard Strudel

When summer and fall growing seasons overlap, it is time to prepare a hot strudel featuring fruits from farm stands and orchards. Throughout the Champlain Valley region you'll find many orchards and farm stands selling the ingredients for this crispy, cinnamon-scented strudel. A perfect place to buy berries is Pray's Farm on Route 9N in Keeseville. For apples, head over to King's Apple Orchard on Mace Chasm Road, off Route 9 in Keeseville.

$^1/_2$ pint fresh raspberries
$^1/_2$ pint fresh blackberries
$^1/_2$ pint fresh blueberries
1 pint fresh strawberries, thinly sliced
4 Granny Smith apples, peeled, cored, and thinly sliced into wedges
$^1/_2$ teaspoon vanilla extract
Juice of 1 lemon
$^1/_4$ cup blackberry brandy
$^3/_4$ cup granulated sugar

2 $^1/_2$ tablespoons cornstarch
$^1/_2$ teaspoon ground cinnamon
$^2/_3$ cup sun-dried cranberries
$^1/_3$ cup finely chopped dried apricots
$^1/_3$ cup coarsely chopped pistachio nuts
1 recipe Cinnamon-Sugar Topping (see below)
Ten 14" x 18" sheets phyllo dough
$^1/_2$ cup melted unsalted butter
Unseasoned bread crumbs as needed

1. In a large plastic bowl, combine the raspberries, blackberries, blueberries, strawberries, apples, vanilla extract, lemon juice, and brandy and carefully fold together to avoid breaking the fruit.

2. In a small bowl, combine the sugar, cornstarch, and cinnamon and mix well. Add the sugar-cornstarch mixture, cranberries, apricots, and pistachio nuts to the fruit mixture and carefully mix. Chill in the refrigerator for 1 hour.

3. Prepare the Cinnamon-Sugar Topping.

4. On a dry, large cloth napkin, place 1 sheet of the dough. Brush with the melted butter, brushing the edges first then working into the center. Lightly sprinkle with the bread crumbs. Repeat the procedure nine times, placing sheet over sheet of dough.

5. Preheat the oven to 350º F. Equally divide the chilled fruit mixture over the length of the dough. Using the edges of the napkin, pull and roll the dough to a round cylinder/log shape. Cut the strudel carefully with a serrated knife crosswise in half (2 equal-sized cylinders). With a large spatula, carefully transfer the two strudels to a greased or parchment paper-lined baking sheet. Brush the strudels generously with the remaining butter and sprinkle with the topping.

6. Place the strudels in the center of the oven and bake for 20–25 minutes or until crispy, brown, and bubbly. Let the strudels rest for 20 minutes before serving warm, accompanied by ice cream and, of course, fresh whipped cream. Serves 8–10.

CINNAMON-SUGAR TOPPING

2 tablespoons granulated sugar   *$^1/_8$ teaspoon ground cinnamon*

Combine both ingredients. Use to sprinkle over strudel before baking.

Roadside Pumpkin-Marmalade Pie

While visiting the local farm stands on your fall foliage trip through the Adirondacks, make sure to pick up some sugar pumpkins, not only for carving, but also to use in this wonderful pumpkin pie recipe. Your neighbors will soon be at your kitchen door!

2 whole eggs
2 egg yolks
$^1/_2$ cup firmly packed light brown sugar
1 $^1/_4$ cups cooked mashed pumpkin
1 cup milk
$^1/_2$ cup heavy cream
$^1/_2$ teaspoon ground cinnamon
$^1/_4$ teaspoon ground nutmeg
$^1/_4$ teaspoon ground ginger
$^1/_2$ teaspoon grated orange peel
2 tablespoons unsalted butter, melted
$^1/_2$ teaspoon salt
One 9" unbaked pie shell*
Orange marmalade as needed
$^1/_4$ cup granulated sugar
2 egg whites

1. Preheat the oven to 475º F. In a large mixing bowl, beat the whole eggs and yolks together. Add all but the last four ingredients and mix thoroughly.

2. Place the pie shell in a pie plate. Pour the mixture into the pie shell and bake for 10 minutes to set the crust. Reduce the temperature to 350º and bake for 20 minutes more, or until the filling is almost set.

3. Remove from the oven when the filling feels slightly firm and spread with a thin layer of the marmalade. Make meringue by beating together the granulated sugar and egg whites until stiff peaks form. (Always use a cold stainless steel or copper bowl with cold egg whites to obtain maximum results.) Cover the marmalade with the meringue.

4. Return the meringue-covered pie to the oven and bake for 15 minutes more, or until the meringue topping is lightly browned. Serve with fresh whipped cream or your favorite ice cream. Makes one 9" pie.

* *See Cooking Basics in the Appendix.*

Orchard Baked Apples with Adirondack Zabaglione

Crates overflowing with a variety of apples welcome us at every food purveyor in the days of September, stirring thoughts of apple pies, apple cider, applesauce, and, yes, baked apples. Fun to make and scrumptious to eat! This recipe is especially for the young at heart!

BAKED APPLES

1/2 cup chopped walnuts
1/3 cup sun-dried cranberries
1/2 cup finely chopped dried pears
Grated peel of 1 orange
4 large Rome apples, washed and cored
Juice of 1 orange
4 teaspoons unsalted butter, divided
3 teaspoons Grade A Adirondack maple syrup

ZABAGLIONE

2 egg yolks
1 tablespoon honey
1 tablespoon Grade A Adirondack maple syrup
1/8 teaspoon ground cinnamon
1/2 teaspoon confectioners' sugar
2 tablespoons plus 2 teaspoons Marsala wine

1. Prepare the baked apples by combining the walnuts, cranberries, pears, and orange peel in a small bowl and mixing well.

2. Preheat the oven to 350° F. Peel a thin strip of skin around the middle of each apple. Place the apples in a buttered baking dish and fill the cavities of each apple with the fruit mixture, pressing down firmly, packing the center of the apple. Pour the orange juice, divided, over each apple.

3. Press 1 teaspoon butter atop each apple. Drizzle 1/2 teaspoon syrup over the butter on each apple. Place the apples in the oven and bake for about 30 minutes. Remove from the oven and set aside.

4. Prepare the zabaglione by combining the egg yolks, honey, syrup, cinnamon, confectioners' sugar, and wine in a stainless steel, medium mixing bowl, held over an equal-sized pan of simmering water. Quickly whisk the egg mixture for 8 minutes or until thick and fluffy. Dollop the zabaglione over each apple and serve immediately. Serves 4.

HARVEST WINE DINNER CELEBRATION

We decided that a Harvest Wine Dinner had to take place at the Friend's Lake Inn in Chestertown, New York. Innkeepers Greg and Sharon Taylor's knowledge of wines and their award-winning wine cellar, combined with the use of local products by Chef Tim Barnok, enhances this celebratory menu.

FIRST COURSE
Trout Mousse
1999 Salmon Run Riesling
Finger Lakes Region

SECOND COURSE
Wild Mushroom & Goat Cheese Beggars Purse
1998 Lamoreaux Landing Reserve Chardonnay
Lodi, New York — Seneca Lake Region

THIRD COURSE
Lobster & Scallop Corn Crêpe with Vanilla Bean Sauce
1998 Millbrook Reserve Pinot Noir
Millbrook, New York — Hudson Valley Region

FOURTH COURSE
Roasted Venison Chop with Pumpkin & Black Truffle Salpicon
1998 Fox Run Vineyards Meritage
Penn Yan, New York — Seneca Lake Region

CHEESE COURSE
New York artisan cheese makers:
    Old Chatham Sheepherding Co., Shepherds Wheel
    Egg Farm Dairy, Wild Ripened Goat Cheddar
    Grafton Farms, Sharp Cheddar
1998 Standing Stone Vineyards Cabernet Franc
Hector, New York — Seneca Lake Region

DESSERT
Chocolate Tower
New York Taylor Port

Trout Mousse

1 smoked trout fillet, skinned and boned
1 ¹/₂ cups cream cheese at room temperature
¹/₄ cup honey
¹/₈ cup whole grain mustard
1 tablespoon minced fresh parsley
2 tablespoons fresh lemon juice
¹/₄ cup sour cream
Salt and black pepper to taste
Crostini (toasted slices French Bread)
Scottish smoked salmon slices
Fresh chive leaves for garnish

1. In a food processor, combine the first seven ingredients and puree until smooth. Taste the mixture and season with the salt and black pepper.

2. On crostini, spread the mousse. Top with 1 slice of the Scottish smoked salmon and garnish with the chive leaves. Serve with a 1999 Riesling from Salmon Run in the Finger Lake Region. Serves 4.

Wild Mushroom & Goat Cheese Beggars Purse

2 tablespoons vegetable oil
¹/₄ cup julienned pancetta
3 cups sliced wild mushrooms (chanterelles, black trumpets, lobster)
1 tablespoon finely chopped shallots
2 scallions, sliced
¹/₄ cup grated Parmesan cheese
¹/₄ cup goat cheese
2 tablespoons white truffle oil*
1 teaspoon salt or to taste
1 teaspoon black pepper or to taste
¹/₄ cup finely chopped fresh parsley
Five 14" x 18" sheets phyllo dough
Melted butter or margarine as needed

1. In a large sauté pan, heat the vegetable oil over high heat and render the pancetta. When the pancetta starts to crisp, add the mushrooms and shallots and sauté until tender.

2. Add the scallions, both cheeses, and truffle oil and cook until the cheeses are melted.

3. Remove from the heat, season with the salt and black pepper, and add the parsley. Chill in the refrigerator.

4. On a dry, large cloth napkin, place 1 sheet of the dough lengthwise on the cloth. Brush the dough with some of the melted butter — just enough to coat. Place another sheet of dough on the top and repeat the procedure until the dough is 5 sheets thick. Cut the dough into 4 equal parts.

5. Preheat the oven to 350º F. In a buttered muffin tin, line four of the wells with the dough. Fill the dough with the chilled reserved mixture. Bring the corners of the dough together and give a light twist to form a purse.

6. Place the tin in the oven and bake the beggars purses for 10–15 minutes, or until they are golden. Serve immediately with a 1998 Reserve Chardonnay from Lamoreaux Landing in the Seneca Lake Region. Serves 4.

* See Food Sources in the Appendix.

Lobster & Scallop Corn Crêpe with Vanilla Bean Sauce

4 Corn Crêpes, warmed (see below)
$\frac{1}{2}$ cup Vanilla Bean Sauce (see next page)
Vegetable oil as needed
12 large fresh scallops, muscle removed
Two 1 $\frac{1}{4}$-pound (chic) lobsters, cooked and shelled
4 teaspoons crushed toasted almonds
4 teaspoons minced fresh chives

1. Prepare the Corn Crêpes.
2. Prepare the Vanilla Bean Sauce.
3. In a large sauté pan, heat $\frac{1}{4}$" vegetable oil over medium heat. Add the scallops and sauté to golden brown on both sides.
4. Cut the lobster tail meat in half lengthwise. Add the four halves and four claws to the pan and sauté until hot.
5. Place 1 warm crêpe on each plate and place $\frac{1}{2}$ lobster tail and 2 scallops on the crêpe. Roll the crêpe and place in the center of the plate. Add the remaining 1 scallop and 1 claw on the top of each crêpe.
6. Spoon 2 tablespoons of the bean sauce over each crêpe. Sprinkle with 1 teaspoon almonds and 1 teaspoon chives. Serve immediately with a 1998 Reserve Pinot Noir from Millbrook Vineyards & Winery in the Hudson Valley. Serves 4.

CORN CRÊPE

2 eggs
$\frac{1}{2}$ cup plus 1 tablespoon milk
$\frac{1}{4}$ cup all-purpose flour
1 tablespoon melted butter
3 tablespoons cooked fresh corn kernels
1 tablespoon minced fresh herbs (parsley, chives, tarragon)

1. In a blender, combine all of the ingredients, except the herbs, and blend for 1 minute. Add the herbs and blend just to combine.
2. Spray a nonstick sauté pan with cooking spray and heat over medium heat until hot. Place $\frac{1}{4}$ cup of the batter in the pan and tilt the pan until the batter is spread evenly around the pan. As soon as the crêpe browns slightly around the edges and becomes dry, turn the crêpe onto a plate with wax paper. Repeat the procedure until the batter is used. Keep warm. Makes ten 6" crêpes. (We have kept the serving amount for 10, in case the first few crêpes should fail or burn.)

VANILLA BEAN SAUCE

1 ¹/₂ shallots, finely diced
5 tablespoons dry white wine
¹/₂ vanilla bean, sliced lengthwise
1 cup heavy cream
¹/₂ teaspoon granulated sugar
¹/₂ pound (2 sticks) unsalted butter at room temperature
¹/₂ teaspoon salt

1. In a medium saucepan, combine the shallots, wine, and vanilla bean. Reduce to almost dry over medium heat.

2. Add the cream and sugar and reduce to one-third over medium heat.

3. Add the butter and whisk until smooth to finish the sauce. Add the salt. Keep warm.

To toast almonds: *Preheat the oven to 350° F. In a baking pan, place the almonds in a single layer and toast in the oven for 5–7 minutes or until golden, stirring frequently. Let the almonds cool completely before using.*

Roasted Venison Chop with Pumpkin & Black Truffle Salpicon

Four 11-ounce venison chops, cleaned
Salt and black pepper as needed
3 tablespoons vegetable oil
¹/₂ cup good red wine
1 ¹/₂ cups demi-glace
6 tablespoons butter
4 cups diced small sugar pumpkin
1 black truffle*, shaved
3 tablespoons black truffle oil*

1. Season the venison chops with the salt and black pepper. In a large sauté pan, heat the vegetable oil over high heat. Add the chops and sear until golden brown. Remove the chops and place in a baking dish.

2. In a small saucepan, reduce the wine by half. Add the demi-glace and reduce by one-third. Add salt and black pepper to taste. Whisk in 4 tablespoons of the butter to give the sauce a shiny appearance. Keep warm.

3. Parcook the pumpkin in boiling water for 12 minutes, or until it is three-fourths cooked. Strain and set aside.

4. Preheat the oven to 350° F. In another sauté pan, melt the remaining butter and add the pumpkin. Cook for 5 minutes and add the black truffle. Add salt and black pepper to taste and the truffle oil. Set aside.

5. Place the venison chops in the oven and cook until desired doneness.

6. Place some of the reserved pumpkin salpicon in the center of each plate. Place 1 venison chop on the top and coat with ¹/₄ cup of the red wine demi-glace. Serve with your favorite vegetable and a 1998 Meritage from Fox Run Vineyards in the Seneca Lake Region. Serves 4.

* *See Food Sources in the Appendix.*

Chocolate Tower

¹/₄ pound semisweet chocolate, melted
1 recipe Chocolate Mousse (see below)

1 recipe Chocolate Leaves (see below)
2 ounces white chocolate, melted

1. Roll and tape an 8" x 4" piece of parchment paper into a tube. Coat the inside of the tube with the semisweet chocolate and freeze.
2. Prepare the Chocolate Mousse.
3. Prepare the Chocolate Leaves.
4. Peel off the parchment paper and fill the tower with the chocolate mousse. Drizzle the white chocolate all over the outside of the chocolate tower and attach the chocolate leaves. Serve with NY Taylor Port. Serves 4.

CHOCOLATE MOUSSE

¹/₂ pound milk chocolate, chopped
1 cup heavy cream
1 tablespoon butter

1 tablespoon granulated sugar
2 cups fresh whipped cream
1 tablespoon vanilla extract

1. Place the chopped chocolate in a stainless steel bowl.
2. In a medium saucepan, bring the cream, butter, and sugar to a boil. Immediately pour the cream mixture over the chocolate and stir until smooth. Let cool to room temperature.
3. Fold in the whipped cream and vanilla extract. Chill until ready to use.

CHOCOLATE LEAVES

10 ounces bittersweet chocolate

1. Have ready a leaf stencil and a 2" pastry brush.
2. In a medium aluminum bowl over boiling water, melt the chocolate, stirring until smooth.
3. Place the leaf stencil on a parchment paper-covered baking sheet. Dip the pastry brush in the melted chocolate and brush the chocolate into the leaf stencil.
4. Place the baking sheet in the freezer. Freeze until the chocolate hardens, but can be easily removed from the baking sheet. Makes 4 leaves.

For the cheese course, serve these great cheeses from New York artisan cheese makers with a 1998 Cabernet Franc from Standing Stone Vineyards in the Seneca Lake Region:
Shephards Wheel from Old Chatham Sheepherding Co.
Wild Ripened Goat Cheddar from Egg Farm Dairy
Sharp Cheddar from Grafton Farms

GLEN FALLS BALLOON FESTIVAL FEAST

Hot-Air Festival Duck Cassoulet

The key to a good cassoulet lies in combining compatible ingredients in one pot, so that they exchange flavors and bring the dish to a splendid finale. Prepare your cassoulet the day before your picnic or outing. It will steep with flavor in its Dutch oven and be delicious when slowly reheated on an outdoor fire or makeshift grill. The "hot-air aroma" of the simmering cassoulet, served with slices of sourdough bread, will quickly bring back the balloons gracing the autumn skies, with their captains sitting in for a bite.

Olive oil as needed
One 5-pound roasted duck, deboned and
  skin reserved
4 slices smoked bacon, coarsely chopped
2 shallots, minced
10 whole garlic cloves, peeled
1 medium onion, diced ¹/₄"
4 celery stalks, diced ¹/₄"
2 medium carrots, diced ¹/₄"
2 teaspoons finely chopped fresh rosemary
2 teaspoons finely chopped fresh thyme
3 teaspoons finely chopped fresh sage
2 cups dry white wine
¹/₄ pound smoked venison sausage*

³/₄ pound smoked andouille sausage*
2 pounds great northern beans, soaked
1 cup drained sauerkraut
6 tablespoons tomato paste
10 cups chicken stock
3 bay leaves
1 ¹/₂ teaspoons black pepper
3 cups julienned leeks
2 cups hot water
¹/₂ cup honey
¹/₃ cup Grade A Adirondack maple syrup
¹/₂ pound (2 sticks) unsalted butter, cut
  into small cubes
Salt as needed

1. In a heavy cast-iron Dutch oven or heavy, deep ovenproof pot, heat ¹/₄" olive oil over high heat. Quickly chop the reserved roasted duck skin into small pieces and add to the oil. Fry the duck skin until crispy. Quickly add the bacon, shallots, and garlic and lightly brown. Add the onion, celery, carrots, rosemary, thyme, and sage and sauté until the onion is transparent.

2. Preheat the oven to 375° F. Add the wine and reduce by half. Add both sausages, beans, sauerkraut, tomato paste, stock, bay leaves, and black pepper and bring to a simmering boil.

3. Coarsely chop the deboned duck meat into bite-sized pieces. Add to the pot. Cover and place in the oven for 1 hour, or until the beans are tender.

4. Once the beans are tender, remove the pot from the oven and place on the stove top, over low heat. Fold in the leeks, hot water, honey, and syrup and simmer for 5 minutes, stirring occasionally. Fold in the butter cubes and add the salt if needed. Stir until melted and smooth. Ready to serve! Serves 10 – 12 hungry balloon observers!

* See Food Sources in the Appendix.

Honey & Thyme Grilled Venison Chops with Foliage Season Salsa

In the Adirondacks, deer-hunting season runs from mid-September through late November. On remote roads, you will spot the parked SUVs of hunting groups who have vanished into the wilderness for a day, hopeful of returning home to stock the freezer with various cuts of venison meat for the holiday table or barbecue. Marinating the venison is a vital part of preparation, to increase the juiciness of the lean meat and to eliminate the gamy flavor. Once marinated, the venison chops in this recipe are perfect to cook on an open grill. After basting and grilling, top them off with a delicious crunchy salsa.

MARINADE
1 cup red wine vinegar
1 cup port wine
2 cups cold water
1 celery stalk, coarsely chopped
1 small red onion, sliced
1 Red Delicious apple, cored and coarsely chopped
2 teaspoons finely chopped fresh thyme
2 bay leaves
6 whole cloves
1/2 teaspoon black peppercorns
1 cinnamon stick
1/4 teaspoon ground ginger
1/4 teaspoon ground coriander
1 tablespoon A-1 sauce

VENISON CHOPS
Eight 8-ounce venison chops, cleaned
1 recipe Foliage Season Salsa (see next page)
1 cup honey
1 tablespoon unsalted butter, melted
1 tablespoon finely chopped fresh rosemary

1. Prepare the marinade by combining all of the marinade ingredients in a medium saucepan. Bring to a simmering boil and simmer for 5 minutes. Transfer the marinade to a plastic bowl and let cool for 1 hour.

2. Prepare the venison chops by placing them in a rectangular glass baking dish. Pour the cooled marinade over the chops. Cover with plastic wrap and marinate in the refrigerator for 3 days. Turn the chops every 8 hours to insure proper marinating.

3. Remove the chops from the marinade and place on a metal rack to drip excess marinade.

4. Prepare the Foliage Season Salsa.

5. In a small saucepan, warm the honey, butter, and rosemary, then remove from the heat.

6. Preheat the grill to high heat. With a basting brush, coat both sides of the chops with the honey-butter mixture. Place the chops on the grill. Quickly mark and sear each side. Lower the heat and continuously baste each chop on both sides. Cook the chops to desired doneness. Serve with the salsa. Serves 8.

FOLIAGE SEASON SALSA

2 Red Delicious apples, peeled, cored, and diced $1/8$"
Juice of $1/2$ lemon
$1/2$ cup cooked fresh corn kernels
1 small red onion, finely diced
$1/4$ cup finely diced scallions
$1/2$ cup quartered seedless red grapes
2 tablespoons finely chopped fresh cilantro
$1/3$ cup red wine vinegar
$1/2$ cup apple cider
$1/2$ cup cranberry juice
3 tablespoons warm honey
4 tablespoons lingonberry preserves
$1/8$ teaspoon salt
$1/4$ teaspoon ground allspice

1. In a medium mixing bowl, combine the apples, lemon juice, corn, onion, scallions, grapes, and cilantro and mix well. Set aside.

2. In a metal mixing bowl, combine the vinegar, cider, cranberry juice, honey, preserves, salt, and allspice. Place the bowl over low heat and stir until the honey is dissolved. Remove from the heat and let cool.

3. Mix the apple salsa with the cooled vinaigrette and let steep for 1 hour before serving. Makes about 3 cups.

Witching Season Fruit Crumble

A beautiful blend of pie-friendly fruits under a crispy crust of rolled oats is a good way to end a day of fun at your Fall Harvest Festival. Eat the crumble before sundown or you might end up with some unexpected visitors flying the friendly autumn skies on broomsticks!

6 ounces strawberries, hulled and halved
$^1/_4$ cup dried Bing cherries
1 Granny Smith apple, cored, peeled, and diced $^1/_2$"
1 pound rhubarb, diced $^1/_2$"
$^1/_2$ cup granulated sugar
$^1/_3$ cup fresh orange juice
1 tablespoon cornstarch
1 cup all-purpose flour
1 cup rolled oats
$^1/_2$ cup firmly packed light brown sugar
$^1/_2$ teaspoon ground cinnamon
$^1/_2$ cup ground almonds
$^1/_2$ cup cold unsalted butter
1 egg, lightly beaten
$^1/_4$ teaspoon vanilla extract

1. Preheat the oven to 350° F. In a large bowl, combine the strawberries, dried cherries, apple, rhubarb, and granulated sugar and mix carefully.

2. In a small bowl, combine the orange juice and cornstarch and mix well. Fold the cornstarch mixture into the fruit and transfer the fruit mixture to a greased baking dish.

3. In a medium bowl, combine the flour, oats, brown sugar, cinnamon, and almonds. With a pastry blender, cut in the butter until the mixture resembles coarse bread crumbs. Add the egg and vanilla extract and mix well.

4. Spoon the oat mixture evenly over the fruit, pressing it down lightly. Place in the oven and bake for 50–60 minutes or until golden brown and bubbly. Serve with fresh whipped cream and perhaps ice cream. Serves 4–6.

THANKSGIVING DINNER ADIRONDACK STYLE

Adirondack Balsam Herb-Roasted Turkey with Wild Mushroom & Herb Gravy

Cooking a perfect Thanksgiving turkey is a daunting task for many cooks. With this recipe, chances are you will achieve "perfect turkey cook" status! A brining technique is used to keep the meat juicy and flavorful down to the bone. In addition, a savory herb butter is applied under the skin to double baste the turkey and to create a crispy skin. If the brining process is too time consuming, you may skip it and still have a delicious turkey. Remember, preparing a day ahead cuts down holiday stress.

BRINE
1 1/2 gallons cold water
1 1/2 cups kosher salt
1 cup superfine sugar
1 teaspoon whole juniper berries
1 teaspoon black peppercorns
1 teaspoon crushed bay leaves

TURKEY
One 14-pound turkey, neck and giblets removed
1 recipe Balsam Green Herb Butter (see next page)
3 Red Delicious apples, washed
1 large onion, coarsely chopped
2 shallots, coarsely chopped
2 medium carrots, coarsely chopped
2 celery stalks, coarsely chopped
1/2 cup mushroom stems (if available)
Melted butter as needed
Kosher salt and black pepper as needed
Water as needed
1 recipe Wild Mushroom & Herb Gravy (see page 39)

1. Prepare the brine by combining the water, salt, sugar, juniper berries, peppercorns, and bay leaves in a large plastic tub. Stir until the sugar and salt are dissolved. Add the turkey to the brine, breast-side down, making sure it is totally immersed in the water. Refrigerate or keep cold for 12 hours.
2. Prepare the turkey by removing it from the brine. Rinse the turkey with cold water and pat the whole turkey dry. Discard the brine.
3. Prepare the Balsam Green Herb Butter.

4. Preheat the oven to 400º F. Loosen the turkey skin by inserting your fingers under the turkey skin and pushing upwards starting at the breast, detaching it from the meat without tearing it. Insert the herb butter under the skin, including the breast, thighs, and legs. Also coat the inside of the turkey cavity.

5. Place the apples inside the cavity. With butcher twine, tie the turkey legs together. Lift the turkey and bring the twine around the turkey, like tying a roast. Finish tying the twine at the breast wing part.

6. In a large roasting pan, scatter the onion, shallots, carrots, celery, and mushroom stems. Place an appropriate size drip rack over the vegetables and place the turkey on the rack breast-side up. Brush the turkey with the melted butter and season with the kosher salt and black pepper.

7. Place the turkey in the oven and roast for 30 minutes. Reduce the temperature to 350º F and roast for 30 minutes more, occasionally brushing with the butter.

8. Add 4 cups of water to the pan. Cover the complete pan with aluminum foil and roast for 1 hour more.

9. Remove the foil from the pan. Cover only the breast part of the turkey with the foil, leaving the thighs and legs exposed. Roast the turkey for 30 minutes more. Add 1 or 2 cups of water if the bottom of the pan with the vegetables appears dry.

10. Remove the foil from the breast. Baste the turkey occasionally while it roasts for 30–45 minutes more, or until the inner thighs read 170º when a meat thermometer is inserted.

11. Transfer the turkey to a large decorated platter or carving board. Remove the twine. Cover the turkey loosely with foil and let rest for 30 minutes.

12. Prepare the Wild Mushroom & Herb Gravy using the pan juices. Serve with the turkey.

BALSAM GREEN HERB BUTTER

1 pound unsalted butter at room temperature
2 tablespoons chopped fresh parsley
2 tablespoons chopped fresh dill
2 tablespoons chopped fresh thyme
2 tablespoons chopped fresh cilantro
2 tablespoons chopped fresh basil
1 teaspoon dried savory
1 teaspoon dried marjoram
1 teaspoon dried rosemary
1 teaspoon black pepper
1 teaspoon kosher salt
3 tablespoons finely chopped red onion
1 tablespoon fresh lemon juice

1. In a medium bowl, combine all of the ingredients and mix well.

2. Leave at room temperature when applying to the turkey. If used for other dishes, wrap in aluminum foil and place in the freezer. This butter is also great when melted atop grilled steaks, chicken, or fish.

WILD MUSHROOM & HERB GRAVY

4 cups water
Olive oil as needed
¹/₂ pound shiitake mushrooms, thinly sliced and stems reserved
¹/₂ pound oyster mushrooms, thinly sliced and stems reserved
1 shallot, minced
Salt and black pepper as needed
¹/₂ cup zinfandel wine
¹/₂ teaspoon finely chopped fresh thyme
¹/₂ teaspoon finely chopped fresh rosemary
¹/₂ cup all-purpose flour
¹/₄ cup heavy cream

1. While the turkey rests, prepare the gravy. Skim the fat from the pan juices and set aside ¹/₄ cup.

2. Place the roasting pan over two burners over medium-to-high heat. Add the 4 cups water to the pan and deglaze the pan by scraping and stirring the bottom. Bring to a boil and simmer for 5 minutes. Pour the pan juices, including the vegetables, into a large strainer set up over a large bowl. Press the vegetables firmly into the strainer, extracting the juices. Set aside 4 ¹/₂ cups juice.

3. In a medium heavy saucepan, heat ¹/₄" olive oil over high heat. Add all of the mushrooms and shallot and sauté until golden brown, adding a pinch of the salt and black pepper. Add the wine, thyme, and rosemary and reduce the wine by half. Add the 4 ¹/₂ cups reserved pan juices and bring to a boiling simmer.

4. Prepare a roux (thickening agent) by combining the reserved ¹/₄ cup turkey fat and flour in a small saucepan. Using a wooden spoon, mix and stir the roux for 3 minutes over medium heat. If the roux is too dry, add a little more fat (roux should be thick and pasty).

5. Add the roux bit by bit to the simmering stock. Thicken the gravy to desired thickness. Stir in the cream. Add more salt and black pepper if needed. Keep warm.

Adirondackana Stuffing Gravy Soppers

Instead of the usual stuffing inside the turkey (a health-risk issue) or a side dish of stuffing, try these hearty muffinlike gravy soppers. Place them warm in a decorative basket on the table, or set one on each plate, and let the sopping begin!

1 ²/₃ cups all-purpose flour
¹/₃ cup yellow cornmeal
¹/₄ cup granulated sugar
2 teaspoons ground mustard
1 ¹/₂ teaspoons baking powder
³/₄ teaspoon salt
¹/₂ teaspoon baking soda
¹/₈ teaspoon ground allspice
¹/₈ teaspoon black pepper
¹/₂ teaspoon caraway seeds
2 teaspoons finely chopped fresh chives
1 cup finely chopped maple-smoked ham*
2 eggs, beaten at room temperature
1 cup buttermilk
¹/₃ cup corn oil
3 tablespoons Dijon mustard

1. Preheat the oven to 400° F. Grease a muffin tin.

2. In a large bowl, combine the flour, cornmeal, sugar, ground mustard, baking powder, salt, baking soda, allspice, black pepper, caraway seeds, and chives and mix well. Stir in the ham and set aside.

3. In a medium bowl, combine the eggs, buttermilk, corn oil, and Dijon mustard and whisk until smooth. Make a well in the center of the reserved dry ingredients and add the egg mixture. Fold together until just moistened.

4. Fill the muffin cups to ³/₄ full and bake for 25 minutes, or until a wooden toothpick inserted in the center comes out clean. Makes 12 – 14 soppers!

* See Food Sources in the Appendix.

Evergreen String Beans with Triple Sec & Tangerine Glaze

The omission of string beans from your holiday table is simply not acceptable! During mid-November, tangerines brighten up the produce stores, to the delight of many — especially hikers and skiers in need of convenient carry-on energy and vitamins for their outings. Tangerines give a new twist to this string bean recipe.

Vegetable oil as needed
1 pound fresh string beans, trimmed and cooked al dente
Salt and black pepper as needed
¹/₄ cup Triple Sec liqueur
Juice of 2 tangerines
2 tablespoons unsalted butter
¹/₂ cup shelled broken walnuts
1 tablespoon Grade A Adirondack maple syrup
Zest of 2 tangerines for garnish

1. In a large skillet, heat ¹/₄" vegetable oil over high heat. Add the beans and mix and toss until hot. Add a pinch of the salt and black pepper.

2. Add the liqueur and flambé or cook down the alcohol for 2 minutes. Add the tangerine juice, butter, walnuts, and syrup and mix well.

3. Transfer the bean mixture to a serving bowl and garnish with the tangerine zest. Serves 4–6.

Smoked Gouda & Apple Wood Bacon Gratinée of Cauliflower

In late October and early November, take advantage of the cauliflower grown locally and displayed at farm stands and produce stores. This new twist on cauliflower au gratin will have holiday guests asking for seconds!

2 small heads or 1 jumbo farm stand-sized head cauliflower
1 teaspoon salt
1 tablespoon vegetable oil
6 strips apple wood-smoked bacon*
1 small onion, finely diced
4 cups shredded smoked Gouda or smoked New York State cheddar cheese*
3 cups heavy cream

1/2 teaspoon salt
Pinch ground nutmeg
1/2 teaspoon black pepper
1 teaspoon onion powder
1/2 teaspoon garlic powder
4 egg yolks
1 tablespoon finely chopped fresh chives for garnish

1. Cut the cauliflower into medium-sized florets, discarding the leaves and core. Place in a large saucepan. Cover with cold water and add the salt. Bring to a simmering boil and simmer for 10 minutes or until cooked but still firm. Place in a large mixing bowl and set aside.

2. In a medium skillet, heat the vegetable oil over high heat and fry the bacon until crispy. Quickly add the onion and sauté for 2 minutes until softened but not brown. Remove from the heat. Fold the mixture into the reserved cauliflower, then fold in 3 cups of the cheese. Set aside and keep warm.

3. In a medium saucepan, place the cream and bring to a boiling simmer. Whisk in the salt, nutmeg, black pepper, onion powder, and garlic powder. Turn off the heat.

4. In a medium mixing bowl, whisk the egg yolks until blended. Slowly temper the egg yolks by adding a little of the hot cream, a spoonful at a time, until all of the cream is incorporated with the egg yolks. (The tempering process avoids curdling the eggs.)

5. Preheat the oven to 325º F. Place the cauliflower in a greased 9 1/2" x 13" baking dish and spread out evenly. Pour the gratin sauce evenly over the cauliflower. Sprinkle the remaining cheese over the top.

6. Place the dish in the oven and bake for 20 minutes, or until the cheese crust is golden brown and the sauce is bubbling.

7. Remove from the oven and garnish with the chives. Serves 4–6.

* See Food Sources in the Appendix.

Dill Billy Potatoes with Red Flannel Glaze

Enhance the holiday spread with these red potatoes, drizzled with a savory butter glaze. Red potatoes are offered in three sizes: A large; B medium-small; C tiny.

3 $^1/_2$ pounds red B potatoes, washed and unpeeled
$^1/_2$ teaspoon salt
$^1/_4$ cup white vinegar
3 sticks unsalted butter
1 teaspoon honey
1 teaspoon yellow mustard
$^1/_2$ teaspoon prepared grated horseradish
1 tablespoon chopped fresh dill
1 tablespoon finely chopped red onion
Salt and black pepper as needed

1. In a large saucepan, combine the potatoes with water to cover, the $^1/_2$ teaspoon salt, and vinegar. Bring to a simmering boil and simmer for 15 minutes, or until the potatoes are fork tender. (Do not overcook.) Drain and keep warm.

2. In a small saucepan, melt the butter over medium heat. Whisk in the honey, mustard, horseradish, dill, and onion until smooth.

3. Pour the warm glaze over the warm potatoes. Toss until mixed, while adding salt and black pepper if needed. Serves 4–6.

Caramelized Pearl Onions with Brussels Sprouts

Crispy Brussels sprouts, straight from the stalk, purchased at a farm stand, are combined with crunchy pearl onions, for a marriage made in culinary heaven!

Vegetable oil as needed
1 pound fresh baby pearl onions, peeled
1/2 cup granulated sugar
1/4 cup white vinegar
1/2 stick unsalted butter
1/4 cup Amaretto liqueur
1 pound fresh Brussels sprouts, peeled, trimmed, and cooked (keep warm)
Salt and black pepper as needed
1 tablespoon diced red bell pepper or pimientos for garnish

1. In a large skillet, heat 1/4" vegetable oil over high heat. Add the pearl onions and toss and brown until slightly softened.

2. Add the sugar and, using a wooden spoon, stir until the sugar caramelizes to a light brown syrup. Quickly add the vinegar. Lower the heat and reduce the vinegar until the onions are coated in a syrupy glaze. Add the butter and liqueur and mix until smoothly incorporated and hot.

3. Carefully fold in the warm Brussels sprouts and mix until glazed and hot. With a slotted spoon, remove the sprouts and onions from the pan and transfer to a serving bowl. Reduce the remaining liquid until syrupy and pour over the sprouts. Garnish with the diced bell pepper. Serves 4–6.

Pilgrim Pumpkin Brûlée

As a final touch to our Adirondack Thanksgiving, may we recommend this delicious pumpkin dessert, which can easily replace the usual pumpkin pie. For best results, prepare the custard twenty-four hours before serving.

CUSTARD

2 cups heavy whipping cream
1 tablespoon dark spiced rum
$1/2$ tablespoon Triple Sec liqueur
$1/8$ teaspoon vanilla extract
$1/8$ teaspoon salt
5 large egg yolks
1 cup canned solid pack pumpkin

$1/3$ cup granulated sugar
1 teaspoon cornstarch
$1/8$ teaspoon ground cinnamon
$1/8$ teaspoon ground ginger
$1/8$ teaspoon ground allspice
Hot water as needed

TOPPING

1 cup granulated sugar
4 tablespoons water

1. Preheat the oven to 350° F. Prepare the custard by combining the cream, rum, and liqueur in a medium saucepan. Bring to a boil. Remove from the heat and add the vanilla extract and salt.

2. In a large bowl, combine the egg yolks, pumpkin, sugar, cornstarch, cinnamon, ginger, and allspice and whisk to blend. In a slow thin stream, whisk in the hot cream mixture.

3. Spoon the mixture among six $1/2$-cup ramekins or ovenproof cups. Place the ramekins in a large, deep ovenproof baking pan. Pour the hot water into the pan, enough to come halfway up the sides of the ramekins.

4. Place the baking pan carefully in the oven and bake for 35 minutes, or until the custard is firm and set.

5. Remove the ramekins from the water and let cool completely. Cover with plastic wrap and refrigerate.

6. Prepare the topping by stirring the sugar and water in a small saucepan over low heat until the sugar is dissolved. Increase the heat and boil, without stirring, until the mixture caramelizes to a golden brown, while swirling the pan occasionally.

7. Remove the ramekins from the refrigerator, discard plastic wrap, and quickly pour the caramel over each ramekin, equally divided. Tilt the ramekins to cover the custard completely. Return to the refrigerator and let cool for 1 $1/2$ hours. Serve with fresh whipped cream. Serves 6.

CHAPTER 2

ADIRONDACK WINTER MAGIC

By November and December, the colors of autumn's foliage have been replaced by the green embrace of pines and other evergreens. Snow will soon provide the dominant color of the season, broken intermittently by dots of color as skiers and hikers take to the hills in their colorful apparel. Chimneys that have lain dormant for most of the year give off puffs of white smoke, as crackling wood fires warm the great rooms of Adirondack lodges and inns.

On the rooftops of vehicles, canoes and camping gear have given way to sleek rows of strapped skis. Summer-season vendors have taken inventory and closed up, relinquishing the winter months to year-round facilities that cater to winter-sports enthusiasts and winter-carnival visitors. Lodges and bed-and-breakfasts await the arrival of weary professionals seeking solitude and refuge from the hustle and bustle of the city and suburbs.

Food pantries are abundantly stocked with nonperishable items, such as beans, grains, syrups, and condiments. Preserved fruits and sealed Mason jars of pickled vegetables, processed from the bounty of the autumn harvest, are checked and labeled. Freezers are stocked with various choice cuts from the past hunting season, to add variety to the dinner fare. Fresh-cut Christmas trees give off the rejuvenating scent of balsam, while pinecones thrown into the fire add crackle and a festive aroma. The winter dinner table is laden with hearty foods to satisfy big appetites and provide the fuel needed to enjoy outdoor activities like Alpine and cross-country skiing, snowmobiling, or ice-fishing.

Winter carnivals, held at popular destinations like Lake George, Saranac Lake, and Lake Placid, bring cheer to the young at heart with sports and games such as snowshoe races, car races on ice, or snowman-building contests. Steaming mugs of hot chocolate and freshly brewed coffee warm the hands and the insides of the snow-stomping festival attendees. A quick bite from the on-site food vendors of hot sandwiches, soups, or fried dough keeps the mind and body going through all the strenuous outdoor activities. At the end of the day, everyone looks forward to gathering around the fire with a hot bowl of soup, or curling up in a blanket with a good book, or sitting down to a filling meal of comfort food at the Adirondack table.

In this chapter, seasonal ingredients are combined with preserves and other nonperishable items to reflect the style of Adirondack winter cuisine. Thick hearty soups and rustic comfort dishes with a gourmet touch are designed to bring you good nourishment and a taste of Adirondack Winter Magic.

Whiteface Mountain Mulled Cider

Warm up with this hot drink in your Adirondack ski lodge after a chilly, exhilarating day on the slopes, or even better, take it with you in a hot Thermos bottle before heading out into Winter Wonderland!

1 quart apple cider
1 tablespoon Adirondack maple sugar
4 cinnamon sticks
1 teaspoon whole cloves
1 teaspoon ground allspice
1 teaspoon orange zest
1 teaspoon lemon zest
1 cup applejack brandy

1. In a medium saucepan, combine the cider, maple sugar, and cinnamon sticks. Combine the cloves, allspice, orange and lemon zest in a cheesecloth bag and tie the bag to seal. Drop the bag into the cider mixture and bring to a simmering boil for 15 minutes.

2. Remove the cinnamon sticks and cheesecloth bag. Add the brandy and mix well. Serve hot. Makes about 5 cups.

ARMAND C. VANDERSTIGCHEL

Ausable Smokestack Mushrooms with Horseradish-Dill Dip

The holiday parties are humming, and it's your turn to cook dinner for a herd of hungry Adirondack aficionados. These awesome "Ausable" smoky mushrooms are perfect to serve as an hors d'oeuvre to keep the "wolves" out of the kitchen while you are coordinating the final touches of your holiday feast. For convenience, prepare the mushrooms the day before; then, just before serving, brush them with butter and a splash of wine and pop them in the oven.

Pinch salt
12 silver dollar-sized mushrooms
Olive oil as needed
1/4 cup finely diced celery
3/4 cup finely diced onions
2–3 strips maple-smoked bacon*
1/2 pound ground pork
Salt and black pepper as needed
1 tablespoon granulated sugar
1 teaspoon finely chopped fresh sage

1 tablespoon finely chopped fresh dill
2 tablespoons crushed pistachio nuts
1/2 teaspoon garlic powder
2 ounces Jack Daniel's whiskey
1/4 cup barbecue sauce
1 egg, beaten
1 cup seasoned bread crumbs
4 tablespoons melted unsalted butter
4 ounces smoked Muenster cheese*
1 recipe Horseradish-Dill Dip (see next page)

1. In a medium saucepan, fill two-thirds with water and bring to a rapid boil. Add the salt and mushrooms and blanch the mushrooms for 2 minutes. Remove the mushrooms from the hot water and cool under cold running water. Shake excess water from the mushrooms and carefully remove the stems. Pat the mushrooms dry with a paper towel. Finely chop the mushroom stems and set aside.

2. In a medium skillet, heat 1/4" olive oil over high heat. Add the celery, onions, and reserved chopped mushroom stems and sauté until the onions are transparent. Remove from the heat and set aside.

3. In another medium skillet, heat 1/4" olive oil over high heat. Add the bacon and sauté until almost crisp. Quickly add the pork and sprinkle with a touch of the salt and black pepper. Sauté the pork until browned, while breaking it up with a fork. Quickly add the reserved celery mixture and mix well. Add the sugar, sage, dill, pistachio nuts, and garlic powder and mix well.

4. Add the whiskey and flambé or cook down the alcohol. Mix in the barbecue sauce.

5. Transfer the mixture to a large mixing bowl and let cool until warm. Add the egg, bread crumbs, 2 tablespoons of the butter, and 2 ounces of the cheese and mix well until the mixture is compact.

6. Prepare the Horseradish-Dill Dip.

7. Preheat the oven to 350º F. Stuff each mushroom generously, pressing the mixture in firmly. Brush each mushroom with the remaining melted butter and top with the remaining cheese. Place in a greased baking dish and bake for 8–10 minutes, or until the cheese is lightly browned and bubbling.

8. Remove from the oven and stack the mushrooms on a platter. Dollop the dill dip atop each mushroom. Serves 4 – 6.

* See Food Sources in the Appendix.

HORSERADISH-DILL DIP

$^1/_2$ *cup sour cream*
1 $^1/_2$ teaspoons prepared grated horseradish
$^1/_2$ *teaspoon yellow mustard*
1 $^1/_2$ teaspoons chopped fresh dill
1 teaspoon granulated sugar
$^1/_2$ *teaspoon black pepper*
$^1/_4$ *teaspoon salt*

In a small mixing bowl, combine all of the ingredients and mix well. Makes almost $^3/_4$ cup.

ARMAND C. VANDERSTIGCHEL

Baby Lima Bean Soup with Cider & Apple Wood Bacon Essence

The snow is relentless, the roads are inaccessible, and the markets are closing early. Every Adirondack family knows that storing a variety of dried beans in the cupboard is a necessity in the heart of winter. In this hearty soup, baby lima beans provide a welcome change from the usual great northern white beans. Why not make a large pot before the first snowfall?

One 16-ounce bag dried baby lima beans
Olive oil as needed
$^1/_4$ pound apple wood-smoked bacon*, finely chopped
1 medium onion, finely chopped
1 teaspoon finely chopped fresh rosemary
2 bay leaves
1 cup apple cider
4 quarts chicken stock or bouillon
1 quart water
1 teaspoon finely chopped fresh sage
$^1/_4$ teaspoon black pepper
Salt as needed
$^1/_2$ cup chopped scallions or fresh chives (optional)

1. Quick soak the beans by placing the beans in a medium deep pot. Add enough water to cover by 2 inches. Bring to a boil and boil for 2 minutes. Remove from the heat. Cover and let stand for 1 hour.

2. In a large saucepan, heat $^1/_4$" olive oil over high heat. Add the bacon and sauté until almost crisp. Quickly add the onion and rosemary and sauté until the onion is transparent. Add the bay leaves and cider. Reduce the liquid in the pan by one-half.

3. Drain the beans. Add the beans, chicken stock, and water to the pan and bring to a simmering boil. Add the sage and black pepper and simmer for 1 $^1/_2$ hours or until slightly thickened and the beans are almost mushy and soft.

4. Taste the soup. Add the salt if needed. Add the scallions or chives right before serving. Serves 6–8.

* See Food Sources in the Appendix.

Tupper Lake Ski Lodge Gourmet Pea Soup

The windows are frosted, the outside ledges are covered with snow, and inside the lodge a large group of hungry ski buddies are warming themselves by the fire. What could be better than to serve them steaming bowls of this thick, healthy, chunky soup, created especially for the cold Adirondack winter. Yielding 16–20 bowls, it is for large gatherings looking for a second helping or to last the entire length of the ski trip. Dig in!

Vegetable oil as needed
$1/3$ pound fatback salt pork, skin removed and pork cubed
3 cups chopped onions
4 celery stalks, finely chopped
1 leek stalk, washed well and finely chopped
1 tablespoon finely chopped fresh rosemary
Three 16-ounce bags dried green split peas
18 cups chicken stock
1 small turnip, peeled and diced $1/2$"
1 small parsnip, peeled and diced $1/2$"
2 small celery root, peeled and diced $1/2$"

1 small rutabaga, peeled and diced $1/2$"
1 pound carrots, diced $1/2$"
6 cups water
$1 1/2$ tablespoons garlic powder
$1/2$ tablespoon dried marjoram
$1/2$ tablespoon celery salt
1 teaspoon black pepper
Salt as needed
2 tablespoons chopped fresh dill
$1/2$ pound Canadian or Irish bacon, smoked ham or sausage*, diced $1/2$"
2 cups diced scallions

1. In a large 2-gallon heavy pot, heat $1/4$" vegetable oil over high heat. Add the salt pork cubes and fry until golden brown. Quickly add the onions, celery, leek, and rosemary and sauté until softened but not browned.

2. Add the split peas and stir to blend the flavors. Add the stock. Bring to a simmering boil and simmer for 10 minutes.

3. Add the turnip, parsnip, celery root, rutabaga, and carrots and return to a simmer.

4. Once the peas are softened, add the 6 cups water, garlic powder, marjoram, celery salt, and black pepper and simmer for 10 minutes more, or until the vegetables are tender. Season with the salt as needed.

5. Add the dill, bacon, and scallions and simmer for 3 minutes. Remove from the heat and serve immediately. Soup should have a slightly thick consistency. Makes 16–20 bowls.

* See Food Sources in the Appendix.

Double-Smoked Bacon & Potato-Cheddar Soup

This sturdy winter soup calls for double-smoked bacon — a salt- and honey-cured bacon slab that is first smoked, then cooked, then smoked again to create a superior hickory taste. A final touch of smoked Colby cheddar whisked into the soup makes it irresistible. Colby cheddar is less oily than regular cheddar, so it melts more uniformly. Smoked cheese is created by smoking at a very low temperature, up to 12 hours for full flavor induction, without the risk of melting. Be prepared to serve seconds.

Olive oil as needed
$1/4$ pound double-smoked bacon*, finely diced
1 medium onion, finely diced
3 celery stalks, finely diced
2 quarts chicken stock or bouillon
4 Idaho potatoes, peeled and diced $1/4$"
2 bay leaves
1 teaspoon onion powder
2 teaspoons garlic powder
$3/4$ teaspoon black pepper
1 cup heavy cream
1 tablespoon cornstarch plus 2 tablespoons water
3 ounces shredded hickory-smoked Colby cheese*
1 cup finely chopped scallions
Salt as needed

1. In a medium saucepan, heat $1/4$" olive oil over high heat. Add the bacon and fry until almost crisp. Quickly add the onion and celery and sauté until the onion is transparent.

2. Add the stock, potatoes, bay leaves, onion powder, garlic powder, and black pepper. Bring to a simmering boil and simmer over low heat for 20 minutes, or until the potatoes are soft. Add the cream and simmer for 10 minutes more.

3. In a cup, combine the cornstarch and water and mix until smooth and pasty. Stir the cornstarch mixture into the soup until well blended and simmer for 5 minutes more. The soup should have a spoon-coating consistency.

4. Remove the soup from the heat. Slowly stir in the cheese, a little bit at a time, until smooth and melted. Add the scallions. Season with a touch of salt if needed. Serve immediately. Serves 6–8.

* See Food Sources in the Appendix.

Wild Greens au Vinaigrette Marmalade with Pan-Seared Herbed Hudson Valley Camembert Cheese

New York State is becoming a nationally famous producer of artisan cheeses, sold in gourmet shops and specially shipped to chefs around the country. Having to rely on our good old French cheese standby is not the order of the day anymore. The Hudson Valley, with its dairy farms and goat cheese producers, is the main producing area. Up in the Adirondacks, the Nettle Meadow Farm produces a fabulous goat cheese, used by many local restaurants. All in all, cheese making is an exciting development in New York State, along with the increasing number of fine wineries.

If Camembert is not available for this recipe, you may substitute a young, firm Brie cheese. Wild mesclun greens are available year-round in all markets. The blend may vary, but it is composed mostly of red oak, green leaf, radicchio, arugula, green oak, mustard greens, watercress, frisée, and dandelion greens. They present beautifully and are very healthy, a good vitamin supply in the cold winter months.

VINAIGRETTE
2 tablespoons minced shallots
1 garlic clove, minced
Drop Tabasco sauce
Pinch salt and black pepper
$1/2$ cup plus 1 tablespoon virgin olive oil
3 tablespoons red wine vinegar
Juice of $1/2$ orange
2 tablespoons orange marmalade

CHEESE
Olive oil as needed
8 ounces Camembert cheese* (preferably Hudson Valley artisan cheese)
2 eggs, beaten
$1/4$ teaspoon black pepper
$1/8$ teaspoon ground nutmeg
$1/2$ teaspoon finely chopped fresh thyme
$1/2$ teaspoon finely chopped fresh rosemary
$1/2$ teaspoon finely chopped fresh dill
All-purpose flour as needed

SALAD

1 pound wild mesclun greens
$^1/_2$ pint cherry tomatoes, halved
1 Red Delicious apple, peeled, cored, and diced $^1/_4$"
$^1/_4$ cup finely diced fresh chives
4 teaspoons toasted almond slivers (see page 30)

1. Prepare the vinaigrette by combining the shallots, garlic, Tabasco, salt, black pepper, olive oil, vinegar, orange juice, and marmalade in a small mixing bowl and whisk until smooth. Set aside.

2. Prepare the cheese by heating $^1/_4$" olive oil in a medium skillet over medium heat. Cut the cheese into 8 slices or pieces.

3. In a small mixing bowl, combine the eggs, black pepper, nutmeg, thyme, rosemary, and dill and mix well. Dip the cheese slices in the egg mixture and coat with the flour. Panfry the cheese slices until golden brown. Drain on a paper towel. Keep warm.

4. Prepare the salad by tossing the mesclun greens with the reserved vinaigrette in a large mixing bowl. Equally divide the greens onto 4 plates. Place 2 slices of the warm cheese atop the greens and sprinkle each plate with the tomatoes, apple, chives, and almonds. Serve immediately. Serves 4.

* See Food Sources in the Appendix.

Horseradish-Crusted Steelhead Salmon with Pickled Cabbage & Watercress Fraîche

Throughout the lakes of the Adirondacks you most likely will catch a truly native fish: steelhead salmon aka landlocked salmon. This smaller version of the Atlantic salmon is a versatile fish to prepare. The distinction between the steelhead and the Atlantic salmon is that the steelhead has a more grayish pink color and a stronger flavor. If steelhead is unavailable, Atlantic salmon is a great substitute! The lakes in the North Country are frequently stocked by the Adirondack Fish Hatchery, which specializes in raising landlocked salmon.

Two $1/2$-pound boneless steelhead salmon fillets
2 tablespoons mayonnaise
1 cup Japanese panko bread crumbs*
$1/4$ cup finely diced scallions
$1/2$ teaspoon prepared grated horseradish
Pinch salt and black pepper
$1/4$ cup melted unsalted butter
1 recipe Pickled Cabbage (see next page)
1 recipe Watercress Fraîche (see next page)

1. Preheat the oven to 350º F. Place the salmon fillets in a greased baking dish. Brush each fillet with 1 tablespoon of the mayonnaise.

2. In a medium mixing bowl, combine the bread crumbs, scallions, horseradish, salt, black pepper, and butter. With your hands, mix and knead the mixture until it is compact. Top and pat each fillet with an equal amount of the bread crumb mixture, pressing firmly onto the fillets.

3. Dab the top of the crusted fillets with more melted butter. Place in the oven and bake for 25 minutes, or until the internal temperature reaches 145º.

4. Meanwhile, prepare the Pickled Cabbage and Watercress Fraîche.

5. Spoon the pickled cabbage onto 2 plates. Place 1 fillet atop each cabbage portion and spoon the fraîche over the salmon crust. Serve immediately. Serves 2.

PICKLED CABBAGE

Olive oil as needed
¹/₂ cup finely chopped onions
1 pound shredded green cabbage
¹/₈ teaspoon ground turmeric
1 teaspoon onion powder
1 teaspoon garlic powder
¹/₂ teaspoon fennel seeds
¹/₂ teaspoon salt
¹/₂ teaspoon black pepper
2 tablespoons confectioners' sugar
2 tablespoons white vinegar
¹/₂ cup white wine
1 teaspoon yellow mustard
1 teaspoon sun-dried cranberries

1. In a large skillet, heat ¹/₄" olive oil over high heat. Add the onions and sauté until transparent. Add the cabbage and sauté until soft and wilted. Add the turmeric, onion powder, garlic powder, fennel seeds, salt, black pepper, and confectioners' sugar and mix and sauté for 2 minutes to develop flavor.

2. Add the vinegar, wine, mustard, and cranberries and mix well. Simmer for 5 minutes over low heat, stirring occasionally. Keep warm.

WATERCRESS FRAÎCHE

1 teaspoon sour cream
1 teaspoon heavy cream
1 teaspoon milk
1 teaspoon fresh lime juice
¹/₂ teaspoon confectioners' sugar
Pinch salt and black pepper
1 tablespoon finely chopped fresh watercress

In a small mixing bowl, combine all of the ingredients and whisk until smooth and silky. Spoon atop the salmon crust before serving.

* See Food Sources in the Appendix.

Wild Buckwheat Honey-Roasted Chicken with Apple & Shiitake Mushroom Stuffing

In farm stands and gift shops around the Adirondacks, you will notice the little plastic squeeze honey bear containing locally produced honey from farms like Gruelick & Sons. Buckwheat honey, a darker version, gives the chicken in this recipe not only a succulent flavor, but also a beautiful, crisp, caramelized outside when drizzled over the skin before roasting. The honey is also inserted under the skin, mixed in a rub of herbs and onions.

1 tablespoon finely chopped fresh rosemary
1 tablespoon finely chopped fresh sage
2 tablespoons finely chopped fresh thyme
1 tablespoon finely chopped fresh tarragon
³/₄ cup finely minced onions
2 tablespoons warm buckwheat honey*
¹/₄ teaspoon white pepper
2 tablespoons melted unsalted butter
1 recipe Apple & Shiitake Mushroom Stuffing (see next page)
One 2 ¹/₂–3-pound chicken
Warm buckwheat honey in a squeeze bottle
Kosher salt as needed
Black pepper as needed

1. In a small mixing bowl, combine the rosemary, sage, thyme, tarragon, onions, honey, white pepper, and butter and mix well. Set aside.

2. Prepare the Apple & Shiitake Mushroom Stuffing.

3. Preheat the oven to 350° F. Place the chicken in a greased roasting pan. Pull the skin of the chicken by inserting fingers under the skin of the breast meat at the cavity opening. Without ripping the skin, proceed to push up the skin all over the chicken including the thighs.

4. Insert equally divided portions of the reserved herb mixture under the skin. Stuff the cavity of the chicken with the mushroom stuffing. With butcher twine, tie the chicken legs together. Lift the chicken and bring the twine around the chicken, like tying a roast. Finish tying the twine at the breast wing part.

5. Using the squeeze bottle, drizzle the warm honey generously over the chicken. Sprinkle with the kosher salt and black pepper.

6. Place the chicken in the oven and roast, uncovered, for 50 minutes. Remove the chicken, cover with aluminum foil, and roast for 20 minutes more. Remove the foil and roast, uncovered, for 20 minutes until a meat thermometer reads 165° when inserted in the center of the chicken. Also check the temperature of the thighs for 165°.

7. Remove from the oven. Carefully remove the twine. Drizzle the chicken with the pan juices before serving. Serves 6–8.

SHIITAKE MUSHROOM STUFFING

Olive oil as needed
³/₄ cup finely diced onions
1 cup finely diced celery
3 ounces sliced shiitake mushrooms, stems removed
1 Red Delicious apple, peeled, cored, and diced ¹/₄"
¹/₂ tablespoon finely chopped fresh rosemary
¹/₂ tablespoon finely chopped fresh tarragon
¹/₂ teaspoon dried marjoram
¹/₄ teaspoon black pepper
¹/₂ teaspoon salt
1 tablespoon buckwheat honey*
4 cups ¹/₂" diced stale bread (about 1 Kaiser roll)
1 egg, beaten
Melted butter as needed

1. In a medium sauté pan, heat ¹/₄" olive oil over high heat. Add the onions and celery and sauté until the onions are transparent. Add the mushrooms, apple, rosemary, tarragon, marjoram, black pepper, salt, and honey and sauté for 3 minutes.

2. Transfer the mixture to a medium mixing bowl. Add the bread cubes and egg and mix well. Add the melted butter if the stuffing appears too dry (should be moist and pliable). Proceed to stuff the chicken cavity.

* See Food Sources in the Appendix.

Steamed Chocolate Mountain Bombs with Wild Blueberry Foam & Amaretto Chocolate Glaze

Steaming this pudding gives it a succulent moist texture and a fruity flavor. Served in a pool of creamy blueberry foam and drizzled with Amaretto chocolate glaze, it is a memorable dessert for all occasions.

BOMBS
1 Anjou pear, peeled, cored, and diced $^1/_4$"
4 tablespoons sun-dried cranberries
$^1/_4$ cup spiced rum
Melted butter as needed
$^1/_3$ cup firmly packed light brown sugar
$^1/_3$ cup superfine sugar
3 tablespoons cocoa powder
2 eggs, beaten
$^2/_3$ cup all-purpose flour
$^1/_2$ cup soft unsalted butter
$^1/_2$ teaspoon baking powder
$^1/_4$ teaspoon ground allspice
Confectioners' sugar for garnish
Fresh blueberries for garnish

BLUEBERRY FOAM
$^1/_2$ pint fresh blueberries
1 tablespoon warm honey
$^1/_4$ teaspoon vanilla extract
2 tablespoons superfine sugar
$^2/_3$ cup heavy cream

CHOCOLATE GLAZE
1 tablespoon Amaretto liqueur
4 tablespoons unsalted butter
4 ounces bittersweet chocolate, chopped into pieces
$^1/_2$ teaspoon vanilla extract
2 tablespoons warm honey

1. Prepare the bombs by combining the pear, cranberries, and rum in a small bowl and mix well. Let the mixture macerate (steep) for 1 hour.

2. Brush 4 ovenproof ceramic cups with the butter or cooking spray. Sprinkle in a little brown sugar, lightly coating all sides. Equally divide the fruit among the 4 cups and set aside. Place a large pan or wide pot on the stove, halfway filled with hot water and bring to a simmering boil. This will be the steam bath to cook the bombs.

3. In a medium bowl, combine the remaining brown sugar, superfine sugar, cocoa, eggs, flour, butter, baking powder, and allspice. With a rubber spatula, mix well until it forms a batter. Equally divide the batter among the cups. Cover the cups with a double layer of aluminum foil and place

in the steam bath. Cook for 45 minutes, occasionally adding a little water to the bath. Chocolate bombs should rise and be firm when done.

4. Meanwhile, prepare the blueberry foam by combining the blueberries, honey, vanilla, super-fine sugar, and cream in a blender. Blend until smooth and foaming. Set aside.

5. Prepare the chocolate glaze by combining the liqueur, butter, chocolate, vanilla, and honey in the top of a double boiler over simmering water. Melt the chocolate and ingredients and mix until smooth. Set aside and keep warm.

6. Spoon 2 tablespoons of the reserved blueberry foam onto each of 4 dessert plates. Insert a knife around the edges of each cup to loosen the bombs. Place 1 bomb bottom-side up in the center of each plate. Spoon or drizzle some of the reserved chocolate glaze over the bombs. Garnish each plate with a dusting of the confectioners' sugar and some blueberries. Serves 4.

AN ADIRONDACK CHRISTMAS FEAST

Château Filet Mignon Chowder

This stick-to-the-ribs chowder is prepared with filet mignon tidbits, available at most butcher shops. Tidbits are the remaining cuts of the beef tenderloin after it is trimmed and cut into medallions. Your guests will welcome this chowder after a chilly day on the holiday road.

Vegetable oil as needed
1 ¼ pounds filet mignon tips, cut into ½" cubes
Salt and black pepper as needed
4 ounces pepper-smoked bacon*, diced ¼"
4 garlic cloves, finely chopped
1 small acorn squash, peeled, seeded, and diced ¼"
4 Idaho potatoes, peeled and diced ¼"
1 bunch celery, diced ¼"
1 medium onion, diced ¼"

1 cup Martini & Rossi red vermouth
3 ½ quarts beef broth or stock
2 cups water
2 bay leaves
2 tablespoons chopped fresh parsley
½ tablespoon chopped fresh sage
2 pounds fresh white mushrooms, diced ½"
4 plum tomatoes, diced ½"
½ cup cooked fresh green peas
¼ cup finely diced fresh watercress
Bunch fresh watercress for garnish

1. In a medium sauté pan, heat ¼" vegetable oil over high heat. Quickly brown the beef cubes and sprinkle with a touch of the salt and black pepper. Set aside.

2. In a large, heavy soup pot, heat ¼" vegetable oil over high heat. Add the bacon and fry until almost crisp. Quickly add the garlic, squash, potatoes, celery, and onion and sauté until the onion is transparent. Add the reserved beef cubes and stir to blend. Add the vermouth and reduce by one-half.

3. Add the broth, water, bay leaves, parsley, and sage. Bring to a simmering boil and simmer for 25 minutes. Add the mushrooms, tomatoes, and peas and simmer for 5 minutes more. Taste the chowder and add salt or black pepper if needed.

4. In large soup bowls, divide the diced watercress. Ladle the chowder into each bowl and garnish with watercress sprigs. Makes 6−8 large soup bowls (and enough for seconds)!

* See Food Sources in the Appendix.

Rudolph's Red Russian Salad

When decoratively assembled and served at room temperature, this Russian salad is perfect for your Christmas dinner table. It is made with fresh beets, which are high in vitamins and iron and available in the winter months, especially at the remaining open local farm stands. Watch the rave reviews pour in with love at first bite.

4 medium cooked fresh beets, diced ¹/₂"
6 large hard-boiled eggs, peeled and diced ¹/₂"
³/₄ cup mayonnaise
¹/₂ cup cooked diced roast beef
1 large dill pickle, diced ¹/₄"
1 teaspoon chopped fresh dill
Pinch salt and black pepper or to taste
6 leaves red leaf lettuce, washed
3 hard-boiled eggs, peeled and halved lengthwise
Mayonnaise as needed
6 fresh dill sprigs
Gold's grated beet-horseradish as needed
6 tomato wedges
6 cucumber slices
12 whole black olives

1. Prepare the salad 1 hour before serving. Cook the beets the same day and do not refrigerate. Keep at room temperature.

2. In a large bowl, gently mix together the diced beets, eggs, mayonnaise, beef, half of the diced pickle, dill, salt, and black pepper.

3. On each of 6 salad plates, place one large leaf of red lettuce. With a medium ice-cream scoop, place a ball of the beet salad in the center of each leaf. Top the salad with 1 egg half flat-side down.

4. With a small cake spatula, cover the top of the egg half with a layer of the mayonnaise. Place 1 dill sprig atop the mayonnaise. With a small teaspoon, place a small drop of the beet/horseradish for decoration.

5. Garnish each plate with 1 tomato wedge, 1 cucumber slice, and 2 olives. Sprinkle a little of the remaining diced pickle over each plate and serve at room temperature. Serves 6.

Weihnacht Christmas Schnitzel

Throughout the North Country, you'll frequently encounter the strong influence of Germans, Swiss, and Austrians in the many restaurants, inns, and food purveyors along the way. As these folks are masters in the celebration of Christmas, what better time to enjoy a hearty and crispy schnitzel on the holiday table, using local Adirondack mushrooms, such as morels, chanterelles, lobster mushrooms, and black trumpets. If these mushrooms are unavailable, substitute a combination of shiitake, oyster, white, and portabella mushrooms. Serve with Holy Smoky German Skillet Home Fries (see recipe on page 65).

SAUCE
Olive oil as needed
$^1/_2$ pound baby pearl onions, peeled
1 tablespoon granulated sugar
1 cup assorted wild mushrooms
1 tablespoon finely chopped fresh rosemary
$^1/_2$ cup port wine
2 cups veal or beef stock
1 $^1/_2$ cups heavy cream
Salt and black pepper as needed

SCHNITZEL
2 cups all-purpose flour
6 large eggs, beaten
3 cups seasoned bread crumbs
Pinch salt and black pepper
Vegetable oil as needed
Four 4-ounce tenderized veal top round cutlets
4 tablespoons unsalted butter, divided
4 fresh rosemary or parsley sprigs for garnish

1. Prepare the sauce by heating $^1/_4$" olive oil in a large skillet over high heat. Add the pearl onions and sauté until golden brown. Quickly add the sugar and stir until the sugar starts to lightly brown. Quickly add the mushrooms and sauté and stir while adding the rosemary.

2. Add the wine and reduce by one-half. Add the stock and reduce by one-half. Add the cream and reduce by one-half. Taste the sauce and add a touch of salt and black pepper if needed. Remove from the heat and keep warm.

3. Preheat the oven to 350° F. Prepare the schnitzel by setting up a breading station by placing the flour, eggs, and bread crumbs in separate bowls. Add the salt and black pepper to the flour and mix well.

4. In a large ovenproof skillet, heat $\frac{1}{4}$" vegetable oil over medium heat.

5. Dredge each cutlet in the flour, then in the egg mixture, and finally in the bread crumbs, pressing and coating each side.

6. Place only 2 cutlets in the hot oil and lightly brown each side. Remove the cutlets and keep warm. Place the remaining cutlets in the pan and lightly brown each side. Remove the pan from the heat and carefully drain the oil. Replace all of the cutlets to the pan and place 1 tablespoon of the butter on each cutlet. Place the pan in the oven and bake for 5 minutes, or until the cutlets are crispy, brown, and puffy.

7. Reheat the mushroom sauce. Remove the skillet from the oven.

8. If serving the schnitzel with the home fries, place each cutlet at an angle on a bed of the home fries. Generously spoon the mushroom sauce over each cutlet and garnish with 1 rosemary or parsley sprig. Serves 4.

JANE McWHORTER

Holy Smoky German Skillet Home Fries

With any hearty meat dish, a good sturdy side dish is vital for the success of the meal. This potato extravaganza is created with the combined flavors of the smoky peppered bacon, the tangy, smoked Colby cheese, and the pungent sweet-and-sour of the sugar and vinegar. Finished in the oven in a heavy cast-iron skillet, you can only wonder — Christmas dreams do come true!

6 Idaho potatoes, unpeeled
Salt as needed
Olive oil as needed
1 cup diced pepper-smoked bacon*
¹/₂ cup diced onions
¹/₄ cup red wine vinegar
2 tablespoons granulated sugar
¹/₂ cup finely chopped fresh parsley
¹/₂ tablespoon garlic powder
¹/₂ tablespoon onion powder
2 teaspoons salt
2 teaspoons black pepper
6 ounces shredded hickory-smoked Colby cheese*

1. In a medium saucepan, place the potatoes, pinch of salt, and enough water to cover over high heat. Bring to a simmering boil and simmer for 20 minutes, or until the potatoes slowly slide off a fork when pierced and lifted.

2. Once cooked, remove the potatoes from the pan and place on a cutting board. Carefully peel and push off the skin of the potatoes while hot. Discard the skin. Slice the potatoes ¹/₂" thick. Set aside and keep warm.

3. Preheat the oven to 375° F. In a large, heavy cast-iron skillet, heat ¹/₄" olive oil over high heat. Add the bacon and fry until almost crisp. Quickly add the onions and sauté until lightly browned.

4. Add the vinegar and sugar and boil until the sugar has dissolved. Quickly add the reserved sliced potatoes, parsley, garlic powder, onion powder, salt, and black pepper. Carefully fold the ingredients together, avoiding mashing the potatoes.

5. Carefully fold in half of the cheese. Once incorporated, sprinkle the remaining cheese on top of the potatoes "pizza style."

6. Place the skillet in the oven and bake for 8–10 minutes, or until the cheese has melted and is lightly browned. Remove from the oven and serve in the skillet on the table. Dig in! Serves 4–6.

* *See Food Sources in the Appendix.*

Wintergreen Spinach Sauté with Pear Tomatoes & Apple Wood Bacon

Celebrate the red and green colors of the winter holidays with this simple but delicious side dish. Pear tomatoes, a new hybrid of the cherry tomato, are colorful and crunchy. It is important that this dish be prepared and served promptly. Fresh spinach wilts quickly and turns bitter when heated too long.

One 10-ounce bag fresh spinach leaves, trimmed
Olive oil as needed
8 ounces apple wood-smoked bacon*, diced 1/4"
2 garlic cloves, thinly sliced
1/2 pint pear tomatoes, halved lengthwise
Pinch salt and black pepper
1 tablespoon unsalted butter

1. In cold water, wash the spinach, sorting out the bad leaves. Dry the spinach by shaking.

2. In a large pot of simmering water, drop in the spinach and cook for 2 minutes or until wilted. Drain and set aside the spinach.

3. In a large skillet, heat 1/4" olive oil over high heat. Add the bacon and fry until almost crisp. Quickly add the garlic and sauté for 2 minutes or until lightly browned. Add the tomatoes and reserved spinach. Sprinkle with the salt and black pepper as needed. Toss in the butter, heat, and mix well. Serve immediately! Serves 6.

* See Food Sources in the Appendix.

Acorn Squash Fruit Ring

Dried fruits are another staple of a typical Adirondack winter pantry — easy to store, nutritious to eat. This simple, colorful side dish will bring cheers to the Christmas table with its presentation, taste, and satisfying flavors. If the 4-inch cake ring mold is unavailable, you can duplicate it by removing the top and bottom lids of a 6-ounce tuna fish can. Be sure to wash and dry the inner and outer rim of the can after removing the lids. (Also remove the tuna . . . ha ha!)

4 teaspoons dried currants
2 tablespoons sun-dried cranberries
1 quart water
4 cups 1/2" diced acorn squash
Vegetable oil as needed
4 teaspoons finely diced dried apricots
1/4 cup honey
1/2 teaspoon ground cinnamon
Salt and black pepper to taste
1/2 cup unsalted butter

1. In a small bowl, soak the currants and cranberries in hot water for 5 minutes. Drain, squeeze out excess water, and set aside.

2. In a large saucepan, bring the 1 quart water to a boil. Add the squash and cook for 5 minutes or until almost tender. Drain and set aside the squash.

3. In a large skillet, heat 1/4" vegetable oil over high heat. Add the reserved squash and sauté until lightly browned. Add the reserved currants and cranberries, apricots, honey, and cinnamon and sauté for 2 minutes. Add the salt and black pepper. Carefully fold in the butter until melted and incorporated.

4. Place each of four lightly greased 4" cake ring molds on small plates. Divide the mixture among the four molds and press down firmly until filled and packed. Carefully remove the rings, leaving a compact mold of squash, resembling a little cake. Serve warm. Serves 4.

High Peaks Chambord & Blackberry Mousse

Whip this irresistible mousse together to its highest peak, and you'll have a declared winner on hand!

1 pint fresh blackberries
¹/₄ cup granulated sugar
¹/₄ cup Chambord liqueur
3 egg whites
5 tablespoons confectioners' sugar
2 cups heavy whipping cream
¹/₂ teaspoon vanilla extract
Chambord liqueur for garnish
¹/₂ pint fresh blackberries for garnish
Fresh mint leaves for garnish

1. In a medium bowl, combine the 1 pint blackberries, granulated sugar, and the ¹/₄ cup liqueur and mix well. Let the berries macerate (steep) for 1 hour to develop flavor.

2. In a cold copper or aluminum bowl, whip the egg whites until stiff peaks form, gradually adding 2 tablespoons of the confectioners' sugar in the final stages. Keep cold.

3. In a separate bowl, whip the heavy cream with the vanilla extract until stiff peaks form, adding the remaining confectioners' sugar in the final stages.

4. In a large bowl, using a rubber spatula, gently fold together the stiff egg whites and the whipped cream. (Do not whip.)

5. Fold in the steeped blackberry mixture until incorporated. Spoon the mousse into tall champagne glasses. Drizzle a little of the liqueur over the top. Garnish with the ¹/₂ pint blackberries and mint sprigs. Serves 10–12.

ADIRONDACK NEW YEAR'S EVE OPEN HOUSE

Mount Marcy Swedish Bites with Gooseberry Sauce

A successful hors d'oeuvre or cocktail snack is always a simple crowd-pleasing dish enhanced with a new twist. These delicious mini Swedish meatballs with a creamy, tangy gooseberry sauce are perfect for your New Year's Eve open house, and perhaps the talk of the following New Year's Day brunch. Gooseberries, a sweet and tangy light green berry, are available at most markets. Along with lingonberries and black currants, they are a Nordic favorite and part of a typical Adirondack sweet tooth pantry, due to the influence of Scandinavian immigrants who are experts in the art of preserving fruits and berries.

Olive oil as needed
1 medium carrot, finely diced
1 celery stalk, finely diced
$^1/_2$ medium onion, finely diced
$^1/_2$ teaspoon curry powder
3 $^1/_2$ pounds ground meat combo mix (beef, veal, pork)
$^1/_2$ teaspoon ground cloves
1 teaspoon white pepper
2 tablespoons A-1 sauce
$^1/_2$ cup drained sauerkraut
3 tablespoons lingonberry preserves
6 large eggs, beaten
2 $^1/_2$ cups seasoned bread crumbs
1 recipe Gooseberry Sauce (see next page)

1. Preheat the oven to 350º F. In a small skillet, heat $^1/_4$" olive oil over high heat. Add the carrot, celery, onion, and curry powder and sauté until the onion is transparent. Set aside and let cool.

2. In a large mixing bowl, combine the meat mix, cloves, white pepper, A-1 sauce, sauerkraut, lingonberry preserves, eggs, and bread crumbs and mix well. Add the cooled carrot mixture and mix well. Cover with aluminum foil and place the bowl in the refrigerator.

3. Prepare the Gooseberry Sauce.

4. Remove the mixture from the refrigerator and roll and form little meatballs the size of cherry tomatoes. Place on greased 1" deep baking sheets and bake in the oven for 12–15 minutes. Remove from the oven and drain the grease.

5. Place the meatballs in a serving bowl and cover with the gooseberry sauce or serve the sauce in a separate bowl and dip the meatballs with a toothpick or small cocktail fork. Makes about 100 minimeatballs.

GOOSEBERRY SAUCE

2 shallots, minced
1 bay leaf
$^1/_2$ cup Triple Sec liqueur
$^1/_2$ quart beef stock or bouillon
$^1/_2$ quart chicken stock or bouillon
$^1/_2$ cup gooseberry preserves
1 $^1/_2$ tablespoons lingonberry preserves
$^1/_8$ teaspoon ground cloves
$^1/_8$ teaspoon white pepper
1 cup heavy cream
Roux as needed*

1. In a medium saucepan over medium heat, combine the shallots, bay leaf, and liqueur and reduce by one-half. Add the beef and chicken stocks and bring to a simmering boil.

2. Add the gooseberry and lingonberry preserves, cloves, and white pepper and return to a simmer. Cook for 5 minutes. Add the cream and return to a simmer. Add enough roux (or cornstarch) to create desired thickness, enough to coat the meatballs. Keep warm.

* See Cooking Basics in the Appendix.

Pepper-Smoked Salmon & Trout Mini-Reubens

If you want to try a new twist on smoked salmon, many ingredients for adding flavor are available by mail order or in specialty stores. How about tequila-cured, pastrami-cured, orange peel-cured, or pepper-smoked salmon, used in this tasty mini-hors d'oeuvre.

4 ounces smoked trout, skinless and boneless
4 ounces cream cheese at room temperature
3 tablespoons fresh lemon juice
2 teaspoons chopped fresh chives
20 slices pumpernickel cocktail bread (2" x 2" squares)
8 ounces pepper-smoked salmon*, sliced
Drained sauerkraut as needed
5 slices Swiss Emmenthaler cheese, cut into 20 squares
Ground paprika as needed
Sour cream for garnish
Fresh chive leaves for garnish

1. Place the trout in a food processor bowl and break it up with your fingers. Add the cream cheese and process until blended and smooth. Add the lemon juice and chives and process quickly one more time to mix. With a rubber spatula, scrape the sides of the processor bowl and process one more short round.

2. With a 2 ¹/₂" round cookie cutter, cut 20 rounds from the pumpernickel. Spread each round with the trout mixture, equally divided, and place on a baking sheet. Place a little piece of the smoked salmon atop the trout mixture. Top the salmon with a little sauerkraut and 1 square of cheese.

3. Sprinkle or dust the mini-Reubens with the paprika. Place them under a hot broiler and melt the cheese. Remove from the broiler and garnish with the sour cream and chive leaves. Serve immediately. Makes 20 mini-Reubens.

* See Food Sources in the Appendix.

SARANAC ICE CASTLE WARM-UP DELIGHTS

Winter Carnival Spiced Hot Chocolate

Nothing is more rewarding than sipping a mug of hot chocolate while braving the elements on a cold February day at the Winter Carnival. If you are willing to invest some time, try this wonderfully rich hot-chocolate concoction, flavored with cloves, cinnamon, vanilla, and tangerine! It is important to let the spices steep just under a simmer to develop flavor.

10 whole cloves
1 tangerine
$^1/_2$ gallon whole milk
1 cup heavy cream
2 cinnamon sticks
8 ounces semisweet chocolate
$^1/_2$ teaspoon vanilla extract
$^2/_3$ cup granulated sugar
Fresh whipped cream for topping
Ground cinnamon for topping

1. Press the sharp stems of the cloves into the tangerine (spiking). In a large pot, combine the spiked tangerine, milk, cream, and cinnamon sticks. Bring the mixture to a simmering boil. Reduce the heat and let the milk remain heated just under a simmer. Steep the milk mixture for 1 hour over the heat. (Do not allow the milk to reduce.)

2. Meanwhile, melt the chocolate by shaving it with a heavy knife into a medium metal bowl. Place the bowl over a pot of simmering water and melt the chocolate while stirring with a rubber spatula. Once melted, keep the chocolate warm.

3. After the milk mixture has steeped for 1 hour, remove the spiked tangerine and cinnamon sticks and discard. Add the vanilla and sugar and stir rapidly until the sugar is dissolved.

4. Using a small ladle, add the milk mixture, a little at a time, to the bowl of warm chocolate, thinning it. Once thin and liquid, slowly pour the chocolate mixture into the pot with the remaining milk mixture, whisking constantly.

5. Reheat the chocolate milk (do not boil). Serve immediately, topped with the whipped cream and a sprinkle of the cinnamon, or pour into a Thermos bottle and take to the Winter Carnival. Makes 6 mugs.

Cross-Country-Style Sparerib & Lentil Soup

Lentils are high in iron and vitamins A and B, perfect for refueling the body during cold Adirondack winter sports and carnival activities. With tender "off the bone" cooked sparerib meat and vegetables, this soup is a powerhouse and easily "outruns" any nutrition bar or drink!

SPARERIBS

Vegetable oil as needed

3 pounds meaty country-style pork spareribs

Salt and black pepper as needed

1 medium onion, diced $1/4$"

3 celery stalks, diced $1/4$"

1 gallon water

2 bay leaves

$1/8$ teaspoon ground cloves

SOUP

One 16-ounce bag dried brown lentils

1 medium carrot, diced $1/4$"

1 cup finely diced leeks

2 Idaho potatoes, peeled and diced $1/4$"

2 cups canned crushed tomatoes

2 garlic cloves, finely chopped

1 cup drained sauerkraut

$1/8$ teaspoon ground cumin

2 teaspoons garlic powder

2 teaspoons onion powder

$1/2$ teaspoon black pepper

$1/2$ teaspoon dried thyme

3 tablespoons granulated sugar

$1/4$ cup red wine vinegar

2 quarts chicken stock or bouillon

$1/4$ cup finely chopped fresh parsley

3 tablespoons unsalted butter

Salt to taste

1. Prepare the spareribs by heating $1/4$" vegetable oil in a large pot over high heat. Add the spareribs and sprinkle with the salt and black pepper. Brown the ribs on all sides.

2. Add the onion and celery and sauté with the ribs until lightly browned. Drain excess oil and add the water, bay leaves, and cloves. Bring to a simmering boil and simmer for 2 hours, or until the ribs are extremely tender and falling off the bone.

3. Remove the ribs from the pot and let cool. Remove the liquid from the pot and set aside.

4. Remove the meat from the cooled ribs. Chop or finely shred the meat and set aside.

5. Prepare the soup by combining 5 cups of the reserved liquid, reserved rib meat, lentils, carrot, leeks, potatoes, tomatoes, garlic, sauerkraut, cumin, garlic powder, onion powder, black pepper, thyme, sugar, vinegar, and stock in a large heavy soup pot and mix well.

6. Bring to a simmering boil and simmer for 45 minutes, or until the lentils are soft and the soup is thick. Add the parsley and carefully whisk in the butter. Add the salt if needed. If soup is too thick, thin it with more chicken stock. Serves 6–8.

Pan-Seared Swedish Potato Sausage with Vodka & Lingonberry Glaze

At Oscar's Adirondack Mountain Smokehouse in Warrensburg, New York, you will find the reach-in refrigerator packed with all kinds of sausages. A truly unique one is the Swedish-style potato sausage, a typical European-inspired sausage, consisting of beef, pork, spices, onion, and potatoes. Pan-seared and served with a vodka and tart lingonberry glaze, it is the way to celebrate the end of another day of Winter Carnival in Winter Wonderland! Serve with Great Camp Yukon Gold Smash with Wilted Kale & Crispy Prosciutto (see recipe on page 75).

Olive oil as needed
6–8 Swedish-style potato sausages*, preboiled or cooked
¹/₂ cup vodka
2 shallots, minced
1 ¹/₂ teaspoons finely chopped fresh rosemary
¹/₄ cup lingonberry preserves
2 tablespoons unsalted butter

1. In a large heavy skillet, heat ¹/₄" olive oil over high heat. Add the sausages and sear and brown on both sides. Carefully drain the oil and return the pan with the sausages to the heat. Add the vodka, shallots, and rosemary and flambé or cook over medium heat until the alcohol is reduced.

2. Remove the sausages from the pan and keep warm on a platter. Add the lingonberry preserves and butter to the pan and whisk until smooth. Glaze the sausages right before serving. Serves 6–8.

* *See Food Sources in the Appendix.*

Great Camp Yukon Gold Smash with Wilted Kale & Crispy Prosciutto

Kale is one of the hardiest members of the cabbage family. Being able to withstand temperatures as low as 5° F, it has always been a popular winter vegetable in European countries, such as Germany, Holland, and Scandinavia. Chefs in the United States are starting to use kale as the Europeans have for years. It has been promoted from a garnishing green to a great flavor maker in stews, soups, and potato dishes. High in vitamins and pungent in flavor, it is a perfect, hearty ingredient. Just imagine a steaming plate of this concoction on the dinner table of a Great Camp, while the cold February winds are shaking the rafters!

MASH
5 pounds Yukon Gold potatoes, peeled and quartered
$1/_2$ teaspoon salt
1 stick unsalted butter, cut into pieces
$1/_3$ cup heavy cream
Salt and black pepper to taste

KALE
3 pounds fresh kale
Pinch salt
Olive oil as needed
6 garlic cloves, thinly sliced
4 ounces prosciutto, thinly sliced and finely chopped
$1/_2$ teaspoon black pepper
4 tablespoons unsalted butter

1. Prepare the mash by covering the potatoes with water in a medium pot. Add the salt. Bring to a simmering boil and boil for 15 minutes, or until the potatoes are fork tender.

2. Drain the water from the pot. Turn off the heat, leaving the potatoes in the pot. Add the butter pieces. Using a hand masher, mash the potatoes until smooth. Add the cream, salt, and black pepper and again mash until smooth. Keep the mashed potatoes warm.

3. Prepare the kale by adding the kale and salt to boiling water in a large saucepan. Boil for 5 minutes or until tender but still bright green (boiling the kale removes its bitterness). Drain the pan and chop the kale into small pieces. Set aside.

4. In a large sauté pan, heat $1/_4$" olive oil over medium heat. Add the garlic and lightly brown. Quickly add the prosciutto and fry until almost crumbly. Add the reserved kale and black pepper and sauté until hot. Add the butter and mix well.

5. Place the mashed potatoes in the center of a serving platter or bowl and surround with the kale. This recipe is also excellent with pork and game dishes. Serves 6–8.

Saranac Powder Snow Apple Beignets

A common feature at most Winter Carnivals, especially on Lake Saranac, is the presence of a fried dough wagon. A flour and egg-based dough is deep-fried and served with confectioners' sugar — a quick, hot, and filling treat, especially liked by children. The apple beignets are marinated apple slices, coated in a special batter and deep-fried crispy. A great sweet treat for the ski or snowmobile trail, or perhaps at an open fire with a cup of hot steaming coffee or cocoa!

$^1/_4$ cup applejack brandy
$^1/_3$ cup granulated sugar
3 Granny Smith apples, peeled, cored, and cut into $^1/_2$" rings
2 cups all-purpose flour
2 large eggs
2 tablespoons corn oil
$^1/_2$ cup pilsner beer
1 teaspoon Grade A Adirondack maple syrup
$^1/_8$ teaspoon ground cinnamon
$^1/_4$ teaspoon salt
3 egg whites
Peanut oil as needed
All-purpose flour as needed
Confectioners' sugar as needed

1. In a small plastic bowl, mix together the brandy and sugar. Place the apple rings in a medium bowl. Drizzle the brandy mixture over the apples and let the apples macerate (steep) for 1 hour.

2. In a another medium bowl, place the 2 cups flour and set aside. In a small bowl, whisk together the eggs, corn oil, beer, syrup, cinnamon, and salt. Slowly pour the egg mixture into the flour and stir until smooth. Cover the bowl with plastic wrap and refrigerate for 1 hour.

3. In a cold copper or aluminum bowl, whisk the egg whites until stiff peaks form. Remove the batter from the refrigerator. With a rubber spatula, carefully fold the egg whites into the batter until combined. Set aside.

4. In a fryer or heavy pot, heat 6 cups peanut oil to 300º–325º F. Dust the steeped apple rings with a little flour and dip into the prepared batter, making sure the apple rings are thoroughly coated. Carefully drop the rings into the hot oil and fry until golden brown.

5. Place the fried beignets on paper towels to drain. Transfer the beignets to a serving dish and dust generously with confectioners' sugar. Makes 10–12 beignets.

Maple BBQ Duck Confit with Wild Rice-Currant Pancakes.

Cranberry Lake Bean & Crawfish Salad.

Farmers' Market Grilled Chicken with Pumpkin Oil-Infused Vegetable Bouquet.

Thendara Pepper-Crusted Filet with Cognac-Merlot Sauce & Scattered Pumpkin Seeds.

*Whiteface Rainbow Trout Napoleon with Idaho Flapjacks & Mustard,
Cream & Tomato Concasse.*

Honey & Thyme Grilled Venison Chops with Foliage Season Salsa.

Harvest Wine Dinner — Wild Mushroom & Goat Cheese Beggars Purse.

Adirondack marshes and towering pines, Wilmington, New York.

ARMAND C. VANDERSTIGCHEL

Harvest Wine Dinner — Trout Mousse.

Harvest Wine Dinner — Lobster & Scallop Corn Crêpe with Vanilla Bean Sauce.

Harvest Wine Dinner — Roasted Venison Chop with Pumpkin & Black Truffle Salpicon.

Harvest Wine Dinner — Cheese Course.

Adirondack summer fun: a good book and an Adirondack chair at Camp Sagamore in Raquette Lake, New York.

Harvest Wine Dinner — Chocolate Tower.

Wintergreen Spinach Sauté with Pear Tomatoes & Apple Wood Bacon.

Tupper Lake Ski Lodge Gourmet Pea Soup.

Wild Greens au Vinaigrette Marmalade with Pan-Seared Herbed Hudson Valley Camembert Cheese.

Weihnacht Christmas Schnitzel with Holy Smoky German Skillet Home Fries.

ADIRONDACK SPRING FEVER

The Gore Mountain ski slope manager stares in disbelief from his office window. The snow is slowly disappearing, leaving bare patches that make the slopes look like a free-form quilt. The weather is warming, the Sun King is retaking his vacated throne, and the birds are reclaiming their nests in droves. Confused waterfowl have found their habitats expanded from the melting snow to flooded land and marshes near the bases of mountains. Mountain springs, brooks, and rivers are regenerated after months of suspended animation in a semi-frozen state. Sport fishermen trade their ice-fishing gear for a fly rod or a spin reel, looking to catch a dozen or so fresh trout, or perhaps a landlocked salmon, a pickerel, or a reluctant bullhead.

The maple syrup-foraging season is ending — gone are the cold nights and warm days that were perfect for tapping the clear, precious liquid. The sap has been boiled down to an amber shade to make its final journey to gift shops and to the breakfast tables of cozy bed-and-breakfasts throughout the region. The last syrup of the season is carefully funneled into bottles and jugs of many sizes and shapes, ready for distribution as a proud Adirondack product of true distinction.

In the kitchens of restaurants, hotels, lodges, and B&Bs, chefs and cooks scroll through their menus, shouting over the disruptive monotone of kitchen exhaust fans as they phone local purveyors in search of the finest ingredients. Because the new breed of artisan food producers and chef-sensitive farmers has raised the quality of food to an all-time high, chefs can rely on the availability of local ingredients to set the culinary direction for the season ahead.

Along the roads throughout the region, farm stands, markets, restaurants, and seasonal lodging facilities are preparing to open shop, gearing up for the busy season and wondering how many visitors this year will bring. This economic infusion is vital for the Adirondack Park's inhabitants, servicing and dependent upon tourism. Throughout metropolitan areas of the Northeast, television and radio commercials, in conjunction with print ads, are reminding millions not to overlook the majestic beauty of the Adirondacks, located within reasonable driving distance. Numerous highway rest stops are restocking their shelves with Adirondack-related paraphernalia and brochures showing what to do and where to do it — true meccas for first-timers needing guidance on their first road trip to vacation wonderland.

Spring in the Adirondacks is a moment of timeless peace, because with the arrival of summer, there is an explosion of movement reaching every outpost. So come and enjoy the special springtime beauty of the Adirondacks.

Spring Onion Potato Focàccia

Watch out for those scallionlike onions with large bulbs and green stalks. They are excellent as appetizers, sautéed and combined with this moist potato-based focàccia bread. Besides being great for sandwiches, you can just tear off a piece and dip it into some virgin olive oil.

4 all-purpose potatoes, washed
2 packages active dry yeast
2 tablespoons granulated sugar
8 cups all-purpose flour
4 teaspoons salt
2 tablespoons virgin olive oil
$^1/_4$ cup finely chopped fresh cilantro
Olive oil as needed
2 spring onions (bulb and stem), thinly sliced, or 2 medium yellow onions, thinly sliced
Salt and black pepper as needed

1. In a medium pot, place the potatoes in 4 cups boiling water to cover and cook until tender. Remove the potatoes from the pot and set aside the cooking water. Peel the skin off the potatoes and mash while hot.

2. In a medium bowl, place 3 cups of the reserved cooking water. When the water is warm (105º–110ºF), add the yeast and 1 tablespoon of the sugar. Let the yeast activate for about 10 minutes.

3. In a large bowl, combine the mashed potatoes, remaining sugar, flour, salt, yeast water, the 2 tablespoons olive oil, and cilantro and mix until blended. Set aside the dough.

4. In a large skillet, heat $^1/_4$" olive oil over high heat. Add the onions and sauté until wilted, but not browned. Add a pinch of salt and black pepper. Remove the onions and place in a small bowl. Carefully fold half of the onion mixture into the dough.

5. Cover the large bowl with a cloth and let the dough rise in a warm spot until doubled in size, about 1 hour.

6. Preheat the oven to 325º F. Brush a 12" x 17" baking pan with olive oil. Flour your hands and place the dough in the pan. Push down the dough slightly to fill the pan and brush the top of the dough with olive oil.

7. Sprinkle the remaining onion mixture evenly over the dough, pressing it in slightly. Lightly sprinkle with salt and black pepper and bake for 30–40 minutes or until golden brown. Makes 1 loaf.

Champagne-Steamed Adirondack Bound Blue Mussels with Maple-Lemon Cream Broth

By the truckload, beautiful dark blue mussels are transported west from the eastern Atlantic shore to the North Country, where chefs eagerly prepare them in many different ways, including this great appetizer. Mussels need to be prepared immediately, the fresher the better. To prepare mussels for cooking, place them in water and remove the floating shells. Brush the shells clean and debeard by removing the beard sticking out of the side of the shell with pliers. Discard any of the mussels that are very light or those that stay open after lightly tapping them. If purchasing farm-raised mussels or Prince Edward Isle mussels, you most likely will not have to debeard any. If not used immediately, place the mussels in a bowl without water and cover with a damp towel.

2 pounds Atlantic Blue mussels, cleaned and debearded
1 shallot, minced
1/4 teaspoon black pepper
1 cup Champagne
1 cup warm heavy cream
Juice of 1/2 lemon
1 tablespoon Grade A Adirondack maple syrup
1/2 cup finely chopped fresh watercress
1 tablespoon unsalted butter

1. Heat a 10" heavy skillet over high heat until hot. Have ready a 10" lid to cover.

2. Place the mussels in the hot skillet and sprinkle with the shallot and black pepper. Add the Champagne and cover immediately. Steam the mussels for 2 minutes, or until the shells open.

3. In a small bowl, quickly whisk together the warm cream, lemon juice, and syrup. Add the mixture to the steamed mussels and steam, covered, for 1 minute more.

4. With a slotted spoon, remove the mussels, leaving the broth and cream in the skillet. Divide the mussels into bowls.

5. Reduce the cream broth to half. Quickly whisk in the watercress and butter until smooth. Pour the cream broth equally over the mussels and serve immediately. Serve with crusty bread and don't forget cocktail forks. Makes 2–4 appetizer portions.

Hemlock Green Scallion Crêpes with Asparagus & Chicken Filling drizzled with Rosemary-Infused Hollandaise

You will enjoy this beautiful bright green crêpe stuffed with crispy asparagus, savory chicken, and shiitake mushrooms, complemented by a rosemary reduction–infused hollandaise — a delicious appetizer celebrating the abundance of asparagus in the spring.

Vegetable oil as needed
1 ³/₄ cups water
1 cup finely diced scallions
3 eggs
2 cups all-purpose flour
¹/₂ teaspoon ground coriander
Pinch salt
Olive oil as needed
1 ¹/₂ pounds skinless boneless chicken breasts, cut into thin strips
1 shallot, minced
¹/₂ cup white wine
¹/₄ cup thinly sliced fresh basil
¹/₃ cup finely diced scallions
1 cup thinly sliced shiitake mushrooms
1 ¹/₃ cups diced red bell peppers
1 recipe Rosemary-Infused Hollandaise Sauce (see next page)
24 cooked fresh asparagus spears
8 fresh watercress sprigs for garnish

1. In an 8-inch nonstick skillet, brush vegetable oil over the entire surface. Set aside.

2. In a blender or food processor, combine the water and the 1 cup scallions and blend on high speed until smooth (mixture will be green). Set aside.

3. In a medium bowl, beat the eggs until frothy. Add the reserved scallion mixture, flour, coriander, and salt and whisk until smooth. (The mixture should have the consistency of liquid heavy cream.)

4. Heat the reserved greased skillet over medium heat until hot. Place ¹/₄ cup of the batter in the pan and tilt the pan until the batter is spread evenly around the pan. As soon as the crêpe browns slightly around the edges and becomes dry, turn the crêpe onto a plate with wax paper. Repeat the procedure until the batter is used, making 8-10 crêpes. Set aside.

5. In a large skillet, heat ¹/₄" olive oil over high heat. Add the chicken strips and brown until cooked through. Drain as much oil as possible from the pan, then add the shallot and wine. Reduce the wine by half. Add the basil, the ¹/₃ cup scallions, mushrooms, and ¹/₃ cup of the bell peppers and sauté for 3 minutes. Remove from the heat and set aside.

6. Prepare the Rosemary-Infused Hollandaise Sauce.

7. Place 1 crêpe in the center of a plate. Place 3 asparagus spears lengthwise in the center of the crêpe and drizzle on 1 teaspoon hollandaise sauce. Top with 3 tablespoons of the reserved chicken mixture. Drizzle again with 1 teaspoon hollandaise sauce and roll up the crêpe like a cigar.

8. Place the filled crêpe in the center of an appetizer plate and drizzle on 2 tablespoons hollandaise sauce. Garnish with 1 watercress sprig and some of the remaining bell pepper. Repeat the procedure to make 8 crêpes. Serves 8.

ROSEMARY-INFUSED HOLLANDAISE SAUCE

2 tablespoons white wine vinegar
3 tablespoons cold water
$^1/_4$ teaspoon salt
Black pepper to taste
3 large egg yolks
2 sticks unsalted butter, melted
2 tablespoons fresh lemon juice
$^1/_8$ teaspoon cayenne pepper
$^1/_2$ teaspoon finely chopped fresh rosemary
$^1/_4$ teaspoon finely chopped shallots
$^1/_3$ cup white wine

1. In a small saucepan, combine the vinegar, 2 tablespoons of the cold water, salt, and black pepper and bring to a boil. Reduce the mixture to 2 tablespoons. Remove from the heat and add the remaining cold water.

2. Transfer the mixture to a medium aluminum bowl. Whisk in the yolks and place the bowl atop a simmering pot of water. As soon as the yolks thicken, slowly pour the melted butter into the yolks, whisking constantly. Continue to whisk until the sauce thickens and appears frothy. Whisk in the lemon juice and cayenne pepper. Set aside.

3. In a small saucepan, combine the rosemary, shallots, and wine and bring to a boil. Reduce to almost dry. With a rubber spatula, transfer the rosemary reduction to the reserved hollandaise and fold in carefully. Remove from the heat and keep warm.

Asparagus Spring Chowder with Boursin Cream

The Northeastern states are known for their various kinds of chowder – a thick, chunky soup that can be a meal all by itself. How about this one, brimming with crisp asparagus pieces, chunks of potatoes, tender chicken pieces, and sweet corn. The key to good chowder is not overcooking the ingredients!

One 3-pound whole chicken, neck and giblets removed
1 gallon cold water
4 bay leaves
12 black peppercorns
1 recipe Boursin Cream (see next page)
Olive oil as needed
2 medium onions, diced ¹/₂"
4 celery stalks, diced ¹/₂"
4 Idaho potatoes, peeled and cut into ³/₄" cubes
1 ¹/₂ pounds fresh asparagus, cut into 1" pieces (tough stem ends removed)
1 cup fresh or frozen corn kernels
Salt to taste

1. In a large soup pot, combine the whole chicken, cold water, bay leaves, and peppercorns. Bring to a low simmering boil and cook for 1 ¹/₂ hours. Remove the chicken and let cool. Strain the stock and set aside.

2. Remove the meat from the cooked chicken, discarding the skin and bones. Cut the chicken into ¹/₂" pieces (yield about 4 cups). Set aside.

3. Prepare the Boursin Cream.

4. In a large soup pot, heat ¹/₄" olive oil over high heat. Add the onions and celery. When the onions and celery start to sweat, add 2 ¹/₂ quarts of the reserved chicken stock. Add the reserved chicken pieces and potato cubes and simmer for 5 minutes, or until the potatoes are almost tender.

5. Add the asparagus pieces, corn, and salt and simmer for 3 minutes, or until the asparagus is bright green and almost soft.

6. Add the boursin cream, while slowly stirring without breaking up the potatoes, and simmer for 3 minutes. (Soup will have a silky and chunky texture with ingredients intact, not overcooked.) Makes about 12 bowls. Good for guaranteed seconds!

BOURSIN CREAM

1 quart heavy cream
One 5-ounce package boursin cheese
¹/₂ teaspoon black pepper
2 teaspoons onion powder

In a small saucepan, warm the cream (do not boil). Slowly crumble the cheese into the cream, while whisking constantly. Add the black pepper and onion powder and mix well. Remove from the heat and keep warm.

ARMAND C. VANDERSTIGCHEL

Eastern Seaboard Pan-Seared Sea Scallops with Dill Sea Foam & Yellow Turnip-Pear Hash

A red-hot trail from the harbors of Maine and Boston runs west to the Adirondacks, where seafood purveyors deliver fresh seafood daily to customers in and around the region. The sea scallop, available on the east coast from fall to midspring, is delicious when served super fresh, a quality recognized by a sweet smell and a fresh moist sheen. Buy "dry" scallops, not those soaked in water or kept in a tripolyphosphate solution as a preserving method. Also use only fresh dill in the Dill Sea Foam, and don't be surprised how good the marriage of savory turnips and sweet Anjou pear works. Use young turnips; they have a sweeter, milder flavor than the stronger flavored aged ones. The peak season for farm stand fresh turnips is from late fall to early spring.

1 recipe Dill Sea Foam (see below)
1 recipe Yellow Turnip-Pear Hash (see next page)
Pomace olive oil as needed (no virgin olive oil)
Two 6-ounce portions dry sea scallops
Kosher or sea salt as needed
Black pepper as needed
2 fresh dill sprigs for garnish

1. Prepare the Dill Sea Foam.
2. Prepare the Yellow Turnip-Pear Hash.
3. In a medium skillet, heat 1/4" olive oil over high heat. Lightly sprinkle the scallops with the salt and black pepper.
4. Carefully place the scallops in the hot oil and quickly brown for 1 minute on each side. Remove the scallops from the pan and set aside.
5. On 2 dinner plates, divide the hash, placing it in the center. Place the scallops atop the hash. Spoon the foam over the scallops and garnish with the dill sprigs. Serves 2.

DILL SEA FOAM
1 medium shallot, minced
1 cup Champagne
2 tablespoons fresh orange juice
1 1/2 tablespoons finely chopped fresh dill
1/4 teaspoon black pepper
1/2 cup heavy whipping cream
Salt as needed

1. In a small saucepan, combine the shallot, Champagne, and orange juice and bring to a boil over high heat. Reduce the liquid to $^1/_4$ cup. Transfer the liquid to a cup and let cool.

2. In a blender or food processor, combine the cooled reduced liquid, dill, black pepper, and cream. Pulse the ingredients a few times to combine.

3. Proceed to blend full power until the liquid starts to foam. Add the salt to taste. Keep the foam in the blender until ready to use. Quick pulse just before topping the scallops. Makes about 1 cup.

YELLOW TURNIP-PEAR HASH

1 pound young yellow turnips, peeled and diced $^1/_2$"
Salt as needed
Olive oil as needed
1 cup finely chopped red onions
1 Anjou pear, peeled and diced $^1/_4$"
2 tablespoons white vinegar
2 tablespoons granulated sugar
$^1/_4$ teaspoon ground cardamom
1 tablespoon honey
2 tablespoons unsalted butter at room temperature

1. In a small saucepan, place the diced turnips in boiling water with a pinch of salt. Boil for 8–10 minutes or until just tender. With a slotted spoon, remove the turnips from the water and cool quickly in the refrigerator.

2. In a large sauté pan, heat $^1/_4$" olive oil over high heat. Add the onions and pear and sauté until the onions are translucent. Add the vinegar and sugar and reduce until almost syrupy.

3. Add the cooled turnips, cardamom, and honey and sauté until mixed and hot. Carefully stir in the butter and add salt to taste. Keep hot. Makes 2 portions.

Early Spring Venison Gumbo with Baby Pearl Onion Mélange

It's early spring. The last snow of the long, cold Adirondack winter is melting, and it's the right time to use the remaining items left in the once-stocked freezer — so why not a venison gumbo with the last venison meat from the fall hunting season.

GUMBO
Vegetable oil as needed
2 1/2 pounds venison stew meat, cut into 1 1/2" cubes
All-purpose flour as needed
Salt and black pepper as needed
1/4 pound bacon, cut into 1/4" strips
4 celery stalks, diced 1"
1 medium onion, diced 1/2"
2 shallots, minced
1 tablespoon minced garlic
2 tablespoons minced fresh gingerroot
4 bay leaves
1/2 cup Cognac or brandy
1 cup port wine
8 cups beef or veal stock or bouillon
4 cups water
1 teaspoon black pepper
1 teaspoon diced fresh thyme
1 teaspoon onion powder
1 cup 1" diced butternut squash

MÉLANGE
Olive oil as needed
Two 10-ounce bags fresh baby pearl onions, peeled
1 teaspoon granulated sugar
1 teaspoon unsalted butter
1/2 pound button-sized mushrooms, washed and stems removed
8 ounces yellow cherry tomatoes, halved
1 cup diced scallions

1. Prepare the gumbo by heating 1/2" vegetable oil in a large heavy pot or Dutch oven over high heat. In a large bowl, dust the venison with the flour and a pinch of salt and black pepper. Shake

off excess flour, carefully place the meat in the hot oil, and brown the venison on all sides.

2. Add the bacon and fry until almost crispy. Add the celery, onion, shallots, garlic, gingerroot, and bay leaves and sauté until the onion is golden brown.

3. Add the Cognac and reduce by half. Add the wine and reduce by half. Add the stock, water, black pepper, thyme, and onion powder. Bring to a simmering boil and simmer, stirring occasionally and scraping the pan, for 45–60 minutes, or until the meat is almost tender.

4. Add the squash and simmer for 8–10 minutes, or until the squash is just tender. Remove the pot from the heat and keep warm.

5. Prepare the mélange by heating $1/4$" olive oil in a large sauté pan over high heat. Add the pearl onions and sauté until golden brown. Add the sugar and stir until the sugar has caramelized. Add the butter and stir until melted. Fold in the mushrooms, cherry tomatoes, and scallions and mix well.

6. Fold the mélange into the warm gumbo, not breaking the meat and squash. Return the pot to the heat. Bring to a slow simmer and simmer for 5 minutes. Serve hot. Serves 6–8.

ST. PATTY'S DAY ADIRONDACK STYLE

Irish Heritage Pepper-Crusted Corned Beef Brisket

In the late 1800s and early 1900s, many Irish immigrants migrated to the Adirondack region to work in the fast-growing mining towns, tannery hamlets, and logging camps. In honor of their hard work and contribution to the development of the North Country, let's celebrate St. Patty's Day "Adirondack Style" with the following regionally influenced Irish favorites. The trick to a perfect, tender corned beef is to simmer it slowly until it is fork tender. This version is enhanced by adding a delicious crust, giving it an extra zing.

8 pounds corned beef brisket
1/4 cup pickling spice
1 shallot, finely minced
1/2 cup finely minced onions
1/2 cup yellow mustard
1/4 cup Grade A Adirondack maple syrup
1/2 teaspoon prepared grated horseradish
1/4 cup cracked black pepper

1. In a large pot, combine the corned beef and cold water to cover. Add the pickling spice. Bring to a simmering boil and slowly simmer, covered, for 3 hours, or until the meat is fork tender (should slide off a large meat fork easily when pierced and lifted).

2. Remove the corned beef from the pot and place on a carving board. Set aside the cooking broth for the Savoy cabbage recipe (see page 90). Trim off all of the fat and remove the attached pickling spices.

3. Preheat the oven to 350º F. In a small bowl, combine the shallot, onions, mustard, syrup, and horseradish and mix well. With a rubber spatula or brush, spread the glaze over the corned beef. Sprinkle the black pepper equally over the glaze, covering the whole brisket.

4. Place the corned beef in a baking dish. Place in the oven and roast for 15 minutes or until lightly browned.

5. Remove the corned beef from the oven and place on a carving board. Let the meat rest for 10 minutes to settle its juices.

6. Slice the brisket thinly against the grain when carving. Serves 6–8. Erin go bragh!

Redskin Irish Buttermilk Mashed Potatoes with Asparagus & Corned Beef Morsels

While carving the corned beef, what do you do with the end pieces and broken small pieces? Chop them up and add them to this delicious corned beef side dish.

4 pounds red (A-sized) potatoes, unpeeled and quartered (see page 43)
Salt as needed
Olive oil as needed
1 cup finely diced onions
1 cup finely diced cooked corned beef brisket (see recipe on page 88)
1 stick unsalted butter at room temperature
$^1/_2$ cup buttermilk
1 tablespoon sour cream
1 teaspoon prepared grated horseradish
$^1/_2$ teaspoon black pepper
1 pound fresh asparagus, cooked and diced $^1/_2$"

1. In a large pot, combine the potatoes and cold water to cover. Bring to a simmering boil, add $^1/_2$ teaspoon salt, and simmer for 20 minutes, or until the potatoes are fork tender. Turn off the heat. Leave the potatoes in the hot water until needed.

2. In a medium skillet, heat $^1/_4$" olive oil over high heat. Add the onions and corned beef and sauté until lightly browned. Set aside.

3. Carefully drain the water from the pot. Leaving the potatoes in the pot, add the butter, buttermilk, sour cream, horseradish, black pepper, and salt to taste. With a potato masher, mash the potatoes until smooth.

4. With a rubber spatula, add the reserved onions and corned beef mixture and asparagus. Carefully fold in and mix (do not overmix). Serve immediately. Serves 6–8.

Braised Spiced Savoy Cabbage with Watercress & Mustard Sauce

The ability to withstand cold weather makes cabbage a perfect vegetable for multiple uses on the Adirondack table. Available throughout the winter months to early spring and high in vitamin C, it is perfect to combat an end-of-winter cold. Savoy cabbage, a crinkly cabbage variety, has an excellent crunchy texture and is a welcome change from the usual green cabbage used on St. Patty's Day.

1 large Savoy cabbage
6 cups strained and skimmed of fat corned beef cooking broth (see recipe on page 88, -step 2.)
1 recipe Watercress & Mustard Sauce (see below)

1. Preheat the oven to 350° F. Remove the outer leaves of the cabbage if dirty and broken. Cut the cabbage into 8 equal wedges, leaving the core attached to prevent the leaves from scattering. Place the wedges in a large baking dish. Pour the cooking broth over the cabbage and cover with aluminum foil.

2. Place in the oven and bake for about 40 minutes. Turn and flip the cabbage after the first 20 minutes to ensure equal heat exposure. Keep the foil tight to create a steam bath.

3. Prepare the Watercress & Mustard Sauce.

4. Once tender, remove the cabbage from the oven. Drizzle the mustard sauce over the cabbage and serve immediately. Serves 6–8.

WATERCRESS & MUSTARD SAUCE
1 cup white wine
1 shallot, minced
2 cups chicken stock or bouillon
1 cup heavy cream
1 teaspoon yellow mustard
1 bunch fresh watercress, finely chopped and stems removed

1. In a medium saucepan, combine the wine and shallot and bring to a simmering boil. Reduce the wine by half. Add the stock and return to a simmering boil. Add the cream and mustard and return to a simmering boil. Add the watercress.

2. Remove the pan from the heat. With a hand blender or in a blender, puree the sauce until green with little specks of watercress.

3. Return the sauce to the heat and bring to a simmering boil. Add a little roux or prepared cornstarch and water to thicken lightly. Remove from the heat and keep warm.

Tannery Hamlet Gourmet Irish Soda Bread

When preparing this new twist on soda bread, be sure to make at least one extra loaf. It will disappear fast.

1 cup whole wheat flour
2 cups unbleached flour
2 teaspoons baking soda
³/₄ cup granulated sugar
1 teaspoon salt
¹/₂ teaspoon dill seeds
¹/₂ stick unsalted butter, cut into small pieces
¹/₂ cup dried black currants or black raisins
¹/₄ cup golden raisins
¹/₄ cup diced dried apricots
1 ¹/₂ cups buttermilk
¹/₄ cup warm honey

1. Preheat the oven to 325° F. In a large mixing bowl, combine the wheat flour, unbleached flour, baking soda, sugar, salt, and dill seeds and mix well.

2. With a pastry cutter, cut the butter into the flour mixture until it resembles a coarse, mealy mixture, distributing the butter evenly to prevent clumps.

3. Make a well in the center of the dry mixture and add the remaining ingredients. With a rubber spatula, fold and mix the ingredients until compact. Flour your hands and place the dough onto a floured board.

4. Knead the dough 2 times, then shape into an 8" diameter ball. Place the dough onto a greased baking sheet. With a knife, cut a shallow X in the top of the loaf and brush with a little buttermilk.

5. Place the loaf in the center of the oven and bake for 30 minutes, or until a wooden toothpick inserted in the center comes out clean. (Adjust the oven temperature if needed.)

6. Remove the bread from the oven and let cool completely. Serve with creamy butter. Makes 1 loaf.

ADIRONDACK EASTER SUNDAY DINNER

Loon Lake Potato-Leek Soup with Crispy Pancetta, Gorgonzola & English Peas

It's late spring, and you are setting up camp or spring cleaning your summer home on pristine Loon Lake. In the distance is the echoing call of the loon, a popular Adirondack lake bird. Why not enjoy all of this beauty with a delicious soup prepared with fresh vegetables from the just re-opened farm stands, along with some meat and cheese from the local meat purveyor. In this recipe, we use fresh English peas, which we remove from the shell. There is a world of difference between these fresh gems and frozen or canned peas. The small amount used in this recipe does not require much shelling time, maybe a fun chore for the kids!

Olive oil as needed
4 ounces pancetta, thinly sliced into strips
4 celery stalks, diced $^1/_4$"
1 large onion, finely chopped
1 pound leeks, washed and finely diced
1 tablespoon finely chopped fresh oregano
1 teaspoon black pepper
$^1/_4$ cup all-purpose flour
3 quarts chicken stock or bouillon
4 bay leaves
1 pound red potatoes, diced $^1/_2$"
1 pound fresh English peas in shell
2 cups heavy cream
4 ounces crumbled Gorgonzola cheese
$^1/_2$ cup finely chopped fresh chives

1. In a large soup pot, heat $^1/_4$" olive oil over high heat. Add the pancetta and fry until crispy. Add the celery and onion and sauté for 3 minutes, or until the vegetables start to sweat. Add half of the leeks and sauté and sweat.

2. Add the oregano, black pepper, and flour. Stir in the flour, while scraping the bottom of the pan for 2 minutes. Add the stock and bay leaves and bring to a simmering boil, stirring constantly.

3. Add the potatoes and cook for 10 minutes, or until the potatoes are almost tender. Add the remaining leeks and simmer for 2 minutes. Add the shelled peas (about 1 cup after shelling) and simmer for 2 minutes. Add the cream and simmer for 2 minutes.

4. Remove the pot from the heat. Carefully stir in the cheese until melted. Mix in the chives. Serve immediately. Makes 10–12 bowls.

Poke-O-Moonshine Baby Beet Salad with Mâche Greens & Goat Cheese Ricotta

Beets have made a tremendous comeback, from unglamorous kitchen staple to a current chef favorite. This is due in part to the wide variety of beets now farmed. The baby beets used in this recipe come in different varieties and colors, such as pink, white, striped, and gold, and are combined with mâche (field greens) and goat cheese ricotta from artisan cheese producers Nettle Mettle Goat Cheese Farm in Thurman, New York.

1/3 cup walnut oil
1 tablespoon white vinegar
2 teaspoons warm honey
1 teaspoon Grade A Adirondack maple syrup
Finely grated peel of 1 lemon
2 teaspoons finely chopped fresh tarragon
Salt and black pepper as needed
1/2 pound golden baby beets, stems removed
1/2 pound red baby beets, stems removed
8 cups fresh mâche (field greens) or mesclun, washed
1/2 cup chopped walnuts
*1 pound goat cheese ricotta**

1. In a small mixing bowl, combine the walnut oil, vinegar, honey, syrup, lemon zest, and tarragon and whisk vigorously until smooth. Add the salt and black pepper to taste. Set aside.

2. Bring a medium pot of water to a simmering boil and add all of the beets. Add a little salt and boil for 10 minutes, or until the beets are just tender.

3. With a slotted spoon, remove the beets from the water and place in a bowl of ice water to cool. Once cooled, peel the beets with a paring knife. Trim off the bottom and top and cut the beets in half. Set aside.

4. In a large mixing bowl, combine the reserved beets, mâche, walnuts, and reserved dressing. Toss all of the ingredients until incorporated.

5. Divide the salad mixture among 6 salad plates. Cut the goat cheese into thin equal slices and divide among the plates, placing the cheese on top of the salad. Sprinkle freshly ground black pepper on top of the salad. Serve immediately. Serves 6.

* See Food Sources in the Appendix.

Shallot-Crusted Leg of Lamb with Roasted Cherry Tomato Jus

What would an Adirondack Easter table be without a roasted leg of lamb accompanied by a natural pan jus? In this recipe, a special flavor-inducing crust is applied inside and outside the netted leg of lamb, resulting in a savory, juicy roast. Be prepared to bring in additional chairs for your next Easter gathering . . . the house will be packed!

CRUST
4 whole shallots, quartered
2 teaspoons finely chopped fresh rosemary
2 1/2 tablespoons gooseberry preserve or orange marmalade
2 tablespoons yellow mustard
2 tablespoons mayonnaise
1 teaspoon prepared grated horseradish

ROAST
2 medium carrots, coarsely chopped
1 medium onion, coarsely chopped
4 celery stalks, coarsely chopped
One 7–8-pound boneless leg of lamb, netted and tied
Kosher salt and black pepper as needed
4 cups white zinfandel wine
2 quarts water
2 bay leaves

SAUCE
1 pint cherry tomatoes, halved
2 red Bermuda onions, thinly sliced
1/4 cup virgin olive oil
Kosher salt and black pepper as needed
1 teaspoon finely chopped fresh rosemary
2 teaspoons balsamic vinegar
Cornstarch as needed
2 sticks unsalted butter, cut into wedges

1. Preheat the oven to 325° F. Prepare the crust by placing the shallots, rosemary, gooseberry preserve, mustard, mayonnaise, and horseradish in a large blender or food processor. Pulse a few times to incorporate the mixture, then turn the blender on high until the mixture is smooth. With a rubber spatula, remove the mixture and place in a bowl. Set aside.

2. Prepare the roast by equally dividing the carrots, onion, and celery in a large roasting pan. Center the lamb roast atop the vegetables.

3. Using a rubber spatula, spread half of the reserved crust mixture inside and outside of the lamb, by pushing the netting aside. Set aside the remaining crust mixture.

4. Sprinkle the lamb with the kosher salt and black pepper. Place in the center of the oven and roast for 1 hour.

5. Deglaze the lamb with the wine. Continue roasting the lamb for 15 minutes more to reduce the wine.

6. Add the 2 quarts water and bay leaves. Increase the temperature to 350º, cover the roast tightly with aluminum foil, and roast for 1 hour.

7. Remove the roast from the oven and discard the foil. Let the lamb cool for 10 minutes. Remove the net carefully and apply the reserved remaining crust mixture. Increase the temperature to 400º, sprinkle again with the kosher salt and black pepper, and roast, uncovered, for 15 minutes, or until the crust is golden brown and the internal temperature reaches 125º–130º.

8. Remove the lamb from the oven and place on a carving board to cool and rest. Keep the oven temperature at 400º.

9. Scrape the bottom of the roasting pan to release the pan flavors. Strain the pan juices. Once the juices settle, skim off the top layer of fat. Set aside 6 cups of the strained pan juices. If you fall short, add additional beef bouillon as a substitute.

10. Prepare the sauce by combining the tomatoes, onions, and olive oil in a small mixing bowl. Place the mixture on a small, rimmed baking sheet, sprinkle with kosher salt, and roast for 10 minutes, or until the tomatoes and onions are lightly browned and wilted. Drain off the oil and set aside the tomato mixture.

11. In a large saucepan, bring the reserved 6 cups strained pan juices to a simmering boil. Add the rosemary, balsamic vinegar, kosher salt, and black pepper to taste and simmer for 3 minutes. Add a prepared cornstarch mixture (water mixed with cornstarch) to the sauce, as needed, just enough to coat the back of a spoon. Turn off the heat.

12. Quickly whisk in the butter until smoothly incorporated. Add the reserved tomato mixture without breaking up the tomatoes. Return the pan to the heat and slowly simmer for 2 minutes.

13. Cut the lamb with a sharp carving knife into thin slices. Serve with the roasted tomato jus. Serves 8–10.

Great Range Pan-Seared Tournedo of Beef with Oyster Mushroom Ragout

Beautiful fan-shaped oyster mushrooms grow cultivated, as well as in the wild, clinging to old tree trunks in clusters. Their meaty texture and slightly peppery flavor make them perfect in stews or ragouts. This thick mushroom ragout is also perfect with pork or chicken dishes. A tournedo is a beefsteak cut from the tenderloin and measures $3/4$"–1" thick and 2"–2 $1/2$" in diameter. They are quick and easy to pan sear.

Vegetable oil as needed
Six 5-ounce beef fillets
Salt and black pepper as needed
1 pound fresh oyster mushrooms, cleaned
Olive oil as needed
2 shallots, minced
1 cup cooked fresh corn kernels
1 cup sparkling apple cider
1 cup heavy cream
$1/2$ teaspoon finely chopped fresh rosemary
1 medium red bell pepper, seeded, deveined, and cut into 4" long thin strips
$1/4$ cup finely chopped fresh chives
Fresh rosemary sprigs for garnish
Fresh chive leaves for garnish

1. In a large heavy skillet, heat $1/4$" vegetable oil over high heat to almost a light haze. Season both sides of the fillets with the salt and black pepper. Carefully place the fillets in the hot oil and sear both sides until browned (2 minutes for rare, 4 minutes for well done). Remove from the heat and let the meat rest for 5 minutes.

2. Remove the bottom roots of the mushrooms. Cut the mushrooms into 2" pieces and set aside.

3. In a large skillet, heat $1/4$" olive oil over high heat. Add the shallots and sauté until soft. Add the reserved mushrooms and sauté until soft. Add the corn and heat through.

4. Add the cider and reduce to one-fourth. Add the cream and the $1/2$ teaspoon rosemary. Cook down to thicken and season with the salt and black pepper. Add the bell pepper and heat through. Add the $1/4$ cup chives and remove from the heat.

5. Place the tournedos on a platter and spoon the mushroom ragout over the top. Garnish the platter with the rosemary sprigs and chive leaves. Serves 6.

St. Regis River Potato Canoes in Lemon & Herb Dressing

These fabulous canoe-shaped potato wedges are truly delicious with any roasted meat. You might turn your back on mashed potatoes after you've tried these "canoes."

7 Idaho potatoes, peeled
1 ³/₄ cups pomace olive oil
Juice of 2 lemons
1 tablespoon finely chopped fresh oregano
1 tablespoon finely chopped fresh rosemary
1 tablespoon finely chopped fresh thyme
1 tablespoon finely chopped fresh sage
1 shallot, cut into quarters
1 teaspoon garlic powder
1 teaspoon black pepper
1 teaspoon dried tarragon
1 teaspoon salt

1. Cut each potato lengthwise into 4 canoelike wedges. Place in a bowl of water.

2. In a large blender or food processor, combine the olive oil, lemon juice, oregano, rosemary, thyme, sage, shallot, garlic powder, black pepper, tarragon, and salt. Turn the blender on high and puree and emulsify all of the ingredients. Set aside.

3. Remove the potatoes from the water and pat dry with a clean kitchen towel. Place the potatoes in a large mixing bowl. Pour the oil mixture over the potatoes and let marinate for 30 minutes, tossing every 10 minutes.

4. Preheat the oven to 375º F. Place the marinated potatoes in a large baking pan and roast for 30 minutes or until crispy and brown.

5. With a slotted spoon, place the potatoes in a serving dish and pour the oil mixture from the pan over the potatoes. Serve immediately. Serves 6–8.

April Vegetable Mélange of Ramp, Cranberry Beans & English Peas in Tarragon Butter

Ramp, a wild leek growing from Canada to the Mid-Atlantic, is becoming increasingly popular as a spring vegetable ingredient, available fresh from March to June. It can be found on the foot-hills of forests, especially in the Catskill region, where it is harvested for green markets in the metropolitan area.

1 ¹/₂ pounds fresh cranberry beans in shell
Salt and black pepper as needed
1 pound fresh English peas in shell
1 medium ramp, washed well and cut into ¹/₂" strips (about 6 ounces)
1 medium yellow squash, cut into ¹/₄" cubes
4 ounces fresh shiitake mushrooms, cleaned
Olive oil as needed
1 shallot, minced
2 sticks unsalted butter at room temperature
¹/₂ tablespoon dried tarragon
1 teaspoon garlic powder

1. Shell the cranberry beans. In a small saucepan, place the beans in boiling water with a pinch of salt. Boil for 5 minutes, or until the beans are just tender. With a slotted spoon, remove the beans and place in a bowl of ice water to cool.

2. Shell the English peas. In a small saucepan, place the peas in boiling water with a pinch of salt. Boil for 3 minutes, or until the peas are just tender. With a slotted spoon, remove the peas and place in a bowl of ice water to cool.

3. In a medium saucepan, place the ramp and squash in boiling water with a pinch of salt. Blanch for 1 minute. With a slotted spoon, remove the vegetables and set aside (do not place in ice water to cool).

4. Remove the stems from the mushrooms and cut the mushrooms into thin strips. Set aside.

5. In a large skillet, heat ¹/₄" olive oil over high heat. Add the reserved ramp and squash and sauté until hot. Add the shallot and reserved mushroom strips and sauté until the shallot is soft. Add the cooled beans and peas and toss and mix until hot. Add salt and black pepper to taste.

6. Add the butter, tarragon, and garlic powder and toss and mix over low heat until well blended. Transfer the mélange to a serving bowl. Serve immediately. Serves 6–8.

Toad Hill Maple Mousse with Apple & Pecan Crunch

Even though the maple syrup-producing season is behind us, there is still plenty of fresh maple syrup available. A smooth velvety maple-infused mousse should change one's mind that syrup is only for pancakes.

6 tablespoons Grade A Adirondack maple syrup
3 egg yolks
Pinch salt
1 1/2 teaspoons orange zest
1 cup heavy cream
1 large Red Delicious apple, peeled, cored, and diced 1/4"
1 1/2 cups coarsely chopped toasted pecans
1 tablespoon light brown sugar
1 teaspoon fresh lemon juice

1. In a medium aluminum bowl, combine the syrup, egg yolks, and salt. Place the bowl over a pot of simmering water and whisk the mixture for 6 minutes, or until it has thickened and the color has changed from dark to light. Make sure that the mixture does not curdle due to overheating. Once thickened, remove the bowl from the heat and place on a bed of ice to cool.

2. Carefully add the orange zest, stirring frequently, while the custard mixture is cooling over the ice.

3. In a separate bowl, whip the cream with an electric mixer until thick and heavy and can hold its shape. Carefully fold the cream into the cooled custard mixture. Divide the mousse into 4–6 dessert glasses and refrigerate for 1 hour.

4. In a medium bowl, combine the apple, pecans, brown sugar, and lemon juice and fold together until the sugar has been absorbed into the apple. Divide the mixture on top of the chilled mousse-filled dessert glasses. Serve immediately. Serves 4–6.

To toast pecans: *Preheat the oven to 350° F. In a baking pan, place the pecans in a single layer and toast in the oven for about 8 minutes, stirring frequently. Let the pecans cool completely before using.*

MEMORIAL DAY ADIRONDACK BBQ

Queen of Lakes Gazpacho with Pumpernickel Log Croutons

Enjoy the convenience of a refreshingly cold and crispy soup, which is easy to prepare and quick to serve. Gazpacho originated in Spain, a cold soup made with pureed vegetables and herbs. Perfect for your Memorial Day barbecue or other spring or summer activities. Now adapted in the U.S., chefs prepare many inspired new variations. Try this one, but prepare a day ahead for flavor infusion and convenience.

1 large seedless cucumber
2 yellow bell peppers
2 red bell peppers
6 ripe plum tomatoes
1 Spanish onion
2 cups zinfandel wine
$^1/_3$ cup tomato ketchup
1 garlic clove, finely chopped
1 tablespoon finely chopped fresh cilantro
1 teaspoon warm honey
2 egg yolks
$^1/_2$ cup extra-virgin olive oil
Salt and black pepper to taste
1–2 drops Tabasco sauce
1 recipe Pumpernickel Log Croutons (see next page)
1 small red onion, finely diced
1 bunch scallions, finely chopped

1. With a vegetable brush, clean all of the vegetables under cold running water.

2. Remove the skin of the cucumber with a vegetable peeler. Finely dice one-third of the cucumber and set aside. Cut all of the bell peppers in half, remove the seeds, and devein. Finely dice one half of each of the yellow and red bell peppers and set aside.

3. In a medium pot, quickly blanch the tomatoes in boiling water for 15 seconds, or until the skins split. With a slotted spoon, remove the tomatoes from the boiling water and plunge into a bowl of ice water. Remove the skin from the tomatoes. Cut 2 of the tomatoes in half and remove the seeds. Finely dice the remaining flesh and set aside.

4. In a small bowl, combine all of the diced vegetables, cover, and refrigerate. This will be part of the salsa to garnish the soup.

5. Coarsely chop the Spanish onion, the remaining cucumber, bell peppers, and tomatoes and place in a large blender or food processor. Add the wine, ketchup, garlic, cilantro, honey, egg yolks, and olive oil and puree until very smooth.

6. Rub the puree through a sieve, using a rubber spatula to push the puree into a large bowl or soup terrine. Season with the salt, black pepper, and Tabasco. Cover the bowl and refrigerate for at least 8 hours or overnight.

7. Prepare the Pumpernickel Log Croutons.

8. In a small bowl, combine the red onion and scallions and mix well. Refrigerate.

9. Remove the bowl from the refrigerator. Mix together the diced vegetables and the onion-scallion mixture to make a salsa. Place the salsa in a small serving bowl with a serving spoon.

10. Ladle the gazpacho into soup bowls and top each serving with the croutons. Use the salsa as individual garnish. Serve cold. Serves 6.

PUMPERNICKEL LOG CROUTONS
6 slices pumpernickel bread
Melted butter as needed
Grated Parmesan cheese as needed

1. Preheat the oven to 325° F. Grease a nonstick baking sheet.

2. Cut three ³/₄" wide x 3" long logs from each slice of bread for a total of 18 logs.

3. Place the logs on the prepared baking sheet and carefully brush the tops with the butter. Lightly sprinkle each log with the cheese and bake in the oven for 10–12 minutes or until crisp.

4. Remove the logs from the oven and let cool on the baking sheet. Makes 18 logs.

Forever Wild Frisée Salad with Haricot Beans & Warm Maple-Smoked Bacon Dressing

Frisée, a member of the chicory family, is a crisp, mildly bitter-flavored green, yellow, or white curly green, always a great accompaniment with pork or hearty meat dishes. Combined with the small, slender, sweet haricot beans, the peppery smooth Hudson Valley Maytag blue cheese, and the tangy smoky dressing, this salad marks a good start for the season to come. The Hudson Valley region in New York State produces wonderful artisan cheese, such as goat, Camembert, and Maytag blue cheese. If these are unavailable, use a similar blue cheese, such as Gorgonzola or Roquefort.

8 tablespoons virgin olive oil
8 strips maple-smoked bacon*, coarsely chopped
1 garlic clove, minced
1 teaspoon red wine vinegar
1 tablespoon Dijon mustard
1 teaspoon honey
1/4 teaspoon black pepper
1/4 cup coarsely chopped hazelnuts
1/2 pound haricot string beans, trimmed
Salt as needed
2 heads fresh frisée, washed and roots removed, or 6 cups torn leaves
1 medium red onion, very thinly sliced
1/2 pound Maytag blue cheese, crumbled

1. In a small saucepan, heat 2 tablespoons of the olive oil over medium heat. Add the bacon and fry until crisp. Add the garlic and lightly brown. Add the vinegar, mustard, honey, black pepper, and remaining olive oil. Whisk until smooth over low heat. Add the hazelnuts and set aside.

2. In a small saucepan, place the beans in boiling water with a pinch of salt. Cook the beans for 5 minutes or until just tender. With a slotted spoon, transfer the beans to a bowl of ice water and let cool.

3. Arrange the frisée on 6 salad plates. Equally divide the cooled beans among the plates. Break up the sliced onion into rings and equally scatter over the salads.

4. Warm the reserved dressing over low heat and stir to mix. Drizzle the warm dressing over each salad, scattering the bacon pieces and nuts. Crumble the blue cheese over the top. Serve immediately. Serves 6.

* See Food Sources in the Appendix.

Saranac Caramel Porter-Marinated & Grilled Rib Eye with Crawfish Butter

Marinating meat before grilling is always recommended for great flavor enhancement. Saranac Brewery in Utica, New York, produces beautiful caramel porter beer, brewed from dark caramel malt, with a smooth yet slightly bitter, roasted flavor — perfect as an ingredient for a marinade. If this beer is unavailable, use a basic porter or amber beer.

*3 bottles Saranac Caramel Porter beer**
³/₄ cup Grade A Adirondack maple syrup
³/₄ cup balsamic vinegar
¹/₂ cup warm honey
1 tablespoon ground coriander
1 ¹/₂ teaspoons ground ginger
Six to eight 20-ounce boneless rib eye steaks
1 recipe Crawfish Butter (see below)
Salt and black pepper as needed

1. In a large mixing bowl, whisk together the beer, syrup, vinegar, honey, coriander, and ginger.

2. In a large plastic container, place the steaks and pour the marinade over them. Marinate for 2 hours in the refrigerator, turning every 30 minutes. To help promote the marinating, pierce little holes in the meat with a fork.

3. Prepare the Crawfish Butter.

4. Preheat the grill to high. Remove the steaks from the marinade and sprinkle with the salt and black pepper. Grill or sear both sides of the steaks until desired doneness.

5. Remove the steaks from the grill. Place on a platter and spoon the crawfish butter over the steaks. Prepare for a feast! Serves 6 – 8.

CRAWFISH BUTTER
2 sticks unsalted butter, softened and cut into cubes
1 tablespoon chopped fresh cilantro
¹/₄ teaspoon black pepper
¹/₄ teaspoon ground paprika
1 teaspoon Grade A Adirondack maple syrup
Olive oil as needed
1 shallot, minced
4 ounces crawfish tails, cut into ¹/₂" pieces
2 tablespoons sherry
Salt and black pepper as needed

1. In a medium mixing bowl, combine the butter, cilantro, the ¹/₄ teaspoon black pepper, paprika, and syrup and mix well. Set aside.

2. In a medium skillet, heat ¹/₄" olive oil over high heat. Add the shallot and sauté until soft. Add the crawfish tails and toss and mix. Add the sherry and reduce to one-fourth. Reduce the heat and add salt and black pepper to taste.

3. Add the warm crawfish mixture to the reserved butter mixture. With a rubber spatula or your hands, squeeze and mix the two mixtures together. (The butter will soften almost to a liquid.) Mix well and keep at room temperature.

* See Food Sources in the Appendix.

PHOTOS: ARMAND C. VANDERSTIGCHEL

Grill-Seared Pork Tenderloin with Sweet Vidalia Salsa

Similar to the beef tenderloin is the smaller tenderloin of pork, attached to the pork loin that produces pork chops. Pork tenderloins are more expensive than the boneless pork loin, but they are easier and quicker to cook and, of course, are super tender. Make sure that your butcher removes all fat and sinew from the tenderloin to insure proper marinating. Vidalia onions have a high sugar content, which surfaces when they are sautéed. Hailing from their namesake town of Vidalia, Georgia, they are harvested only in May and June.

3 tablespoons fresh lemon juice
2 tablespoons apple cider vinegar
1/2 cup dry vermouth
1/2 teaspoon Tabasco sauce
2 teaspoons Grade A Adirondack maple syrup
1/2 teaspoon sesame oil
1/2 teaspoon virgin olive oil
2 teaspoons finely chopped fresh sage
1 teaspoon finely chopped fresh rosemary
4 garlic cloves, minced
1 bay leaf
1 teaspoon freshly ground black pepper
4 pounds boneless pork tenderloin, trimmed of fat and sinew
Salt as needed
1 recipe Sweet Vidalia Salsa (see next page)
Fresh rosemary sprigs for garnish

1. In a small bowl, combine the lemon juice, vinegar, vermouth, Tabasco sauce, syrup, sesame oil, and olive oil and whisk until smooth. Add the sage, rosemary, garlic, bay leaf, and black pepper and whisk well.

2. Place the pork in a shallow glass or plastic container and spread out. Pour the marinade over the pork and marinate overnight in the refrigerator, turning the pork every 4 hours.

3. Preheat a grill with a lid to high heat. Have ready a handful of apple or cherry wood chips soaked in a little apple cider. Remove the pork from the marinade, shaking off excess liquid. Set aside the marinade.

4. Place the pork on the hot grill and sprinkle salt on all sides. Quickly sear both sides over high heat. Remove the pork from the grill and set aside. Reduce the heat to a slow smolder. Toss in the soaked wood chips. (The chips will create smoke.)

5. Return the pork to the grill, cover with the lid, and slowly grill the pork for 1 hour, turning occasionally, until cooked in the center (165ºF).

6. Prepare the Sweet Vidalia Salsa.

7. Remove the pork from the grill and let rest for 15 minutes. Thinly slice the pork onto a platter. Top with the salsa and garnish with a few rosemary sprigs. Serves 6.

SWEET VIDALIA SALSA
Olive oil as needed
1 large Vidalia onion, diced ¹/₄"
1 small red bell pepper, seeded, deveined, and diced ¹/₄"
4 fennel stalks, diced ¹/₄"
2 tablespoons balsamic vinegar
¹/₂ teaspoon salt
¹/₂ teaspoon black pepper
1 tablespoon granulated sugar

1. In a large sauté pan, heat ¹/₄" olive oil over high heat. Add the onion and sauté until lightly browned. Add the bell pepper and fennel and sauté until soft.

2. Add the vinegar, salt, black pepper, and sugar and simmer for 1 minute. Remove the pan from the heat and keep warm. Makes about 1 ¹/₂ cups.

New York State Cheddar & Tomato Sandwich with Herb Garden Mayonnaise

For the vegetarian in the crowd, this sandwich should be a welcome addition to the spread. To prevent sogginess, do not prepare the sandwich too far in advance. Nicely arranged on a platter with some loose watercress as garnish, this sandwich could become the main attraction.

1 recipe Herb Garden Mayonnaise (see below)
12 thick slices sourdough bread
12 thin slices mild New York State or Vermont cheddar cheese
12 slices ripened beefsteak tomatoes
24 peeled thinly cut cucumber slices
1 large red onion, very thinly sliced
1 bunch fresh watercress, washed and dried
Salt and black pepper as needed
12 small radishes, bottom and top caps removed

1. Prepare the Herb Garden Mayonnaise. Have ready 12 long wooden cocktail toothpicks.

2. Prepare each sandwich by spreading the herb mayonnaise on top of 1 slice of bread. Layer the sandwich with 2 slices of cheese, 2 slices of tomato, 4 slices of cucumber, scattered rings of red onion, and sprigs of watercress. Sprinkle the vegetables with a little salt and black pepper.

3. Spread the herb mayonnaise on the top slice of bread, face down. Place the mayonnaise side of the bread on top of the vegetables and secure with 2 toothpicks on each side of the sandwich. Place 1 radish on top of each toothpick as a decorative garnish.

4. With a sharp knife, slice the sandwich in half. Repeat the procedure for the remaining sandwiches. Place the sandwiches on a decorative platter and cover with plastic wrap until ready to serve. Makes 6 sandwiches (12 half sandwiches).

HERB GARDEN MAYONNAISE

1 cup mayonnaise
1 garlic clove, minced
2 tablespoons finely chopped fresh basil
1 tablespoon finely chopped fresh dill
1 tablespoon finely chopped fresh tarragon
1 tablespoon finely chopped fresh chives
2 tablespoons finely chopped fresh parsley
1/2 teaspoon black pepper

In a small mixing bowl, combine all of the ingredients. With a rubber spatula, fold and mix together well. Set aside.

Adirondack Forest-Style Grilled White Asparagus with Mustard & Chive Dressing

Asparagus is a celebrated spring vegetable and what better to use than the white asparagus. Once only available in Europe, white asparagus is now also enjoyed in America. This delicacy is grown underground like Belgian endive to prevent it from greening and is preferred for its smoothness and thick stalk.

24 white asparagus stalks
Salt and black pepper as needed
2 teaspoons Dijon mustard
2 tablespoons heavy cream
2 egg yolks
2 tablespoons vegetable oil
1 tablespoon finely chopped fresh chives
Virgin olive oil as needed
24 thin slices Black Forest ham*

1. With a vegetable peeler, carefully trim each stalk 2" from the tip down, then cut 1" off the end. Discard the ends.

2. In a large saucepan, place the asparagus in boiling water with a pinch of salt. Cook the asparagus for 3 minutes or until almost tender (al dente). Transfer the asparagus and liquid to a large bowl placed on another large bowl of ice. Let the asparagus cool in its cooking liquid. Once cooled, transfer the bowl to the refrigerator for 1 hour.

3. In a medium mixing bowl, combine the mustard, cream, and egg yolks and whisk well. Set aside.

4. In a small saucepan, combine the vegetable oil and $^1/_2$ cup of the asparagus liquid (from refrigerator) and bring to a boil. Remove from the heat and slowly pour the mixture into the reserved cream mixture, while vigorously whisking until smooth. Add salt and black pepper to taste. Add the chives and refrigerate to cool slightly.

5. Preheat a grill or broiler. Remove the asparagus from its remaining liquid and pat dry with a clean kitchen towel. Brush the asparagus with the olive oil and sprinkle with salt and black pepper.

6. Place the asparagus on the grill or under the broiler. Lightly brown and grill mark the stalks, avoiding breaking or overcooking. Remove and carefully place on a platter to cool slightly.

7. Wrap each asparagus stalk lengthwise with 1 slice of the ham, leaving the tip to stick out. Arrange the wrapped asparagus on a large platter. Drizzle the cooled dressing over the asparagus. Be prepared for a delicacy! Serves 6–8 (3–4 asparagus per person).

* See Food Sources in the Appendix.

Apple Pear Hobo Bags with Buckwheat Honey Drizzle

A newcomer at fruit stands and farmers' markets is the apple pear, also known as the Asian pear. Originally grown in Japan, it is now grown in the U.S. in a version called "Twentieth Century." Its flowery fragrance, mild, sweet flavor, and crunchy texture paired with its extreme juiciness have made the fruit an instant hit statewide. The apple pear maintains a little firmness when ripe and has a longer shelf life than regular pears. In the following recipe, the pears are sautéed with savory ingredients and encased in a hobolike pastry bag.

4 ¹/₂ cups all-purpose flour
1 ¹/₂ cups vegetable shortening (preferably Crisco)
¹/₄ teaspoon ground cinnamon
³/₄ teaspoon salt
³/₄ cup ice-cold water (place water in freezer for 20 minutes)
Corn oil as needed
8 apple pears (Asian pears), peeled, cored, and cut into ¹/₂" cubes
¹/₂ cup toasted almonds (see page 30)
¹/₄ teaspoon ground ginger
¹/₂ cup firmly packed light brown sugar
¹/₂ cup unsalted butter at room temperature
¹/₄ cup Calvados or applejack brandy
1 recipe Buckwheat Honey Drizzle (see next page)

1. Set aside ¹/₂ cup of the flour. In a large mixing bowl, combine the remaining flour, shortening, cinnamon, salt, and ice water and mix with an electric mixer at slow to medium speed until all of the ingredients are incorporated.

2. On a flat, clean surface, sprinkle ¹/₄ cup of the reserved flour. Flour your hands and place the dough on the floured surface. Sprinkle the remaining reserved flour on top of the dough.

3. Pat down the dough to flatten. Divide the dough into 2 equal pieces and roll each piece with a rolling pin to a ¹/₄" thickness. Using a round 6" diameter cookie or pastry cutter, punch 4 rounds out of each dough section for a total of 8 rounds.

4. In a large nonstick sauté pan, heat ¹/₄" corn oil over high heat. Add the pears and sauté for 3 minutes to soften. Add the almonds, ginger, brown sugar, and butter, mix to coat, and sauté for 3 minutes more.

5. Remove the pan from the heat and pour in the brandy. Return the pan to the heat and let the brandy ignite or reduce. Once burned or reduced, remove from the heat and transfer to a bowl to cool slightly for 5 minutes.

6. Preheat the oven to 375º F. Using a slotted spoon, measure ¹/₂ cup of the apple pear mixture and place in the center of each dough round.

7. Create a purselike bag by pulling up the east-north-west-south corners together until sealed tightly on top. Repeat the procedure with the remaining dough rounds.

8. Place the hobo bags on a greased or parchment paper-lined baking sheet, 2 inches apart (making room for expansion), and bake for 15–20 minutes, or until the crust is golden brown.

9. Prepare the Buckwheat Honey Drizzle.

10. Place 1 hobo bag on each dessert plate or together on a decorative platter. Equally divide the drizzle over the bags. Serve immediately. Serves 8.

BUCKWHEAT HONEY DRIZZLE

³/₄ cup buckwheat honey
1 ¹/₂ tablespoons unsalted butter at room temperature
¹/₈ teaspoon vanilla extract
¹/₂ teaspoon lemon zest

In a small saucepan, slowly warm the honey. Whisk in the butter until smooth. Whisk in the vanilla and lemon zest. (Do not boil.) Remove from the heat and keep warm. Makes ³/₄ cup.

CHAPTER 4

ADIRONDACK SUMMER FUN

Memorial Day is over. It is the beginning of the long summer holiday season in the Adirondack State Park. You can feel the mixture of excitement, anticipation, and restlessness among proprietors of the hospitality industry. B&B owners and innkeepers are up early, checking the daily flood of e-mail from all corners of the world, answering requests for information and confirming reservations.

Adirondack furniture craftsmen are reviewing their stock and fine-tuning their spring production schedules, to accommodate the summer sales to come. Their craft has gained tremendous popularity due to lifestyle magazine coverage, successful furniture publications, the Internet, and word of mouth. Homeowners of new vacation dwellings are all too eager to proudly furnish them with the hottest interior style around — Adirondack Style.

Hiking and canoe outfitters make their final safety inspection for the adventurous hikers and watersport enthusiasts seeking a change of pace from the city life — perhaps inspired by the many survival shows on major networks. It is also a good time to use that SUV for what it was intended — riding rough dirt roads that have finally dried out after mud season.

Chefs and restaurant owners have finished their new summer menus, which offer both ground-breaking recipes using the summer's bounty of fresh produce and older standbys to appeal to the less adventurous. Aboard the *W. W. Durant* of the Raquette Lake Navigation Co., Captain Pohl is tuning up his engines and checking his supplies, for the summer season means many cruises for this popular restaurant on the water. He schedules Sunday brunches, lunches, dinners, and moonlight cruises, and plans for the many guests who will enjoy the gourmet food served from the ship's galley.

On the wooded hillsides around Chestertown, you might glimpse a white-clad chef from the Friend's Lake Inn gathering wild mushrooms for the nightly special or picking wild berries for a dessert creation. Greg Taylor, proprietor of the inn, is considered the region's top wine specialist. He knows the season will bring many wine aficionados to his restaurant, so the wine list must perfectly pair with the summer menu offerings.

At the Bark Eater Inn in Keene, owner Joe-Pete Wilson has doubled the production of pancakes in his antique kitchen, and they are eagerly devoured by his recently arrived guests of the season. Kathy Hohemeyer, chef extraordinare of the popular Lodge at Lake Clear is doubling her production of sauerbraten — the famous pickled beef dish that is loved by many but not available everywhere. For that reason alone, she will do brisk business in her German/Adirondack-style restaurant, which is surrounded by a beautiful property and lodging facilities.

Around the eastern perimeter of the park, farm stands are loaded with fresh vegetables, fruits, pies, preserves, and cheeses. Down at the Lakeside Farms Cider Mill in Ballston Lake, the press is in full production, turning out summer cider. Fresh cider doughnuts are prepared by the hundreds, for they are irresistible to the lunch crowd, always ready to take a dozen back to the office or family coffee clutch.

On the southern border of the Adirondack State Park lies Saratoga Springs. Some call it the "Gateway to the Adirondacks." Thousands of visitors, enjoying the horse races and spa, will be drawn by curiosity and hearsay to the majestic Adirondack Park to the north. They will discover a region unimagined elsewhere in New York State, just as yours truly once did. Soon they will combine their yearly Saratoga visit with a trip to the Adirondacks. Since Saratoga is a great restaurant town with fine gourmet shops, it has been a springboard for many great chefs inspired to participate in the evolution of regional cuisine. For this reason, Saratoga restaurants and chefs are featured in this chapter and throughout the book.

Following Labor Day, the racetrack will fall silent again, just as it has each autumn for decades. Long streams of cars will head south, full of campers with wonderful summer memories. Adirondack authors and artists will have enjoyed their yearly gathering at the Hoss's Country Corner Author Picnic/Signing in Long Lake. All are looking forward to next year's meet, some for a new book, others for a juicy hamburger from the open grill.

The summer has brought new friends to the region, who will tell others about the wonderful summer paradise they discovered. Drawn by the mountains, clear sparkling lakes, and miles of dense, balsam-scented forests, they will follow a tradition dating back a hundred years, when famous names like Presidents Roosevelt and Coolidge discovered what we have — the rustic charm of the Adirondack wilderness, forever wild and always good in taste.

Trappers Pan-Seared Steak over Russet Potato & Lobster Hash with Lobster Claw-Scallion Butter

If Surf n' Turf is too light a "wave" for you, have a sturdy Adirondack trappers steak. Use an old-fashioned, cast-iron skillet for best results, plus the skillet is also perfect to use over a hot grill or open campfire. Canadian or Maine Lobsters are available throughout the region, even sold roadside during the summer, as seen on Route 86 in Raybrook, New York.

Olive oil as needed
Two 16-ounce New York sirloin strip steaks
Kosher salt and black pepper as needed
$1/2$ cup diced onions
2 large russet potatoes, peeled, cooked, and cut into $1/2$" cubes
One $1 1/4$-pound lobster, cooked and meat removed from shell
$1/4$ cup white vinegar
1 tablespoon granulated sugar
2 tablespoons finely chopped fresh chives
2 bunch scallions, coarsely chopped
2 tablespoons unsalted butter

1. In a heavy skillet, heat $1/4$" olive oil over high heat. Generously season the steaks with the salt and black pepper. Sear the steaks on both sides until desired doneness.

2. In a separate, large heavy skillet, heat $1/4$" olive oil over high heat. Add the onions and sauté until lightly browned. Add the potatoes and sauté until browned.

3. Cut the tail meat from the lobster into $1/2$" pieces. Add the pieces to the pan and heat all ingredients through. Add the vinegar, sugar, and chives and mix carefully to avoid breaking up the potatoes. Heat all ingredients through and keep warm.

4. In a medium skillet, heat $1/4$" olive oil over high heat. Add the scallions and quickly fry until almost crispy. Add the lobster claw meat to the pan and heat through. Add the butter to melt and mix with the scallions.

5. Divide the potato mixture between 2 plates. Place 1 steak on each serving of potatoes and spoon the scallion butter over the steaks. Garnish with the lobster claws. Serves 2.

Lumberjack Roasted Pork Cakes in Lemon-Rosemary Sauce

These roasted pork cakes are delicious and easy to make. They even taste good the next day, served cold on a roll with a little mustard! The extensive ingredient list infuses a spectrum of great flavors. Freshly ground pork is best purchased at your local butcher. If this dish is prepared and eaten near a tree line, be prepared to share with the lumberjacks coming out of the "woodwork!" Serve the pork cakes on a large platter with Wilted Escarole in Garlic-Shallot Butter with Roquefort Cheese Crumble and Marjoram Pesto New Potatoes (see recipes on pages 122–23).

Olive oil as needed
1/4 pound bacon, finely diced
1 medium onion, thinly sliced
4 garlic cloves, minced
1 medium carrot, finely minced
Salt and black pepper as needed
3 pounds ground pork
4 eggs, beaten
1/2 cup finely chopped fresh Italian parsley
2 tablespoons tomato paste
2 tablespoons honey
1 tablespoon onion powder
1/2 tablespoon garlic powder
1 teaspoon black pepper
1/2 teaspoon curry powder
1/4 teaspoon ground cloves
1/2 teaspoon salt
2 cups seasoned bread crumbs
1 recipe Lemon-Rosemary Sauce (see next page)

1. Preheat the oven to 350º F. In a medium skillet, heat 1/4" olive oil over high heat. Add the bacon and fry until almost crispy. Quickly add the onion, garlic, and carrot and sauté until the onion is wilted. Add a little salt and black pepper. Remove from the heat and let cool.

2. In a large mixing bowl, combine the pork, cooled onion mixture, eggs, parsley, tomato paste, honey, onion and garlic powders, the 1 teaspoon black pepper, curry powder, cloves, the 1/2 teaspoon salt, and bread crumbs and mix thoroughly until compact. Add more bread crumbs if too loose. Form about 16 oval-shaped cakes. Place the cakes on a greased baking sheet and bake for 25 minutes or until cooked through. Keep warm.

3. Prepare the Lemon-Rosemary Sauce.

4. Place 4 cakes on each plate. Ladle the sauce over the cakes and serve immediately. Serves 4.

LEMON-ROSEMARY SAUCE

Olive oil as needed
1 shallot, minced
8 garlic cloves, sliced
1 1/2 cups chardonnay wine
6 cups chicken stock
1 teaspoon minced fresh rosemary
1/2 teaspoon black pepper
Juice of 1/2 lemon
1 stick unsalted butter, cut into pieces

1. In a large saucepan, heat 1/4" olive oil over medium heat. Add the shallot and garlic and lightly brown. Add the wine and reduce to one-half.

2. Add the stock, rosemary, black pepper, and lemon juice. Bring to a simmering boil and simmer for 5 minutes. Turn off the heat. Whisk in the butter pieces until smooth. Keep warm.

ARMAND C. VANDERSTIGCHEL

Balsamic Lemon Thyme Honey-Grilled Chicken with Wild Blueberry Glaze over Silver Dollar Yam Cakes

From late spring to late summer, blueberries are abundant throughout the Adirondack region, both domestic (large) or wild (smaller and sweeter), and are usually available at farmers' markets. Used in pies and cakes, it is also a wonderful berry paired with poultry — chicken, duck, pheasant, or quail. Pick a pint of these berries, make sure they are dark blue with a powdery white bloom, and prepare this fun dish with your family and friends. Beware of the blue tongue!

1 ¹/₂ cups balsamic vinegar
³/₄ cup olive oil
³/₄ cup warm honey
1 ¹/₂ tablespoons finely chopped fresh lemon thyme
Four 6-ounce chicken breasts, pounded flat to ¹/₂" thick
1 recipe Blueberry Glaze (see below)
1 recipe Silver Dollar Yam Cakes (see next page)
Fresh lemon thyme sprigs for garnish

1. In a small bowl, combine the vinegar, oil, honey, and thyme and whisk well. Place the chicken in a flat container. Pour the marinade over the chicken and marinate in the refrigerator for 3 hours, turning the chicken occasionally.

2. Prepare the Blueberry Glaze.

3. Prepare the Silver Dollar Yam Cakes.

4. Preheat the grill to very hot. Remove the chicken from the marinade and set aside the marinade. Place the chicken on the hot grill and quickly grill and mark both sides. Reduce the heat to very low and slowly cook the chicken, basting with the reserved marinade, until firm and cooked through.

5. Remove the chicken from the heat. On each plate, place 1 chicken breast atop 3 yam cakes and drizzle the reserved blueberry glaze over the top. Garnish with the lemon thyme sprigs. Serves 4.

BLUEBERRY GLAZE
1 tablespoon unsalted butter
1 pint domestic or wild blueberries
¹/₄ cup Sloe Gin liqueur
1 tablespoon granulated sugar
¹/₈ teaspoon salt

1. In a large skillet, melt the butter over medium heat. Add the blueberries and sauté for 2 minutes.

2. Add the liqueur, sugar, and salt and reduce the glaze to almost syrupy. Set aside.

SILVER DOLLAR YAM CAKES
1 pound yams, peeled, grated, and pressed dry in paper towels
2 eggs, beaten
2 teaspoons Grade A Adirondack maple syrup
½ teaspoon black pepper
¼ teaspoon ground coriander
5 tablespoons all-purpose flour
½ teaspoon salt
Vegetable oil as needed

1. In a medium bowl, combine the yams, eggs, syrup, black pepper, coriander, flour, and salt and mix well.

2. In a medium skillet, heat ½" vegetable oil over medium heat. Measure ¼ cup of the yam mixture at a time, pat into a silver dollar size, and place in the hot oil. Fry the cakes for 2 minutes on each side and place on paper towels to drain. Keep warm. Makes 12 cakes.

Grits-Crusted Soft-Shell Crabs with Roasted Corn Aïoli & Chiffonade of Purple Basil

Nothing is more anticipated by food lovers, than the arrival of fresh soft-shell crabs in early summer. Before they reach their full maturity, blue crabs shed their hard shell several times. In this period when their shells are soft, they are quickly harvested and sent all across the nation to anxious chefs, ready to offer this delicacy to their distinguished guests. Panfrying is the favorite method, as in this recipe where the grits create a super crispy crust. Combined with aïoli, made from fresh, local summer corn and the powerful perfume from purple basil, this dish will surprise your guests! Aïoli is a homemade, garlic-flavored mayonnaise — very easy to prepare. Purple basil, also known as opal basil, has small leaves and a spicy taste; it can be purchased at farm stands and garden centers as a plant.

4 medium soft-shell crabs
2 cups all-purpose flour
6 eggs, beaten
4 cups Quaker Quick Grits
2 teaspoons Cajun blackening seasoning
2 teaspoons onion powder
1/2 teaspoon salt
1 recipe Aïoli (see next page)
Vegetable oil as needed
Fresh purple basil leaves for garnish

1. Clean and prepare the crabs by washing them with cold water. Snip off the mouth part with scissors. Pull back the shell and remove the gills (spongy filterlike pieces) on each side of the shell. Dry the crabs with paper towels and set aside.

2. Set up a breading station by placing the flour, eggs, and grits in separate bowls. Add the Cajun seasoning, onion powder, and salt to the flour and mix well.

3. Bread the crabs individually by dipping them in the flour first, eggs second, and grits third. Press the crabs firmly into the grits to coat thoroughly. Place the breaded crabs in the freezer for 30 minutes to adhere the coating before frying.

4. Prepare the Aïoli.

5. In a large heavy skillet, heat 1/2" vegetable oil over medium heat. Remove the crabs from the freezer and fry 2 at a time in the oil. Fry each crab for 3 minutes on each side until crispy and brown. Repeat with the remaining crabs. Drain the crabs on paper towels.

6. Place 1 crab on each plate and drizzle with the reserved aïoli. Garnish with the purple basil leaves. Serves 4.

AÏOLI

2 large ears fresh corn, shucked
Vegetable oil as needed
4 egg yolks
1 teaspoon white vinegar
1 garlic clove
2 cups pomace olive oil
$^1/_4$ teaspoon salt
$^1/_4$ teaspoon black pepper
1 $^1/_2$ teaspoons fresh lime juice
12 fresh purple basil leaves or sweet basil, thinly sliced

1. Preheat the oven to 450° F. Brush the corn lightly with the vegetable oil. Place the ears on a baking sheet and bake for 12–15 minutes or until lightly roasted a golden brown. Remove from the oven and let cool. With a sharp knife, cut off the corn kernels into a bowl. Set aside.

2. In a food processor, combine the egg yolks and vinegar. Turn the processor on medium speed. Add the garlic and reserved roasted corn and puree until almost smooth. Slowly pour in the olive oil, pureeing and creating an emulsion. Add the salt, black pepper, and lime juice and puree until smooth.

3. With a rubber spatula, transfer the aïoli to a small bowl. Fold in the basil strips and set aside. Makes about 2 cups.

Log Chalet of Grilled Monkfish Bunked with Charred Vine-Ripened Tomatoes & Roasted Yellow Pepper Puree

A favorite fish among discerning chefs is monkfish. This white flesh, meaty, sweet-flavored fish used to be called the poor man's lobster. The recent demand for monkfish has driven the price up to almost the lobster average. Chefs prefer the fish because it's perfect to grill, broil, or sauté. In this recipe, it is marinated, grilled, and paired with farm stand fresh tomatoes and yellow bell peppers, with a hint of fresh thyme.

1 cup extra-virgin olive oil
Juice of 2 lemons
3 teaspoons white vinegar
1 1/2 tablespoons minced fresh thyme
1 1/2 teaspoons black pepper
Four 12-ounce monkfish fillets
16 whole vine-ripened red plum tomatoes
Olive oil as needed
1 recipe Roasted Yellow Pepper Puree (see next page)
1/2 cup finely diced fresh chives
Fresh thyme sprigs
Fresh chive leaves

1. In a small mixing bowl, combine the 1 cup olive oil, lemon juice, vinegar, thyme, and black pepper and mix well. Set aside.

2. Slice each fillet into four 1/2" medallions for a total of 16 medallions. Place the medallions in a large bowl and cover with the reserved marinade. Marinate in the refrigerator for 1 hour.

3. Preheat the grill or broiler to very hot. Place the tomatoes on the grill and brush lightly with oil. Char the skin of the tomatoes until black. Remove from the grill and place in a bowl filled with ice water. Shock for 5 minutes. Remove the tomatoes and carefully peel off the charred skin. Set aside.

4. Prepare the Roasted Yellow Pepper Puree.

5. Remove the monkfish medallions from the marinade and place on a preheated hot grill or broiler. Grill the fish until firm and brown on both sides.

6. On each of 4 plates, spoon 2 tablespoons reserved puree in the center. Place 3 medallions in the center of the puree. Top the medallions with 3 charred tomatoes. Place 1 medallion atop the tomatoes. Top with 1 tablespoon puree, then top with 1 charred tomato. Sprinkle with 2 tablespoons of the chives. Garnish with the thyme sprigs and chive leaves. Serves 4.

ROASTED YELLOW PEPPER PUREE

4 whole yellow bell peppers
Olive oil as needed
1 cup diced onions
8 garlic cloves, peeled
¹/₂ teaspoon black pepper
1 teaspoon kosher salt or as needed
1 cup heavy cream

1. Brush the bell peppers with a little oil and place on a preheated hot grill or broiler. Char the outside skin of the peppers until black. Remove from the grill and place in a bowl. Cover with plastic wrap and sweat for 5 minutes. Remove the charred skins and seeds under cold running water and coarsely chop the pepper flesh. Set aside.

2. In a medium skillet, heat ¹/₄" olive oil over medium heat. Add the onions and garlic and sauté until golden brown. Set aside.

3. In a food processor, combine the reserved bell peppers, onions and garlic, black pepper, and salt and puree and pulse the mixture until smooth. At full speed, slowly add the cream until the mixture is smooth. Add more salt or black pepper if needed. Set aside.

Wilted Escarole in Garlic-Shallot Butter with Roquefort Cheese Crumble

Hearty in flavor, slightly bitter, and high in nutrients, escarole is delicious when sautéed in oil or butter. Topped with crumbles of Roquefort cheese, a moist, strong sheep's milk cheese from France, we have a perfect side dish. Prepare this dish right before serving.

3 pounds fresh escarole
Virgin olive oil as needed
1 shallot, minced
10 garlic cloves, thinly sliced
1 stick unsalted butter, cut into pieces
Salt and black pepper as needed
$^1/_3$ cup crumbled Roquefort or Gorgonzola cheese*

1. Wash the escarole in plenty of water. Cut off the roots and tear the leaves into 2" pieces. Place in a colander and rinse again with cold water.

2. Fill a large pot halfway with hot water. Add a pinch of salt and bring to a rolling boil. Place the escarole in the hot water and wilt for 1 minute. With a strainer, remove the escarole from the water and squeeze out the excess water.

3. In a large skillet, heat $^1/_4$" olive oil over high heat. Add the shallot and garlic and sauté until browned. Quickly add the escarole and sauté and mix well. Add the butter pieces to melt and flavor. Sprinkle with the salt and black pepper to taste.

4. Transfer the escarole to a serving bowl. Pour the pan juices over the top and sprinkle with the cheese. Serve immediately. Serves 6–8.

* *See Cheese Glossary in the Appendix.*

Marjoram Pesto New Potatoes

New potatoes are immature potatoes, usually from the round white or red variety. In this recipe, we use the new white potato. Available in the spring and early summer, these potatoes have thin skins, making them perfect for boiling whole. Fresh marjoram is delicious, and when combined with flat leaf Italian parsley, which has a strong peppery flavor, it is perfect to coat these potatoes in a pesto.

4 pounds new white potatoes with skins
Kosher salt as needed
6 garlic cloves
2 small red onions, diced
¹/₂ cup coarsely chopped fresh Italian parsley
3 tablespoons finely chopped fresh marjoram
¹/₄ teaspoon prepared horseradish
Juice of ¹/₂ lemon
¹/₂ teaspoon black pepper
¹/₂ teaspoon salt
3 cups extra-virgin olive oil

1. Place the potatoes in a large pot of water, add a pinch of kosher salt, and bring to a boil. Boil the potatoes for 12 minutes or until fork tender (potato slowly slides off the fork). Drain the potatoes and place in a large bowl. Keep warm.

2. In a food processor, combine the garlic, onions, parsley, marjoram, horseradish, lemon juice, black pepper, and the ¹/₂ teaspoon salt. Pulse the processor until all of the ingredients are chopped. Turn to full speed, while slowly adding the oil. Blend until smooth.

3. Pour the pesto over the warm potatoes and toss gently. Add the kosher salt for flavor if needed. Serve immediately. Serves 6 – 8.

Great Adirondack Truffle Creamed Spinach

When the steaks are sizzling on the grill, a good creamed spinach as a side dish (like in steak houses) comes to mind. This recipe has been taken to an exceptional flavor level with ingredients such as bacon, eggs, and aromatic white truffle oil — no wonder we call it great! Extra-virgin olive oil infused with the powerfully scented white truffle, found in Piedmont, Italy, or domestically in the state of Oregon, is a wonderful combination of flavors. Truffle oil is available at most gourmet shops or by mail order*.

Olive oil as needed
¼ pound smoked bacon, finely chopped
1 shallot, minced
1 small onion, finely chopped
1 garlic clove, minced
2 tablespoons all-purpose flour
1 cup chicken stock
2 cups heavy cream
1 ½ pounds frozen spinach, thawed and drained
1 teaspoon baking soda

1 teaspoon black pepper
½ teaspoon dried tarragon
½ tablespoon granulated onion powder
½ tablespoon granulated garlic powder
¼ teaspoon ground cloves
½ teaspoon salt or as needed
2 hard-boiled eggs, finely chopped
2–3 tablespoons white truffle extra-virgin olive oil (depending on strength or personal taste)

1. In a heavy medium pot, heat ¼" olive oil over high heat. Add the bacon and fry until almost crispy. Quickly add the shallot, onion, and garlic. Reduce the heat to medium and lightly brown the onion mixture. Add the flour to bind, creating a little roux mixture.

2. Add the stock and stir into the roux until it thickens and bubbles. Add the cream and mix well until it lightly thickens. Add the spinach, baking soda, black pepper, tarragon, onion and garlic powders, cloves, and salt and mix well. (Baking soda keeps the color bright green!)

3. Bring the spinach mixture to a low simmer over low heat. Let the mixture bubble, stirring constantly, for about 5 minutes.

4. Turn off the heat and add the chopped eggs and mix well. Add the truffle oil and mix well. Add salt if needed. If the spinach is too thick, thin with chicken stock. If desire, top the spinach with croutons, chopped eggs, or shaved white truffle. Serves 6–8.

* See Food Sources in the Appendix.

Algonquin Apple Cake

Indulging in a fine cake sure beats eating bark! (A bark eater is the English translation of the Algonquin word *adirondack.*) Easy to make and plenty to share, this cake is a true delight for large gatherings.

4 Jonathan or Granny Smith apples, peeled, cored, and diced ¹/₂"
2 cups granulated sugar
2 tablespoons warm honey
2 tablespoons Grade A Adirondack maple syrup
1 cup vegetable oil
2 large eggs, beaten
2 teaspoons vanilla extract
1 ²/₃ cups coarsely chopped unsalted pistachio nuts
3 cups all-purpose flour
2 teaspoons baking soda
1 teaspoon baking powder
2 teaspoons ground cinnamon
¹/₂ teaspoon ground cardamom
¹/₄ teaspoon ground nutmeg
1 teaspoon salt
Confectioners' sugar for garnish

1. In a large mixing bowl, combine the apples and sugar and mix well. Let the apples macerate for about 1 hour.

2. Preheat the oven to 350° F. In a small bowl, combine the honey, syrup, oil, eggs, and vanilla extract and mix well. Fold the honey mixture into the apple mixture, then fold in the nuts.

3. In another large bowl, combine the flour, baking soda, baking powder, cinnamon, cardamom, nutmeg, and salt and mix well. Fold and mix the flour mixture into the apple-honey mixture until you have a smooth batter.

4. Scrape the batter from the bowl onto a greased, rimmed 12" x 17" baking sheet or into a greased 9" x 13" x 2" baking dish. Smooth out the batter and bake for about 1 hour.

5. Remove the cake from the oven and let cool for 1 hour. Cut the cake into 2" x 2" squares. Place the squares on a platter and with a sifter, sprinkle the confectioners' sugar over the top. Serves 8–10.

Yellow Sugar Plum Napoleon Rafts with Blackberry Brandy-Steeped Wild Blueberries & Lemon Verbena Cream

While driving through Keene Valley on Route 28N, my eye caught the Rivermeade Farm Store, known for its extensive selection of locally grown produce from its main farm and greenhouses on Beede Road. Beautiful, yellow baby sugar plums were the immediate inspiration for a summer dessert. Combined with plump wild blueberries and lemon verbena, a pleasant lemon-scented herb, which is available at most farm stands and garden centers, and we have a delicious, seasonal dessert, crispy and refreshing.

3 sheets phyllo pastry
¹/₂ stick unsalted butter, melted
Granulated sugar as needed
1 recipe Yellow Sugar Plum Compote (see next page)
1 recipe Wild Blueberries (see next page)
1 recipe Lemon Verbena Cream (see next page)
¹/₄ cup confectioners' sugar
Fresh lemon verbena leaves for garnish

1. Preheat the oven to 350º F. Lay 1 phyllo sheet on a clean working surface. Carefully brush the entire sheet with the melted butter. Lightly sprinkle with the granulated sugar.

2. Fold the sheet forward, lengthwise, creating a long narrow rectangle. Brush the top with butter. Fold the rectangle from left to right and brush with butter. Fold again from left to right, creating a 6 ¹/₂" x 4 ¹/₂" rectangle and brush with butter.

3. Repeat the procedure with the remaining 2 sheets. Place the 3 rectangles on a greased or parchment paper-lined baking sheet and bake for 8 minutes, turning the rafts over after 4 minutes to equally brown both sides. Remove from the oven and let cool.

4. Prepare the Yellow Sugar Plum Compote.

5. Prepare the Wild Blueberries.

6. Prepare the Lemon Verbena Cream.

7. Equally spread a layer of plum compote on each phyllo raft. Cut each raft in half for a total of six 4" x 3" pieces.

8. Assemble each napoleon by layering 3 pieces each with the blueberries and lemon verbena cream. When both are assembled, sprinkle generously with the confectioners' sugar through a sieve. Garnish with the lemon verbena leaves. Serves 2.

YELLOW SUGAR PLUM COMPOTE

2 tablespoons unsalted butter
1 pound yellow baby sugar plums, pitted and quartered
Zest and juice of $1/2$ lemon
3 teaspoons Grade A Adirondack maple syrup
1 tablespoon honey
3 tablespoons granulated sugar
$1/8$ teaspoon salt
4 teaspoons cornstarch mixed with $2 1/2$ tablespoons cold water

1. In a medium skillet, melt the butter over medium heat. Add the plums and sauté until softened. Add the lemon zest and juice, syrup, honey, sugar, and salt and sauté until the sugar is melted.

2. Add the cornstarch mixture and mix well. Simmer for 3 minutes or until thickened. Remove the compote from the heat and let cool for about 20 minutes. The compote should be thick and spreadable.

WILD BLUEBERRIES

1 pint wild or domestic fresh blueberries
$1/3$ cup granulated sugar
3 tablespoons blackberry brandy
$1/8$ teaspoon salt
Juice of $1/2$ lemon

In a medium bowl, combine the blueberries, sugar, brandy, salt, and lemon juice and mix carefully without breaking the blueberries. Let the blueberries steep for 1 hour.

LEMON VERBENA CREAM

2 cups heavy whipping cream
1 teaspoon minced fresh lemon verbena or mint leaves
4 tablespoons confectioners' sugar
$1/4$ teaspoon vanilla extract
Zest of $1/2$ lemon

In a cold medium bowl, whip the cream until lightly thickened. Add the verbena, sugar, vanilla extract, and lemon zest and continue to whip the cream until stiff peaks form. Chill immediately until ready for use.

ADIRONDACK FOURTH OF JULY BARBECUE

Mountain Medley Roadside Strawberry Lemonade

Pick up those beautiful, super sweet, locally grown summer strawberries sold at farm stands in every corner of the Adirondacks and indulge in this refreshing, thirst-quenching lemonade!

1 cup freshly squeezed lemon juice (about 6 lemons)
1 1/2 cups hulled and sliced fresh strawberries
4 fresh lemon verbena or mint leaves
1/2 cup good-quality honey (no buckwheat or dark)
1 cup ice
3 cups cold water
Fresh lemon verbena or mint sprigs for garnish

1. In a large good-quality blender, combine the lemon juice, strawberries, lemon verbena, and honey and blend until the mixture is smooth. Add the ice and blend until smooth. Add the water and blend until smooth and frothy.

2. Pour the lemonade into glasses with ice cubes. Garnish with a lemon verbena or mint sprig. Makes about 2 quarts.

Kettle of Cider-Scented Steamer Clams in Summer Savory Herb Butter Broth

Summer holidays in the Northeast are often celebrated with clambakes. If you want a great appetizer and a simple way to prepare delicious clams, try this recipe prepared with super sweet steamers. A steamer is a delicate soft-shelled clam from the Atlantic Ocean and is 3"–4" long. If unavailable, you can use cherrystone or littleneck clams.

When selecting clams, avoid open clams; when tapped on the shell, they should close if alive. Steamer clams have a neck protruding from the shell; when tapping the shell, the neck should pull back toward the shell.

The next step is soaking (purging) the clams before cooking to make the clams purge any sand caught in their shells. Place the clams in a large tub covered with fresh seawater or dissolve 6 tablespoons of salt per gallon of tap water. (A chef's secret is to add a little cornmeal to the water.) Discard any floating clams and soak the remaining clams in the refrigerator for 3 hours. Drain and rinse with cold water.

¼ bushel or two 1-gallon buckets fresh steamer clams
4 shallots, minced
One 32-ounce bottle sparkling apple cider
½ pound andouille sausage, thinly sliced
½ pound or 3 cups julienned leeks
1 cup fresh corn kernels
1 medium red bell pepper, seeded, deveined, and diced ¼"

1 bunch scallions, finely diced
1 tablespoon finely chopped fresh summer or winter savory or thyme
1 teaspoon dried tarragon
1 teaspoon black pepper
1 pound unsalted butter
Kosher salt as needed
Lemon wedges
Baguette bread

1. Select, purge, soak, and rinse the clams according to the recipe introduction. Place a large heavy kettle or cast-iron pot over high heat and heat until very hot.

2. Place the clams in the pot and sprinkle the shallots over the clams. Quickly pour the cider over the clams, cover, and let steam over high heat, occasionally turning the clams until they open.

3. With a wire mesh ladle or large slotted spoon, transfer the clams to a large serving bowl, leaving the remaining broth in the pot. Cover the clam bowl with aluminum foil to keep warm.

4. Remove the pot from the heat. Strain the clam broth through cheesecloth or a fine strainer into a bowl. Wipe the pot clean and return the strained clam broth to the pot. Return the pot to high heat and bring the broth to a boil.

5. Add the sausage, leeks, corn, bell pepper, scallions, savory, tarragon, and black pepper to the broth. Reduce the heat to a low simmer and cook for 3 minutes. Remove the pot from the heat and whisk in the butter until smooth. Add the salt if needed.

6. Pour the broth over the bowl of clams and serve immediately with the lemon wedges and slices of baguette bread. Dig in and enjoy! Serves 6–8.

Adirondack Clam Chowder

You have New England, Rhode Island, and, of course, Manhattan clam chowder. Now you can have your own Adirondack version, a very chunky, filling concoction in a silky broth prepared with fresh garden vegetables and chopped quahog clams from the eastern seaboard. When purchasing clams for this recipe, visit your local fish store and ask for freshly shucked chopped clams in clam liquor (liquid). They are sold in pint, quart, or 1/2-gallon tubs. This is the best bet for your money and time, and you will be getting a fresh and quality product, instead of using canned or frozen clams or of having to steam, shuck, and chop your own.

When preparing the clams, drain off and reserve the clam liquor for use in the chowder. Clam liquor is also sold in cans, and it would be advisable to have some on hand in case you run short of fresh clam liquor. This recipe makes a large pot, perfect for a large family gathering, considering many will go for seconds.

Prepare the chowder a day ahead to let it cure. Curing the chowder means developing more flavor while it sits overnight. Transfer the chowder to a large pot or caldron and place it on the grill or open fire to heat up. Who knows, Uncle Sam might pay a visit to savor this delicious chowder on this Fourth of July.

Olive oil as needed
6 strips apple wood-smoked bacon*, diced 1"
1 medium onion, diced 1"
4 celery stalks, diced 1"
3 medium carrots, cut into ³/₄" cubes
2 bay leaves
1 cup white wine
2 quarts reserved or canned clam liquor, juice, or broth
2 pounds B-sized red potatoes, cut into 1" cubes (see page {00})
2 teaspoons onion powder
1 teaspoon black pepper
1 teaspoon dried thyme
¹/₂ teaspoon Cajun blackening seasoning
1 teaspoon granulated sugar
¹/₂ cup cooked fresh corn kernels
1 medium leek stalk (¹/₂ pound), washed and cut into 2" long thin strips
¹/₂ pound green cabbage, diced 1"
1 quart heavy cream
5 cups chopped fresh clams
Salt and black pepper to taste
Chopped fresh parsley for garnish
Oyster crackers

1. In a large, heavy soup pot, heat $1/4$" olive oil over high heat. Add the bacon and fry until almost crispy. Quickly add the onion, celery, carrots, and bay leaves and sauté until the onion is transparent. Add the wine. Reduce the wine to one-half.

2. Add the clam liquor and bring to a simmering boil. Add the potatoes, onion powder, black pepper, thyme, Cajun seasoning, and sugar and return to a simmering boil.

3. Once the potatoes are almost cooked (al dente), add the corn, leek, and cabbage. Bring to a simmering boil and cook for 4 minutes, or until the vegetables are wilted.

4. Add the cream. Return to a simmering boil and simmer for 3 minutes. Add the clams. Return to a simmering boil and cook for 3 minutes. Add the salt and black pepper.

5. Remove from the heat. Ladle the chowder into bowls and garnish with the parsley. Serve with the oyster crackers. Makes 16–20 bowls.

* See Food Sources in the Appendix.

Chef's Tip: *The key to perfect chowder is not to overcook it, especially the clams. Chopped clams cook quickly and turn rubbery when cooked longer than 3 minutes.*

Crown Point Grilled Pork Tenderloin Medallions with Lavender-Scented McIntosh-Peach Salsa

In June, farm stands are abundant with fresh peaches, good for a quick snack or perfect for a salsa. French lavender, a distinctive tasting herb can be purchased dried or the much preferred fresh lavender. Purchase fresh lavender as a potted plant and transfer it to your herb garden or to a larger pot. Place it in a sunny spot, give it plenty of water, and watch the beautiful purple flowers bloom. Perfect as a plate garnish — just snip off the leaves and place on your prepared recipes. Enjoy!

MARINADE & PORK

3/4 cup white vinegar

Juice of 3 oranges

1 1/2 tablespoons honey

1 1/2 teaspoons mustard

1 1/2 tablespoons teriyaki sauce

1 1/2 cups pomace olive oil

1 1/2 tablespoons minced fresh lavender

Three 12-ounce pork tenderloins, trimmed and cut into twelve 3-ounce medallions

SALSA

2 peaches, pitted and diced 1/2"

2 McIntosh apples, peeled, cored, and diced 1/4"

Juice of 1 lime

Juice of 1 orange

1/4 cup minced red onions

2 tablespoons diced scallions

1 teaspoon minced fresh lavender

2 tablespoons white vinegar

1 tablespoon granulated sugar

1/8 teaspoon salt

1/4 teaspoon black pepper

1. Prepare the marinade by combining the vinegar, orange juice, honey, mustard, teriyaki sauce, olive oil, and lavender in a medium bowl and mix well.

2. Place the pork medallions in a plastic container. Pour the marinade over the pork and marinate in the refrigerator for 24 hours.

3. Prepare the salsa 2 hours before serving. In a medium bowl, combine the peaches, apples, lime juice, orange juice, onions, scallions, lavender, vinegar, sugar, salt, and black pepper and mix well. Let the salsa steep for 2 hours before serving.

4. Remove the pork from the marinade and set aside the marinade. Turn the grill to the highest heat. Place the pork on the hot grill and sear the pork quickly on both sides. Turn the heat to the lowest setting and slowly cook until the medallions feel firm and the internal temperature is 160° F.

5. Place the medallions on a large platter and sprinkle with the salsa. Serve family style. Serves 6.

SARATOGA RACES FAMILY PICNIC

Grandstand Red Beet Slaw

Beets are in fashion on today's menus for their flavor, color, and health benefits. You will certainly become fashionable when you serve this slaw to friends and family before heading to the grandstand at the Saratoga races with a betting slip in your hand. The combination of savory beets with crunchy carrots and sweet coconut is a finish line winner! Tip: Be sure to use a box grater to shred the beets and carrots.

3 pounds fresh beets, peeled and shredded
3 large carrots, shredded
2 cups shredded coconut
3 tablespoons warm honey
3 tablespoons Grade A Adirondack maple syrup
4 tablespoons lingonberry preserves
$^1/_2$ cup white vinegar
1 cup cranberry juice
Juice of 1 lime
2 tablespoons poppy seeds
$^1/_2$ teaspoon salt

1. In a large mixing bowl, combine the beets, carrots, and coconut and mix well.

2. In a medium mixing bowl, combine the honey, syrup, preserves, vinegar, cranberry juice, lime juice, poppy seeds, and salt and whisk vigorously until combined.

3. Pour the vinaigrette into the beet mixture and mix well. Serves 6–8.

Congress Park Market Square Salad Mélange au Basil Vinaigrette

Next to beautiful Congress Park in downtown Saratoga is a market square famous for its weekly farmers' market, where you might most anything: fresh baked goods, bottled preserves, fresh vine-ripened tomatoes, crispy green and yellow string beans, colorful yellow tomatoes, local scallions, fresh basil — all winning ingredients for this delectable salad. From the local gourmet shop, we add some Feta cheese and super sweet black mission figs. When purchasing figs, select those that are soft to the touch, not wrinkled, mushy, or bruised. It is also recommended that you hide the figs before making the salad; they are a great snack.

2 ¹/₂ cups Basil Vinaigrette (see below)
2 ¹/₂ pounds firm, ripe, or vine-ripened red
  tomatoes
2 pounds firm, ripe yellow tomatoes
¹/₂ pound fresh green string beans,
  trimmed

¹/₂ pound fresh yellow wax beans, trimmed
Kosher salt and black pepper as needed
1 bunch scallions, coarsely diced
¹/₂ pound Feta cheese, crumbled
2 pints fresh black mission figs, halved
  lengthwise

1. Prepare the Basil Vinaigrette.

2. Wash all of the tomatoes, trim off ends, and cut into medium-sized wedges (half moons). Place in a large mixing bowl.

3. In a large saucepan, combine all of the beans with water to cover and a touch of salt. Bring to a boil and cook for 2–3 minutes or until still bright and almost tender.

4. With a slotted spoon, remove the beans from the pan and place in a bowl of ice water to cool. Remove the beans from the cold water and add to the tomatoes.

5. Add the scallions, cheese, and figs and gently mix together. Add the vinaigrette and mix carefully. Add salt and black pepper if needed. Serves 6–8.

BASIL VINAIGRETTE

¹/₂ cup white vinegar
2 tablespoons warm honey
¹/₂ teaspoon fresh lemon juice
¹/₄ teaspoon black pepper
¹/₄ teaspoon salt

¹/₄ teaspoon ground coriander
12 large basil leaves, washed and torn into
  pieces
2 cups olive oil

1. In a food processor, combine the vinegar, honey, lemon juice, black pepper, salt, and coriander and pulse and mix. Add the basil and pulse and chop.

2. On full speed, slowly add the oil until the vinaigrette is smooth and bright green. Makes 2 ¹/₂ cups.

Saratoga Patriot Potato Salad with Scallion Oil

Where most potato salads can look dull, globbed in mayonnaise and using only one type of potato, enter a new creation, which features four different types of potato, available at most gourmet shops or even some upscale supermarkets. By using a light, colorful scallion oil, we keep the beautiful colors of the potatoes; the thin skin is left on for flavor and color variation. Enjoy your patriotic red, white, and blue potato salad! (These potatoes were purchased at Rivermeade Farms in Keene Valley, New York.)

1 pound blue or purple Peruvian potatoes, unpeeled
1 pound cranberry red or B-sized red potatoes, unpeeled
1 pound rose finn, rose fir, or yellow fingerling potatoes, unpeeled

1 pound California long white or Yukon gold potatoes, unpeeled
Vegetable oil as needed
1 pound andouille sausage*, diced ½"
3 cups Scallion Oil (see below)
1 cup finely diced scallions
Kosher salt and black pepper as needed

1. In a large pot, combine all of the potatoes in salted boiling water to cover and cook until fork tender. Because potatoes have different cooking times and sizes, watch the potatoes after 5 minutes and remove the fork tender potatoes when cooked. (Do not overcook.) Place the cooked potatoes in a bowl and chill in the refrigerator for 1 hour.

2. In a medium skillet, heat ¼" vegetable oil over high heat. Add the sausage and fry until almost crispy. Drain and set aside the sausage.

3. Prepare the Scallion Oil.

4. Cut the chilled potatoes into 1" wedges and place in a large mixing bowl. Add the reserved sausage, scallions, and scallion oil and gently mix without breaking the potatoes. Add the salt and black pepper to taste. Serves 6–8.

SCALLION OIL

4 garlic cloves
¼ teaspoon white pepper
¼ teaspoon salt
1 tablespoon granulated sugar

⅓ cup white vinegar
1 bunch scallions, diced
2 ⅔ cups olive oil

1. In a food processor, combine the garlic, white pepper, salt, sugar, and vinegar and pulse until almost smooth. Add the scallions and pulse until mixed.

2. On full speed, slowly add the oil and pulse until smooth and silky. Makes 3 cups.

* *See Food Sources in the Appendix.*

Traver's Day Ale-Marinated Grilled Turkey Fillets with Goose Raspberry Salsa

In the third week of August, Traver's Day fever hits Saratoga Springs, the busiest week of the August meet. Chefs are gearing into overdrive to accommodate the hungry crowds, and fast-food joints have long lines, so why not relax and enjoy a picnic on the racetrack grounds. Try this grilled turkey, which can be served cold and grilled the day before at home.

1 bottle Saranac Pale Ale beer or
  compatible brand
1 shallot, minced
³/₄ cup balsamic vinegar
Juice of 2 oranges

¹/₂ cup honey
¹/₂ tablespoon finely chopped fresh rosemary
¹/₂ tablespoon pickling spice
Six to eight 5-ounce turkey breast fillets
3 cups Goose Raspberry Salsa (see below)

1. In a medium saucepan, combine the beer, shallot, vinegar, orange juice, honey, rosemary, and pickling spice and bring to a quick boil. Transfer the marinade to a plastic bowl and place in the refrigerator to cool.

2. Place the turkey fillets in the cooled marinade and return to the refrigerator for 6 hours, turning occasionally.

3. Prepare the Goose Raspberry Salsa.

4. Preheat the grill to very hot. Remove the turkey from the marinade and grill both sides. Reduce the heat and cook until firm and cooked through. Transfer the turkey to a large platter and spoon the salsa generously over the top. Serves 6–8.

GOOSE RASPBERRY SALSA

¹/₂ pint fresh raspberries
¹/₂ pint fresh gooseberries, small white
  grapes, or white currants
1 small yellow bell pepper, seeded,
  deveined, and diced ¹/₄"
¹/₂ cup finely diced red onions

2 tablespoons finely chopped fresh cilantro
¹/₄ cup white vinegar
Juice of 2 oranges
3 tablespoons granulated sugar
Dash Tabasco sauce

1. In a medium bowl, combine the raspberries, gooseberries, bell pepper, onions, and cilantro and gently mix together.

2. In a small mixing bowl, combine the vinegar, orange juice, sugar, and Tabasco sauce and whisk together.

3. Pour the vinegar mixture over the raspberry mixture and gently mix without breaking the berries. Let the salsa steep before serving. Makes about 3 cups.

"Hot Bet" Cajun Ham Sandwich with Smoked Gruyère & Beefsteak Tomatoes on Dark Pumpernickel with Purple Sage Mayonnaise

Every picnic deserves a good hearty sandwich, so why not pile high with some wonderful local ingredients, like Cajun ham, bacon, and smoked Gruyère cheese from Oscar's Adirondack Mountain Smokehouse*, large beefsteak tomatoes from the farmers' market, and hand-cut pumpernickel from the local bakery. Purple sage is available at farmers' markets and garden centers (substitute with green sage, if unavailable). Indulge . . . and pick the right horse!

1 cup Purple Sage Mayonnaise (see below)
1 bakery loaf dark pumpernickel bread, thickly cut into 16 slices
2 pounds Cajun cooked ham*, very thinly sliced
8 ounces smoked Gruyère cheese*, thinly sliced
16 beefsteak tomato slices
1 red onion, very thinly sliced
16 strips apple wood-smoked bacon*, cooked crisp

1. Prepare the Purple Sage Mayonnaise.

2. Prepare each sandwich by spreading 2 tablespoons of the mayonnaise divided on 2 slices of bread. Pile 4 ounces of ham, 2 ounces of cheese, 2 tomato slices, sliced onion to taste, and 2 bacon strips on the bottom slice of bread.

3. Place the other slice of bread on top and secure with 2 toothpicks. Slice in half and serve. Makes 8 sandwiches.

PURPLE SAGE MAYONNAISE
1 shallot, minced
1 tablespoon chopped fresh purple sage or green sage
$^1/_2$ cup chopped fresh watercress
2 egg yolks
2 teaspoons white vinegar
$^1/_4$ teaspoon salt
$^1/_2$ teaspoon onion powder
1 cup olive oil

1. In a food processor, combine the shallot, sage, watercress, egg yolks, vinegar, salt, and onion powder and pulse until well chopped.

2. Slowly add the oil in a thin stream at full speed until well mixed and smooth. Makes 1 cup.

* See Food Sources in the Appendix.

Royal Blackberry Scones with Ruby Port-Plum Butter

Scones are considered Scottish quick bread by origin. For centuries, this triangular-shaped oats and griddle back favorite was a standard at teatime in the British Isles. In the last decade, though, scones have become a popular breakfast, brunch, or picnic item in the United States and come in various shapes and flavors. Blackberries are available fresh from spring through early autumn; when using fresh, make sure that they are completely black, at their sweetest peak! As scones are a dry quick bread, it is important to eat or serve them with preserves, marmalades, or butter. This plum butter is delicious on scones, toast, or a thick piece of country bread. Juicy fresh plums in many shapes and colors are available — yellow sugar plums, green plums, dinosaur plums, red plums, and purple plums. Use a good-quality port, like Tawny Ruby Port for great results.

3 ¹/₂ cups all-purpose flour
3 ³/₄ teaspoons baking powder
3 ¹/₂ tablespoons granulated sugar
1 teaspoon salt
6 tablespoons vegetable shortening
³/₄ cup milk
2 eggs, slightly beaten
¹/₄ teaspoon ground cardamom
¹/₄ teaspoon ground cinnamon
¹/₈ teaspoon almond extract
2 tablespoons dried black currants
¹/₂ cup quartered fresh blackberries
1 tablespoon confectioners' sugar
All-purpose flour as needed
1 egg, beaten (for brushing)
Dried black currants as needed
Granulated sugar as needed
1 recipe Ruby Port-Plum Butter (see next page)

1. Preheat the oven to 375º F. In a large mixing bowl, combine the flour, baking powder, the 3 ¹/₂ tablespoons granulated sugar, and salt and stir to blend. With a pastry blender or a fork, cut the shortening into the flour until it resembles fine bread crumbs. (Do not overmix.)

2. Slowly add the milk, the 2 eggs, cardamom, cinnamon, almond extract, and the 2 table-spoons black currants to the dry mix and blend until smooth and moistened. (Do not overmix.)

3. In a small bowl, combine the blackberries and the confectioners' sugar. With a rubber spatula, carefully blend the blackberry mixture into the dough without breaking the berries too much.

4. Fold the dough together until you form a large ball. Place the ball on a floured work surface. Dust both sides of the ball with flour and flatten to ¹/₂". With a biscuit cutter or a glass, cut

out about 12 rounds. Place the rounds 1" apart on a greased baking sheet.

5. Brush the scones with the beaten egg and sprinkle with a few dried currants and some granulated sugar. Place in the oven and bake for 10–12 minutes. Serve with the plum butter. Makes about 12 scones.

RUBY PORT-PLUM BUTTER

2 tablespoons unsalted butter
1 1/2 pounds purple or red plums, pitted and cut into 1/2" cubes
1/3 cup Tawny Ruby Port
Juice of 1 orange
Peel of 1 orange
4 tablespoons honey
2 tablespoons granulated sugar
1/4 teaspoon salt

1. In a medium skillet, melt 1 tablespoon of the butter over medium heat. (Do not burn the butter). Add the plums and sauté until soft. Increase the heat and add the port, orange juice and peel, honey, sugar, and salt.

2. Reduce the mixture over high heat, stirring constantly, for about 8 minutes until the consistency is the thickness of applesauce. Remove from the heat and stir in the remaining butter until smooth. Let cool before serving. Makes 1 1/2 cups.

CHAPTER 5

FOOD PURVEYORS OF THE ADIRONDACKS

The renaissance of American regional cuisine and the immensely popular Food Network have spurred the growth of producers of artisan products. Responding to the needs of chefs, Northeastern farmers have turned their potato fields and cornfields into gardens of Eden, producing rare exotic greens, potatoes, and vegetables, specially grown for chefs and farmers' markets in the metropolitan areas. Regional wines and cheeses have experienced enormous growth due to clever marketing, Internet sales, and backing from chefs and restaurateurs. We have become what European countries have been for decades — fascinated with fresh, locally produced food.

I clearly remember as a child, while living in Holland, my frequent outings with my grandmother, who shopped every day for the evening supper. Her refrigerator was as small as an average microwave. Her attitude was — eat fresh daily, cook from scratch daily. Our morning trip would consist of visiting strictly artisan specialty stores for every component of the meal. Beautiful, cracking fresh bread from the bakery, loaves still hot, freshly trimmed meat from the butcher shop, fresh produce at the vegetable stand, and daily delivered milk, brimming with a layer of cream in the glass milk bottles. On Friday, she would take me to Scheveningen, the seaside fishing village, only a ten-minute tram ride way. She would fill her basket with freshly caught flounder or codfish. Smoked eel and mackerel, wrapped in yesterday's newspaper, were purchased for the Saturday night dinner, consisting simply of smoked fish, cold cuts, Dutch split pea soup, and brick heavy pumpernickel bread slathered with dairy-fresh butter and draped with hand-cut slices of the local aged Gouda cheese, purchased by the wheel. These are great memories that still haunt me in a pleasant way. They remind me of the importance of promoting, buying, and sharing the wonderful products of our local food purveyors and farmers.

More than ever, the Adirondack region is flourishing with artisan food purveyors and stores selling such goods as sweet maple syrup, wild honey, goat cheese, and much more. Chefs are planning their menus around the farmers' crops, which provides a two-way service: The consumer enjoys the freshest product available, and the producer stays in business. This great development will catch your eye as you travel the region and visit the many farmers' markets. We applaud all of the farmers and food artisans for their hard work and vision. We encourage chefs to continue their quest to use the best the region has to offer. We thank you, the home cook and food lover, for supporting this cause. Bon Appétit!

ADIRONDACK BUFFALO COMPANY

If you think you've seen it all in the Adirondacks, head over to Blue Ridge Road in North Hudson, just a few miles west off the Northway, I-87 exit 29. Enter the Adirondack Buffalo Company, where besides enjoying the spectacular sight of fifty or more buffalos in the valley below, you can visit an on-premise gift shop and a farm stand offering fresh local produce, buffalo meat, and incredibly delicious, inexpensive pies and cakes. Here are two favorite recipes from Steve and Doreen Ossekop.

Buffalo Pot Roast

1 tablespoon olive oil
3–4 pounds bison chuck or bottom round roast
5 garlic cloves
2 tablespoons Worcestershire sauce
¼ cup Chablis wine
1 teaspoon granulated garlic
1 teaspoon granulated onion
¼ cup water
Salt and black pepper as needed
6 medium carrots, cut into chunks
6 medium potatoes, peeled and cut into chunks
3 medium onions, quartered

1. Preheat the oven to 275º F. (Because buffalo meat is very lean, it is very important to cook the meat at a very slow temperature.) Coat the bottom of a large roasting pan or Dutch oven with the olive oil.

2. Cut small slits in the meat and insert the garlic cloves. Place the roast in the roasting pan and sprinkle with the Worcestershire sauce, wine, and granulated garlic and onion. Pour the water in the bottom of the pan and sprinkle the roast with a little salt and black pepper.

3. Tightly cover the pan and bake for 1 hour. After 1 hour, remove the pan from the oven and add the carrots, potatoes, and onions. Cover and continue baking for 2 hours, or until the meat is fork tender (slides off the fork).

4. Transfer the meat to a serving platter and let rest for 20 minutes. Keep the vegetables and pan juices warm.

5. Slice the meat and surround with the vegetables. Drizzle the pan juices over the meat. Serves 6.

Rhubarb Bread

BREAD

1 ¹/₂ cups firmly packed brown sugar
²/₃ cup vegetable oil
1 egg
1 cup sour milk (mix 1 teaspoon vinegar with 1 cup lukewarm milk)
2 teaspoons vanilla extract
1 teaspoon baking soda
1 teaspoon salt
1 teaspoon ground cinnamon
2 ¹/₂ cups all-purpose flour
1 ¹/₂ cups thinly sliced fresh rhubarb

TOPPING

¹/₃₄₄
* cup granulated sugar*
1 tablespoon unsalted butter at room temperature

1. Preheat the oven to 325º F. Grease and flour two 9" x 5" (1 ¹/₂-pound) loaf pans.

2. Prepare the bread by combining the sugar, oil, egg, sour milk, and vanilla extract in a large mixing bowl and mixing well. Add the baking soda, salt, cinnamon, and flour and mix until smooth. Fold in the rhubarb.

3. Prepare the topping by combining the sugar and butter in a small bowl and mixing until crumbly.

4. Pour the batter into the prepared loaf pans. Sprinkle with the topping and bake for 1 hour, or until the top is firm and springy and a toothpick inserted in the center comes out clean. Makes 2 loaves.

ADIRONDACK BUFFALO COMPANY
Blue Ridge Road
North Hudson, New York 12855
518-532-9466

COOPER'S CAVE ALE COMPANY

What do you do when you love brewing beer at home, you are fascinated by the motion picture *The Last of the Mohicans,* and your corporate employer of eleven years leaves the area? You guessed it — open a microbrewery, unique to the area, on St. Patrick's Day and launch it as the Cooper's Cave Ale Company, a name inspired by a scene from that same movie, featuring a hidden cave under a waterfall, a now historic site in the center of Glens Falls. Ed and Patty Bethel, along with son Adrian, are the owners of a full-time operation, brewing various English-style ales and servicing the Adirondack region's finest restaurants. This beer-friendly recipe is great with one of Cooper's Cave Porter, Red, Brown, or Pale Ales, or Sagamore Stout. Be sure to visit the Bethels during operating hours for a tour and a sampling of ales!

Cooper's Cave Cheddar-Ale Dip

One 8-ounce package cream cheese at room temperature
8 ounces extra-sharp cheddar cheese, shredded
$^1/_3$ cup Cooper's Cave Pale Ale or Tavern Ale
$^1/_2$ cup sautéed minced onions
1 tablespoon Worcestershire sauce
1 tablespoon honey
$^3/_4$ teaspoon ground paprika
$^1/_4$ teaspoon Tabasco sauce
Assorted crackers as needed

In a food processor, combine all of the ingredients, except the crackers, and process until smooth. Transfer to a serving bowl and refrigerate overnight. Serve with the crackers and beer, while watching a great sports game! Makes about 3 cups.

COOPER'S CAVE ALE COMPANY
2 Sagamore Street
Glens Falls, New York 12801
518-792-0007
E-mail: brewers@cooperscaveale.com

FO CASTLE FARMS

The people of the town of Burnt Hills consider themselves a lucky bunch. They have it all on Kingsley Road — a farm stand, a gift shop, a country-style coffee shop, and an apple orchard, known as Fo Castle Farms. Once an apple stand established in 1908, the business has grown to what it is today. The on-premise bake shop is notorious for turning out homemade breads, doughnuts, pies, and wonderful breakfast muffins.

Fo Castle Cranberry-Nut Muffins

4 large eggs
1 ³/₄ cups canola oil
1 tablespoon vanilla extract
1 tablespoon orange extract
1 ¹/₂ cups fresh orange juice
¹/₂ cup milk
6 cups all-purpose flour
2 cups granulated sugar
1 tablespoon baking powder
2 teaspoons salt
3 cups sliced fresh cranberries
1 cup chopped walnuts

1. Preheat the oven to 350º F. In a large mixing bowl, beat the eggs until fluffy. Add the oil, vanilla extract, orange extract, orange juice, and milk and beat well.

2. In another large bowl, combine the flour, sugar, baking powder, and salt and mix well. Stir in the cranberries and walnuts. Add the egg mixture to the flour mixture and mix until just combined. (Do not overmix.)

3. Grease or paper line muffin tins (12 supersized or eighteen 2" size) and fill muffin cups ²/₃ full.

4. Place in the oven and bake for 30–40 minutes, or until a toothpick inserted in the center comes out clean. Muffins must feel firm. Serve warm with a slab of country butter and don't forget to brew the coffee! Makes 12 supersized muffins and eighteen 2" muffins.

FO CASTLE FARMS
166 Kingsley Road
Burnt Hills, New York 12027
518-399-8322

HOSS'S COUNTRY CORNER

When driving through Long Lake, it is impossible to miss the large bark-decorated building of Hoss's Country Corner on the corner of Routes 30/28 North. A great black bear welcomes you into the store, which is packed with Adirondack gifts, books, and various food items from local Adirondack artisans. Across the street, check out their roadside food stand with ice cream and great chili dogs. Every second Tuesday in August, a large tent is erected next to the building, and Adirondack authors participate in Hoss's Author Night. Hundreds of locals and vacationers flock to this event, enhanced with live country music, to have their favorite Adirondack books autographed. Before the evening's event, the authors are treated to a huge barbecue and cookout, compliments of John and Lorrie Hosley. Charming host Lorrie submitted her favorite Adirondack cookie recipe for our book. Thanks!

Maple Syrup Cookies with Maple Sugar Frosting

3 ¹/₂ cups all-purpose flour
1 teaspoon baking powder
1 teaspoon baking soda
1 cup Grade A Adirondack maple syrup
¹/₄ cup firmly packed light brown sugar
1 cup unsalted butter at room temperature
3 eggs, beaten
¹/₂ cup chopped walnuts
¹/₂ cup chopped dates
1 recipe Maple Sugar Frosting (see next page)
All-purpose flour as needed

1. Preheat the oven to 350º F. In a large mixing bowl, combine the 3 ¹/₂ cups flour, baking powder, baking soda, syrup, sugar, butter, eggs, walnuts, and dates. With a rubber spatula, mix together until smooth. Chill the dough in the refrigerator for 1 hour.

2. Prepare the Maple Sugar Frosting.

3. Transfer the chilled dough from the bowl to a floured work surface. Flatten the dough to ¹/₂", dusting both sides with flour. With a desired cookie cutter, cut out the cookies.

4. Place the cookies on a greased baking sheet ¹/₂" apart and bake for about 15 minutes. Let the cookies cool. Top with the frosting. Makes about 4 dozen cookies.

MAPLE SUGAR FROSTING
2 egg whites
¹/₃ teaspoon cream of tartar
1 cup Grade A Adirondack maple syrup

1. In a cold bowl, beat together the egg whites and cream of tartar until stiff peaks form.

2. In a small saucepan, heat the syrup to 238º F (temperature can be measured with a candy thermometer).

3. Beat the hot syrup into the stiffened egg whites. Set aside. (This frosting is also great on cakes.)

HOSS'S COUNTRY CORNER
Routes 30/28 North
Long Lake, New York 12847
518-624-2481

ARMAND C. VANDERSTIGCHEL

LAKESIDE FARMS CIDER MILL

For the best apple cider doughnuts in the Northeast, head over to Lakeside Farms in Ballston Lake, New York. Fresh apple cider is produced on the premises and infused into the doughnuts. The farm store has a large variety of locally grown produce and artisan-produced products, such as honey and maple syrup. Lunch is served with three-mile-high stack sandwiches on various breads and delicious hot soups like the one submitted here by the chef and the Pearce family, who are going into their fifty-fourth year of business.

Squashy Apple Bisque

12 cups chicken stock
4 butternut squash, seeded, peeled, and diced ¹/₂"
6 large Fuji apples, peeled, cored, and quartered*
4 medium onions, coarsely chopped
1 teaspoon minced fresh rosemary
1 stick plus 7 tablespoons unsalted butter
³/₄ cup plus 3 tablespoons all-purpose flour
3 cups half-and-half
Salt and black pepper to taste
Apple cider as needed

1. In a large, heavy soup pot, combine the stock, squash, apples, onions, and rosemary and bring to a boil. Reduce the heat and simmer over low heat for 2 hours or until tender.

2. In a small saucepan, melt the butter over medium heat. Add the flour to bind and stir with a wooden spoon for 3 minutes, creating a roux. Turn off the heat.

3. With a food processor or a handheld blender, puree the squash mixture until smooth. Add the roux (butter/flour mixture) and mix until smooth.

4. Return the bisque to a simmering boil. Add the half-and-half, salt, and black pepper. Add a little cider to smooth out the bisque and simmer for 5 minutes. Enjoy! Makes 8 – 12 bowls.

* *See Fruit Glossary in the Appendix.*

LAKESIDE FARMS CIDER MILL
336 Schauber Road
Ballston Lake, New York 12019
518-399-8359

MAIN STREET ICE CREAM PARLOR

With fond memories of our childhood excursions to old-fashioned ice-cream parlors and luncheonettes, gleaming with shiny mixers, blender cups, and silver-footed cake and doughnut displays, we can only applaud the Robbins family for maintaining this Adirondack landmark that reflects a special era gone by. Besides ice cream, they serve breakfast, lunch, and early dinner with a strong emphasis on homemade, especially their famous soups. For Adirondack souvenir hunters, a gift shop is in a neighboring room. The following recipes highlight Main Street Ice Cream Parlor's typical signature dishes.

Main Street Country-Style Creamy Chicken Soup

4 tablespoons butter
1 medium onion, diced ¹/₄"
3 celery stalks, diced ¹/₄"
2 medium carrots, diced ¹/₄"
2 pounds skinless boneless chicken breast,
  diced ¹/₄"
4 cups chicken stock or bouillon

2 cups light cream
1 cup half-and-half
1 ¹/₂ cups cooked fresh peas
Cornstarch and water as needed
Salt and black pepper as needed
Ground nutmeg as needed
Chopped fresh parsley as needed

1. In a heavy soup pot, melt the butter. Add the onion, celery, and carrots and sauté for 4–5 minutes. Add the chicken and sauté until lightly browned. Slowly add the stock and simmer until the chicken and vegetables are tender.

2. Add the cream, half-and-half, and peas and heat through. If a thicker soup is preferred, mix together a little cornstarch and cold water and blend into the soup until desired thickness. Add the salt and black pepper to taste.

3. Ladle into soup bowls and garnish each bowl with a dash of nutmeg and a sprinkle of parsley. Serves 4–6.

Adirondack Maple & Walnut Sundae

"What a pity this is not a sin!" said Mr. Stendal, on first tasting this ice-cream sundae!

1 recipe Maple & Walnut Topping (see below)
2 scoops vanilla bean ice cream
Fresh whipped cream as needed
Grade A Adirondack maple syrup as needed
Chopped walnuts as needed

1. Prepare the Maple & Walnut Topping.
2. In a large glass sundae cup, place 1 scoop of the ice cream. Top with 1 tablespoon of the topping. Add a second scoop of ice cream and top with the remaining topping. Add the whipped cream, drizzle with the syrup, and sprinkle with the walnuts. Makes 1 sundae.

MAPLE & WALNUT TOPPING
1 tablespoon Grade A Adirondack maple syrup
1 tablespoon chopped walnut halves

In a small cup, combine all of the ingredients. Let stand for 2 hours.

MAIN STREET ICE CREAM PARLOR
Main Street
Chestertown, New York 12817
518-494-7940

ARMAND C. VANDERSTIGCHEL

NETTLE MEADOW GOAT CHEESE FARM

We are pleased to announce the existence of an artisan goat cheese farm in the Adirondacks that produces fantastic varieties sought after by local chefs and gourmet food markets as far away as New York City. Laurie Goodhart and husband Raynald Hebert commit to a seven-day work week to tend their goats, which are milked twice a day for ten months. On the fifty-acre farm, the goats are fed natural ingredients like nettle, raspberry bush, and even pine needles. This is important to the final flavor of the cheese, which many consider creamy, flavorful, and not too strong like most goat cheese. Cheeses offered are Fromage Blanc, Chèvre, Garlic Herb, Mixed Herbs, Tellicherry Pepper, and Lemon Verbena, as well as a beautiful firm goat cheese Ricotta. Here are a couple of Laurie's recipes using goat cheese.

Summer Tomato Salad

1 cup 1"-diced ripe plum tomatoes
2 cups 1"-diced cucumbers
²/₃ cup chèvre cheese
¹/₃ cup olive oil
2 garlic cloves, minced
¹/₄ cup chopped fresh basil
2 teaspoons balsamic vinegar
1 teaspoon tamari (thick soy sauce) or regular soy sauce

1. In a medium bowl, combine the tomatoes and cucumbers. In a separate medium bowl, combine the cheese, oil, garlic, basil, vinegar, and tamari and whisk until well mixed.

2. Pour the mixture over the tomatoes and cucumbers and mix to coat. Serve immediately. Serves 2–4.

Nettle Meadow Hot Potato Salad

2 cups 1"-diced new potatoes
1 ¹/₂ cups trimmed string beans
²/₃ cup chèvre cheese
¹/₃ cup olive oil
2 garlic cloves, minced
¹/₂ tablespoon coarsely cracked black pepper (preferably tellicherry)
1 teaspoon dried thyme
Kosher salt to taste

1. In a medium saucepan, cook the potatoes and beans in boiling water until tender. With a slotted spoon, remove the hot potatoes and beans from the water and place in a mixing bowl.

2. In a separate bowl, combine the cheese, oil, garlic, black pepper, thyme, and salt and whisk until almost smooth. Pour into the hot potato and bean mixture and carefully mix to dress. Serve immediately. Serves 2–4.

NETTLE MEADOW GOAT CHEESE FARM
South Johnsburg Road
Thurman, New York 12885
518-623-3372
www.foodstores.com

Laurie's Dessert Tip: *Fill fresh purple figs with Fromage Blanc cheese, then dip the figs in melted bittersweet chocolate.*

ARMAND C. VANDERSTIGCHEL

OSCAR'S ADIRONDACK MOUNTAIN SMOKEHOUSE

If you are a frequent diner at Adirondack restaurants and wonder why the phrase "we use Oscar's meats and products" often pops up on the menu, go visit the source! This cozy butcher shop and smokehouse, nestled on a hill off the main drag in Warrensburg, New York, smokes incredible hams, sausages, chicken, trout, and cheeses. Diners, restaurants, and bed-and-breakfasts swear by their nitrate-free breakfast sausage and bacon, which comes in many flavors. The homemade beef jerky is a big hit among hikers and trailblazers seeking lightweight, tasty, and nutritious backpack food. Fresh, on-premise-made cold cuts and wursts are plentiful. Besides a successful retail and wholesale business, Oscar's does a tremendous mail-order business, especially around Christmas, when the slogan is, "Order your hams early!" Here are two very simple Oscar's recipes, using their products!

Smoked Chicken Salad

1 cooked whole skinless boneless smoked chicken breast, diced $^1/_4$"
$^3/_4$ cup mayonnaise
1 teaspoon chopped fresh dill
Salt and black pepper to taste
$^1/_4$ cup finely diced red bell pepper
$^1/_4$ cup finely diced green bell pepper

In a medium bowl, combine the chicken, mayonnaise, dill, salt, black pepper, and both bell peppers and mix well. (Equal amounts of sweet country relish can be substituted for the bell peppers.) Serve on your favorite bread! Serves 2.

Warren County-Style Smoked Pork Chops

One thing the Quintal family knows for sure is how to smoke pork the right way. These popular center-cut pork chops (known in Germany as "Kasseler Rippchon") are best roasted with sauerkraut.

1 pound bag (not canned) sauerkraut
1 Red Delicious apple, peeled, cored, and diced ¹/₄"
¹/₄ cup whole fennel seeds
Two 12-ounce smoked pork chops
1 bottle beer

1. Preheat the oven to 350º F. In a small roasting pan, combine the sauerkraut, apple, and fennel seeds and mix well. Place in the oven for about 10 minutes, stirring frequently.

2. Remove the pan from the oven and place the pork chops atop the sauerkraut. Pour the beer over all and roast the chops in the oven for 8–10 minutes or until hot. Serve immediately. Serves 2.

OSCAR'S ADIRONDACK MOUNTAIN SMOKEHOUSE
22 Raymond Lane
Warrensburg, New York 12885
800-627-3431

ARMAND C. VANDERSTIGCHEL

PUTNAM STREET MARKET PLACE

Located in the heart of downtown Saratoga Springs, Putnam Market is the place to find gourmet foods, needed ingredients, and a large variety of fine wines and exotic beers. Catherine Hamilton and her sister Gloria Hamilton Groskowitz surprise their loyal customers daily with deliciously prepared foods and scrumptious baked treats, like these cookies.

Triple Ginger Cookies

³/₄ cup unsalted butter at room temperature
1 cup firmly packed dark brown sugar
¹/₄ cup molasses
1 egg, beaten
2 ¹/₄ cups all-purpose flour
2 teaspoons ground ginger
2 teaspoons baking soda
¹/₂ teaspoon salt
1 ¹/₂ tablespoons crushed fresh gingerroot
3 ounces crystallized ginger, chopped

1. In a large mixing bowl, cream together the butter and sugar. Beat in the molasses, then the egg. Set aside.

2. In a separate large bowl, sift together the flour, ground ginger, baking soda, and salt. Stir the dry ingredients into the molasses mixture and mix with a wooden spoon until blended.

3. Add the gingerroot and crystallized ginger and stir until well mixed and blended. Cover and refrigerate for at least 2 hours or overnight.

4. Preheat the oven to 350º F. Shape the dough into 1" balls. Place 2" apart on a greased cookie sheet and bake for 10 minutes or until browned. Let cool for 30 minutes. Makes 5 dozen cookies.

PUTNAM STREET MARKET PLACE
435 Broadway
Saratoga Springs, New York 12866
518-587-3663

TOAD HILL MAPLE FARM

As we traveled throughout the Adirondack region, it was evident that Toad Hill Maple Farm is the most popular maple syrup producer and packer in the region. In gift shops and bed-and-breakfasts, Randy Galusha's syrup is sold in many attractive bottles, jugs, and tins. We had the privilege of touring his facility in Athol, New York, and witnessing the process of maple syrup tree tapping, boiling, and packaging. Randy and his wife Jill know that in late winter/early spring when the nights are cold, the days are warm, and the maple starts running at its peak, it is time to roll up their sleeves and get to work.

When Randy was eleven years old, he started hanging coffee cans on maple trees to retrieve the clear sap. In a borrowed, large pan, he boiled the sap down to syrup over a fire between cement blocks. (It takes forty gallons of maple sap to produce one gallon of maple syrup!) As time went by, his passion for maple syrup grew into a lucrative part-time business. The traditional method of drilling a 2"–5" deep tap hole in a maple tree and inserting a pipeline spout over a hanging bucket has now been replaced by a tubing system. Randy's sugar bush consists of 100 acres of 2,500 trees.

The trees are tapped traditionally with a hard plastic or nylon sap spout connected to a plastic pipeline, which runs to a collection tank. From there it is put onto a truck, where it is hauled to

the sugarhouse to be fed into the evaporator, which is wood fired. A whopping 500 gallons is evaporated per hour, producing twelve or more gallons of maple syrup. The syrup is then filtered, checked for density, and packaged at 180º F (hot packing). The bacteria and yeast growth determine the grade. Fresh, cold sap makes the preferred Grade "A" light colored, the more expensive finer tasting syrup. Bacterial action on sap converts the tree's natural sucrose to glucose and fructose, which tend to darken when heated, resulting in a darker color syrup.

The lighter syrup is perfect as a topping on pancakes, waffles, and ice cream. It is more expensive due to its high-maintenance production process that calls for pristine sap, clean pipelines, and immediate boiling to avoid bacteria growth. For that reason alone, tubing has become the new collection method because it eliminates dragging heavy buckets of sap through the snow.

ARMAND C. VANDERSTIGCHEL

The darker syrup is actually more flavorful with a deep caramel taste, making it better for cooking. Once packaged into various bottles, jugs, and cans, the pure syrup is distributed throughout the region, ready to fly off store shelves or be poured generously onto the pancakes of hungry guests at lodges and bed-and-breakfasts.

The following classic recipe was prepared by Jill Galusha.

Jack Wax (Sugar on Snow)

2 cups Grade A Adirondack light amber maple syrup
Pristine fresh snow

1. In a heavy medium pot, boil the syrup over medium heat to 234º–238º F (use a candy thermometer to measure).

2. Place a mound of snow into each of 4 bowls. Immediately, evenly divide the syrup onto the snow in each bowl. The syrup will immediately stiffen to a taffylike candy and can be peeled off with a fork or fingers. Some northeastern maple syrup-producing communities have "Sugar on Snow Parties," where children enjoy the maple candy poured onto the snow.

TOAD HILL MAPLE FARM
766 Zaltz Road
Athol, New York 12810
518-623-2272
E-mail: toadhill@global2000.net

USDA Grades

Light Amber
Medium Amber
Dark Amber

Vermont Grades

Fancy
Grade A/Medium Amber
Grade A/Dark Amber
Grade B

Maple syrup by USDA standards has 3 grades; Vermont has 4 grades.

Throughout this book, you will find many recipes using pure maple syrup as an important ingredient, either as a flavor maker or a natural sweetener. For many of you, maple syrup is a comfort food condiment, usually poured over pancakes and waffles for breakfast. Unfortunately, most of the maple syrup found in pantries is an imitation made of corn syrup flavored with artificial maple extract. Adirondack/New York State maple syrup achieves the same level of quality as Vermont maple syrup. Because Vermont leads New York State as a production state, Vermont syrup is more popular. The following chart shows the overall production in America.

Top 10 Maple Syrup Production/Amount of U.S. Gallons of Syrup

1. Quebec   4,222,000
2. Ontario   592,000
3. Vermont   570,000
4. New York   400,000
5. Maine   153,000
6. New Brunswick   109,000
7. Wisconsin   100,000
8. Pennsylvania   95,000
9. New Hampshire   94,000
10. Michigan   85,000

* Sources: USDA, Agriculture Canada

CHAPTER 6

B&B, HOTEL & RESORT RECIPES

Since the first stagecoach made its way over the rough roads of the Adirondacks, there has been a need for inns to provide food and sleep for the weary traveler.

Today, this need has grown into a million-dollar business. Staying at an Adirondack bed-and-breakfast, inn, lodge, hotel, or resort is a treat for visitors. Why stay in a generic hotel chain, when you have the option of sleeping in a cozy, beautifully decorated country- or Adirondack-style guest room in a quiet setting,

to be awakened by the aromas of freshly brewed coffee, savory bacon, and the whiff of cinnamon-scented French toast. These little touches make this lodging industry tick — the mix of local charm and personal service.

In this chapter, we have assembled a very interesting array of recipes from Adirondack lodging facilities. These recipes showcase the variety of the lodgings' menus and their desire to send you on your way with a hearty, freshly prepared meal. Have a great stay!

ADIRONDACK HOTEL ON LONG LAKE

The Adirondack Hotel on Long Lake, originally built in 1853, is one of the oldest hotels in the region. The unique, four-story structure has been renovated, and today it provides great accommodations in rooms featuring a unique blend of rustic Adirondack and Victorian design. The hotel boasts two restaurants: The Lake Street Café specializes in light fare and casual dining, and The Victorian Room offers regional cuisine with a great wine list. Executive Chef Joseph Thompson, a seven-year veteran of the hotel, prepares hearty Adirondack dishes like this bacon-wrapped filet mignon submitted by Chef Thompson and owner Carol Young.

Bacon-Wrapped Filet Mignon

Vegetable oil as needed
Two 8-ounce Black Angus filets mignon
Salt and black pepper as needed
2 slices hickory-smoked bacon
4 medium fresh portobello mushrooms, cleaned
1 cup brown sauce*
2 fresh rosemary sprigs

1. Preheat the oven to 350º F. In a large sauté pan, heat ¼" vegetable oil over high heat. Sprinkle the filets with the salt and black pepper. Pan sear the filets quickly on both sides until golden brown. Remove from the pan.

2. Wrap 1 slice of the bacon around the sides of each filet and secure with a wooden toothpick. Place the filets in a baking dish and roast in the oven to desired internal temperature and doneness.

3. Slice 2 of the mushrooms into thin strips and set aside. Heat ¼" vegetable oil in a medium skillet over high heat. Place the remaining 2 whole mushrooms in the oil and sear on both sides until cooked. Remove from the pan and set aside.

4. Place the reserved sliced mushrooms in the pan and sauté in the pan juices. Add the brown sauce to the sliced mushrooms and cook over a low simmer for 3 minutes.

5. Remove the filets from the oven. Place 1 whole mushroom in the center of each plate. Place 1 filet atop each mushroom. Ladle the mushroom sauce over the filets and garnish with the rosemary sprigs. Serves 2.

* See Cooking Basics in the Appendix.

ADIRONDACK HOTEL ON LONG LAKE
P.O. Box 355, Route 30
Long Lake, New York 12847
518-624-4700
www.theadirondackhotel.com

ALL TUCKED INN

To watch the sunrise over the Vermont Green Mountains and Lake Champlain, while enjoying a full country breakfast seems one of the things that Adirondack dreams are made of. Located in the historic village of Westport is the cozy bed-and-breakfast All Tucked Inn. Innkeepers Claudia Ryan and Tom Haley are known for providing their guests with delicious food, especially showcased during their "Golf Stay & Play Getaway," in which golf outings at the Westport Golf Club are combined with breakfast, lunch, dinner, and a comfortable stay at the inn. For the colder months, the following dish from Tom is a real crowd pleaser.

Stilton Chicken with Port Wine Sauce

4 ounces Stilton cheese at room temperature
4 ounces cream cheese at room temperature
2 tablespoons port wine
Four 8-ounce skinless boneless chicken breasts
All-purpose flour as needed
3 eggs, beaten
1 cup plain bread crumbs
Salt and black pepper as needed
1/2 cup unsalted butter
1 recipe Port Wine Sauce (see next page)

1. In a small bowl, mash together the Stilton and cream cheese with a hand potato masher. Add the wine and mix well.

2. Place 1/4 cup of the cheese mixture in the center of each chicken breast. Fold the meat around the cheese like a jelly roll. Secure with wooden toothpicks, if necessary.

3. Set up a breading station by placing the flour, eggs, and bread crumbs in separate bowls. Add the salt and black pepper to the flour and mix well.

4. Dredge the chicken first in the flour, then the eggs, and then the bread crumbs. Press the bread crumbs firmly onto the chicken. Place the breaded chicken in the refrigerator for 30 minutes.

5. Preheat the oven to 350° F. In a large skillet, slowly melt the butter over medium heat. Add the chilled chicken rolls and sauté until the bread crumb exterior is light brown on all sides.

6. Transfer the chicken to a greased baking dish. Place in the oven and bake for 40 minutes, or until the internal temperature reaches 160°. Remove from the oven and keep warm.

7. Prepare the Port Wine Sauce.

8. Place 1 chicken breast on each plate and lightly coat with the wine sauce. Serves 4.

PORT WINE SAUCE

1 tablespoon unsalted butter
1 shallot, minced
¹/₄ cup port wine
¹/₂ cup chicken stock or bouillon
¹/₂ cup heavy cream
Salt and black pepper to taste

1. In a small saucepan, melt the butter over low heat. Add the shallot and sauté until soft.

2. Add the wine and stock. Bring to a simmering boil and reduce to ¹/₂ cup. Add the cream and cook, stirring constantly, until the sauce is slightly thickened. Season with the salt and black pepper. Keep warm.

ALL TUCKED INN
53 South Main Street (Route 22)
P.O. Box 324
Westport, New York 12993
888-ALLTUCK
www.alltuckedinn.com

ALYNN'S BUTTERFLY INN BED & BREAKFAST

Nestled at the foot of Moon Mountain in Warrensburg, New York, is Alynn's Butterfly Inn, a quaint bed-and-breakfast with a French Country aura. With hiking, biking, and cross-country skiing nearby, Innkeepers Al and Lynn make sure that a fantastic country breakfast is waiting for you before you head out for the day. The authors are pleased to declare that this quiche is the best they ever had!

Marcia's Spinach Feta Quiche

One 8" unbaked pie shell*
6 large eggs
1 cup light cream
1 tablespoon finely chopped onions
¹/₂ cup crumbled Feta cheese
¹/₂ cup chopped frozen spinach, thawed and drained
¹/₂ teaspoon salt
1 teaspoon black pepper
¹/₄ teaspoon garlic powder
Dash ground nutmeg

1. Preheat the oven to 325º F. Place the pie shell in a pie plate. With a fork, pierce some holes in the bottom.

2. In a medium mixing bowl, whisk the eggs and cream until frothy. Fold in the remaining ingredients.

3. Pour the mixture into the pie shell. Place the quiche in the oven and bake for 40 minutes, or until a wooden toothpick inserted in the center comes out clean, and the quiche is firm. Serves 6–8.

* *See Cooking Basics in the Appendix.*

ALYNN'S BUTTERFLY INN BED & BREAKFAST
P.O. Box 248, Route 28
Warrensburg, New York 12885
518-623-9390; 800-221-9390
www.alynnsbutterflyinn.com

BARK EATER INN

Those looking to partake in a piece of history through lodging should visit the Bark Eater Inn, a former stagecoach stop dating back 150 years. It is now a country inn run by Joe-Pete Wilson and his friendly staff. The breakfast here is legendary. After breakfast, guests can enjoy horseback riding from the adjoining stables or, in the winter, go cross-country skiing on the many miles of trails. Here is a breakfast favorite from Chef Pat and her accomplice Chris.

Outrageous Banana Pancakes

1 cup all-purpose flour
1 tablespoon orange zest
¹/₂ cup plain yogurt
1 tablespoon baking powder
¹/₂ teaspoon salt
2 egg whites
¹/₂ cup whole milk
2 cups sliced bananas

1. In a medium mixing bowl, combine the flour, orange zest, yogurt, baking powder, salt, egg whites, and milk and mix until smooth.

2. Grease and heat a griddle until very hot. Ladle the pancake batter onto the griddle. Flip the pancakes when bubbly and brown around the edges and continue to cook until firm and brown on both sides.

3. Top the pancakes with the sliced bananas and if desire, sprinkle walnuts and brown sugar over the top and drizzle with Grade A Adirondack maple syrup. Makes 6 pancakes.

BARK EATER INN
Alstead Hill Road (off Route 73)
Keene, New York 12942
518-576-2221
www.barkeater.com

BOATHOUSE BED & BREAKFAST

Located in the town of Bolton Landing, overlooking Lake George — "The Queen of the American Lakes" — is the Boathouse Bed & Breakfast. Built in 1917 as the summerhouse of speedboat racer and Gold Cup recipient George Reis, it enjoyed a complete renovation in 1997. At the Boathouse, situated on Millionaires Row with breathtaking views, guests enjoy a full breakfast prepared by Chef Patty Grambery and hosted by Innkeeper Joe Silipigno. Try this Italian-style omelette pie, prepared with fresh local vegetables.

Vegetable Frittata

2 tablespoons vegetable oil
1 cup sliced fresh button mushrooms
²/₃ cup ¹/₄"-diced onions
²/₃ cup ¹/₂"-diced green bell peppers
1 cup ¹/₂"-diced zucchini
1 teaspoon minced garlic
5 large eggs
¹/₃ cup light cream or milk
¹/₂ teaspoon salt
Dash black pepper
1 ¹/₂ cups soft bread crumbs
One 8-ounce package cream cheese, cut into ¹/₂" cubes
1 cup shredded cheddar cheese

1. Preheat the oven to 350° F. In a large skillet, heat the vegetable oil over high heat. Add the mushrooms, onions, bell peppers, zucchini, and garlic and sauté until crisp and tender. Remove from the heat.

2. In a large bowl, beat together the eggs, cream, salt, and black pepper. Add the vegetable mixture, bread crumbs, cream cheese, and cheddar cheese to the egg mixture and stir thoroughly, but lightly so cream cheese cubes are intact.

3. Pour the mixture into a well-greased 9" pie plate. Place in the oven and bake for 45 minutes or until set in the center and browned. Let cool for 5–10 minutes before cutting into wedges. Serves 6–8.

BOATHOUSE BED & BREAKFAST
44 Sagamore Road
Bolton Landing, New York 12814
518-644-2554
www.boathousebb.com

THE CHESTER INN

Chestertown's cozy main street features The Chester Inn, a beautiful home dating back to 1832 and listed on the National Register of Historic Places. It is owned by our Main Street Ice Cream Parlor friends Bruce and Suzanne Robbins. Guests are treated to a hearty breakfast of homemade corn bread, fresh fruit with vanilla sauce, sausage, ham or bacon, juice, and coffee or tea, or a special of the day like this heavenly cheese and vegetable breakfast soufflé.

Cheese & Vegetable Breakfast Soufflé

8 large eggs
3 cups milk
1 teaspoon salt
1 teaspoon ground mustard
5 slices white bread, cubed
Olive oil as needed
1 red bell pepper, seeded, deveined, and thinly sliced
1 green bell pepper, seeded, deveined, and thinly sliced
1 medium onion, thinly sliced
9 fresh button mushrooms, cleaned and thinly sliced
1 cup shredded cheddar cheese
1 tablespoon finely chopped fresh tarragon or chervil

1. Preheat the oven to 350º F. In a medium mixing bowl, beat the eggs. Add the milk, salt, and ground mustard and mix well. Set aside.

2. In 8 buttered ramekins*, equally divide the bread cubes.

3. In a medium skillet, heat $1/4$" olive oil over high heat. Add both bell peppers, onion, and mushrooms and sauté until caramelized.

4. Equally divide the mixture among the ramekins. Equally divide the cheese among the ramekins. Pour the reserved egg mixture into the ramekins until $3/4$ full.

5. Sprinkle the tarragon over the tops. Place the ramekins on a baking sheet and bake for 40 minutes or until cooked and firm. Serve immediately. Serves 8.

* See Cooking Basics in the Appendix.

THE CHESTER INN
Main Street (Route 9)
Chestertown, New York 12817
518-494-4148
www.chesterinn.com

THE COPPERFIELD INN

Located in the charming town of North Creek, adjacent to Gore Mountain Ski Resort, is The Copperfield Inn. With many amenities suited to a ski resort, this inn has a great restaurant serving regional fare, as well as a cozy drinking spot, Trappers Tavern. Brian Sterner, Executive Chef, is fond of roasted and grilled duck, as showcased in this recipe that he contributed; he also has an Adirondack Surf n' Turf, consisting of duck and trout!

Grilled Breast of Duck with Maple & Currant Demi-Glaze

4 tablespoons red wine vinegar
1 ¹/₂ tablespoons ground walnuts
5 tablespoons Grade A Adirondack maple syrup
¹/₂ cup canola oil
Three 11-ounce boneless duck breasts
1 recipe Maple & Currant Demi-Glaze (see below)

1. In a medium mixing bowl, combine the vinegar, walnuts, syrup, and oil and mix well. Add the duck breasts and marinate in the refrigerator for 1 hour.
2. Prepare the Maple & Currant Demi-Glaze.
3. Remove the duck breasts from the marinade and place on a hot grill or broiler and cook until desired doneness. Remove the fat and cut into thin slices. Fan the slices on each plate and spoon the demi-glaze over the top. Serves 2.

MAPLE & CURRANT DEMI-GLAZE
6 cups veal stock*
³/₄ cup Grade A Adirondack maple syrup
2 tablespoons red currant jelly

In a large saucepan, combine the stock, syrup, and jelly. Reduce, stirring constantly, over medium-high heat to one-half. Keep warm.

* See Cooking Basics in the Appendix.

THE COPPERFIELD INN
Main Street
North Creek, New York 12853
518-251-2500
www.copperfieldinn.com

CORNERSTONE VICTORIAN BED & BREAKFAST

The Cornerstone Victorian is a recent addition to the great lodging facilities in the Adirondacks. Formerly known as The Bent Finial Manor, it is now under the new ownership of Doug and Louise Goettsche, two hospitality veterans who have managed properties in the Catskills. The beautiful Victorian-style manor is back in full force to accommodate travelers seeking a comfortable stay in charming Warrensburg and a delicious breakfast prepared by the gracious hosts. This is a wonderful variation on French toast that perhaps could win an award for a perfect Valentine's Day breakfast . . . food for thought versus food for lovers!

Strawberries & Cream French Toast

½ cup vanilla yogurt
½ cup half-and-half
3 large eggs, beaten
1 teaspoon vanilla extract
1 cup finely ground toasted almonds (see page 30)
Two 1" thick slices challah bread
2 tablespoons unsalted butter
2 cups hulled and halved strawberries
Fresh whipped cream as needed
Confectioners' sugar as needed
Grade A Adirondack maple syrup

1. In a medium bowl, combine the yogurt, half-and-half, eggs, and vanilla extract and mix well. Put the almonds into a shallow bowl.

2. Dip the bread slices into the egg mixture and coat well. Dip the battered bread into the almonds and coat well.

3. In a medium nonstick skillet, melt the butter over medium heat. Place the coated bread in the pan and lightly brown on both sides.

4. Remove the bread from the pan. Cut in half and stand the slices on their edges, forming a starlike structure on the plate. Fill the corners with the strawberries and whipped cream. Dust with the confectioners' sugar and serve with the maple syrup. Serves 1.

CORNERSTONE VICTORIAN BED & BREAKFAST
3921 Main Street (Route 9)
Warrensburg, New York 12885
518-623-3308
www.cornerstonevictorian.com

COUNTRY ROAD LODGE BED & BREAKFAST

At the end of a country road, bordering the almighty Hudson River, lies the Country Road Lodge, a cozy ski lodge and bed-and-breakfast on thirty-five acres of secluded property bordering State lands. With the Hickory Hill Ski Center next door and plenty of cross-country skiing available, Innkeepers Steve and Sandi Parisi are always ready to welcome their guests with a cup of steaming coffee and some of these already famous muffins.

Lemon-Ginger Muffins

2 cups all-purpose unbleached flour
1 teaspoon baking powder
1 teaspoon baking soda
¹/₂ teaspoon salt
2 large eggs, beaten
1 ¹/₄ cups plain yogurt
¹/₄ cup unsalted butter, melted

¹/₄ cup granulated sugar
1 tablespoon grated lemon zest
1 ¹/₂ tablespoons crumbled or grated
   candied ginger
Juice of 1 lemon
2 tablespoons granulated sugar

1. Preheat the oven to 375º F. Grease a nonstick 2" x 16" muffin tin.

2. In a medium mixing bowl, combine the flour, baking powder, baking soda, and salt and mix well. In a large mixing bowl, lightly whisk the eggs, then whisk in the yogurt, butter, the ¹/₄ cup sugar, lemon zest, and ginger.

3. With a rubber spatula, gently mix the dry ingredients into the wet ingredients. Spoon the batter into the muffin cups ²/₃ full and bake for about 18 minutes, or until the muffins show just a tinge of brown.

4. Meanwhile, combine the lemon juice and the 2 tablespoons sugar in a small bowl and stir until the sugar is dissolved.

5. Remove the muffins from the oven and brush on the glaze. Let the muffins cool in the tin for 2 minutes, then lift out to cool completely. Makes 12 muffins.

COUNTRY ROAD LODGE BED & BREAKFAST
Steve and Sandi Parisi
115 Hickory Hill Road
Warrensburg, New York 12885
518-623-2207; fax: 518-623-4363
www.countryroadlodge.com

Baking Hint: *If muffins (or breads or cakes) don't lift out easily, your tin is not seasoned adequately. Soak the tin only in cold water to soften residue, wipe out with a wet dishcloth, and dry with a paper towel. Your muffins should release with the slightest touch. Never use soap or detergent on baking tins.*

FRIEND'S LAKE INN

Even though we introduced you to Friend's Lake Inn in Chapter 1, Adirondack Fall, it was impossible to omit this fabulous recipe that has been an inn favorite for the last few years. Chef Tim Barnok is a master at using native Adirondack ingredients with a touch of the gourmet. Innkeepers Greg and Sharon Taylor, who have received many national awards for their inn, will dazzle you with their very large wine cellar and their expertise at recommending the perfect wine for your dinner. The inn has many rooms furnished in Adirondack Style, recreating the perfect Adirondack spirit for the guest. The inn's proximity to the adjacent cross-country ski trails and ski center is a great convenience for those seeking refuge during the winter months.

Vegetarian Delight

Olive oil as needed
1 small eggplant, cut into $1/2$" slices
$1/2$ cup red wine
2 tablespoons honey
$1 1/4$ cups balsamic vinegar
$1/2$ cup granulated sugar
2 whole plum tomatoes, halved

1 fresh beet, peeled and thinly sliced
3 sweet potatoes, peeled
$1/2$ cup destemmed and julienned fresh
*   shiitake mushrooms*
$1/2$ cup destemmed and julienned fresh
*   oyster mushrooms*
3 oyster mushroom petals for garnish

1. In a large skillet, heat $1/4$" olive oil over high heat. Add the eggplant slices and pan sear until light brown. Add the wine, honey, and $1/4$ cup of the balsamic vinegar and cook until reach a syrupy consistency. Set aside.

2. In a small saucepan, combine the remaining vinegar and the sugar and reduce until reach a syrupy consistency. (This is the balsamic reduction.) Set aside.

3. Preheat the oven to 350º F. Toss the tomato halves in olive oil and place in a baking dish. Roast in the oven for 5 minutes or until soft. Remove from the oven and set aside.

4. Increase the temperature to 375º. Place the beet slices on a greased baking sheet and bake for 10 minutes or until crisp.

5. In a medium saucepan, combine the potatoes and water to cover and boil for 12 minutes or until tender. Drain and rice or mash the potatoes.

6. In a medium skillet, heat $1/4$" olive oil over high heat. Add the mushrooms and sauté until cooked through. Fold the mushrooms into the riced or mashed potatoes. Coat the oyster mushroom petals in oil and broil until lightly browned. Set aside and keep warm.

7. Divide the potato mixture in half and place in the center of each plate. Successively top with the eggplant mixture (confit), tomatoes, beets, and a drizzle of the balsamic reduction. Garnish the plate with the reserved oyster mushroom petals. Serves 2.

Toasted Fennel & Porcini-Dusted Lamb Chop

1 tablespoon toasted fennel seeds
2 teaspoons porcini powder*
One 1–1 ¹/₂-pound rack of lamb, cleaned and trimmed by butcher
2 Idaho potatoes, peeled and quartered
Vegetable oil as needed
1 medium white onion, thinly sliced
2 shallots, minced
3 garlic cloves, minced
¹/₂ cup thinly sliced fresh morel mushrooms
1 pint heavy cream

1. Preheat the oven to 350° F. Grind the toasted fennel seeds in a coffee grinder. In a small bowl, mix together the ground fennel seeds and porcini powder.

2. Dust the lamb with the powder mixture and pan sear in an ovenproof sauté pan. Place the lamb in the oven and roast for 15 minutes or until desired doneness.

3. While the lamb is roasting, place the potatoes in water to cover and boil until fork tender. Drain and set aside. Keep warm.

4. In a small sauté pan, heat ¹/₄" vegetable oil over high heat. Add the onion and cook until caramelized.

5. Rice the reserved warm potatoes. Fold the caramelized onions into the potatoes and keep hot.

6. In another sauté pan, heat ¹/₄" vegetable oil over high heat. Add the shallots and garlic and cook until the shallots are translucent. Add the morels and sauté until soft. Add the cream and reduce by one-half.

7. Divide the potato mixture and place in the center of each plate. Slice the rack of lamb into chops and place the chops atop the potatoes, bone-side up. Spoon the morel sauce over the chops. Serve immediately. Serves 2.

* See Food Sources in the Appendix.

Spaghetti Squash with Fresh Peas, Ham & Parmesan Cream

1 spaghetti squash, halved and seeded
2 tablespoons butter, divided
2 cups water
3 tablespoons roasted minced garlic
2 cups heavy cream
³/₄ cup julienned ham
¹/₂ cup blanched fresh peas
³/₄ cup grated Parmesan cheese
Salt and black pepper to taste

1. Preheat the oven to 350º F. In a shallow baking pan, place the squash skin-side down. Put 1 tablespoon of the butter into each of the squash halves. Pour the water into the pan and cover with aluminum foil. Roast in the oven for 1–1 ¹/₂ hours, or until the squash is almost cooked but not overcooked.

2. When cooked, scrape out the squash into strands and set aside.

3. In a sauté pan, combine the garlic and cream and reduce by one-fourth. Add the ham, peas, and cheese and return to a simmer. Stir in the reserved squash, salt, and black pepper and heat through. Serve hot. Serves 4.

Cranberry & Chartreuse Sorbet Intermezzo

8 cups (64 ounces) cranberry juice
1 ¹/₂ cups Chartreuse liqueur
2 cups confectioners' sugar
Juice of 3 lemons

In a large mixing bowl, whisk together all of the ingredients. Place the mixture in an ice-cream maker and spin until it reaches sorbet consistency. Serve immediately. Serves 4–6.

FRIEND'S LAKE INN
Friend's Lake Road
Chestertown, New York 12817
518-494-4751; fax: 518-494-4616
www.friendslake.com

GREAT CAMP SAGAMORE

Great Camp Sagamore is a nonprofit educational facility. The camp, dating from the Gilded Age of the late 1800s, once served as a summer retreat for the Vanderbilt and Emerson families. Today, from May to October, the Great Camp offers learning programs, conferences, and tours. Wonderful food is served in the beautiful dining hall, where before meals, the chef rings the large outside bell to call in the guests. Enjoy these delicious pancakes from a recipe submitted by Chef Yiva Fisher.

Adirondack Raspberry Granola Pancakes

3 cups all-purpose flour
3 tablespoons granulated sugar
1 teaspoon salt
2 ¼ teaspoons baking powder
2 teaspoons baking soda

3 eggs, beaten
3 ½ cups buttermilk
3 cups fresh Adirondack raspberries
2 cups quick-cooking oats
½ cup granulated sugar

   1. In a large mixing bowl, sift together the flour, the 3 tablespoons sugar, salt, baking powder, and baking soda. Whisk in the eggs and buttermilk.

   2. In a separte bowl, toss together the raspberries, oats, and the ½ cup sugar. Set aside.

   3. Ladle the batter onto a lightly greased hot griddle to form 4"–5" circles. Before flipping the pancakes, scatter the reserved raspberry mixture over the tops, then turn and cook until golden brown. Makes about 24 pancakes.

GREAT CAMP SAGAMORE
Sagamore Road (off Route 28)
Raquette Lake, New York 13436
315-354-5311
www.sagamore.org

ARMAND C. VANDERSTIGCHEL

Saranac Powder Snow Apple Beignets.

Horseradish-Crusted Steelhead Salmon with Pickled Cabbage & Watercress Fraîche.

Toad Hill Maple Mousse with Apple & Pecan Crunch.

Eastern Seaboard Pan-Seared Sea Scallops with Dill Sea Foam & Yellow Turnip-Pear Hash.

Saranac Caramel Porter-Marinated & Grilled Rib Eye with Crawfish Butter.

Great Range Pan-Seared Tournedo of Beef with Oyster Mushroom Ragout.

Balsamic Lemon Thyme Honey-Grilled Chicken with Wild Blueberry Glaze over Silver Dollar Yam Cakes.

Crown Point Grilled Pork Tenderloin Medallions with Lavender-Scented McIntosh Peach Salsa.

Log Chalet of Grilled Monkfish Bunked with Charred Vine-Ripened Tomatoes &
Roasted Yellow Pepper Puree.

Trappers Pan-Seared Steak over Russet Potato & Lobster Hash with Lobster Claw & Scallion Butter.

Grits-Crusted Soft-Shell Crabs with Roasted Corn Aïoli & Chiffonade of Purple Basil.

Outrageous Banana Pancakes at the Bark Eater Inn, Keene, New York.

Serenity at Camp Sagamore, Raquette Lake, New York.

Friend's Lake Inn Toasted Fennel
& Porcini-Dusted Lamb Chops.

The Friend's Lake Inn,
Chestertown, New York.

Stilton Chicken with Port Wine Sauce at All Tucked Inn, Westport, New York.

Port Bay Chop at the Wawbeek Resort, Tupper Lake, New York.

Friend's Lake Inn Cranberry & Chartreuse Sorbet Intermezzo.

HOTEL SARANAC OF PAUL SMITH'S COLLEGE

The historic ninety-two-room Hotel Saranac in downtown Saranac Lake is considered by many to be the culinary heartbeat of the Adirondacks. Besides the typical "Adirondack Style" interior, the hotel is a gathering point for culinary students from nearby Paul Smith's College, as they apprentice alongside the professional staff. The college has been known to develop many prominent chefs of the North Country. Enter Anthony Lynarolakis, Executive Chef of Hotel Saranac, who is responsible for these typical Adirondack recipes, using local ingredients. When you dine in the A. P. Smith's Restaurant or the Boathouse Lounge within the hotel, you can find these specials on the ever-changing menu.

Landlocked Salmon Cakes with Dill & Caper Aïoli

2 pounds landlocked salmon (steelhead) or Atlantic salmon, deboned and cooked
1/3 cup minced red bell pepper
1/4 cup minced green bell pepper
1 tablespoon minced fresh cilantro
2 cups Japanese panko bread crumbs*
1/3 cup green Dijon mustard
2 eggs, beaten
1/4 cup rice wine vinegar
1/2 cup mayonnaise
1 tablespoon Tabasco sauce
Salt and black pepper to taste
2 cups crushed cornflakes
1 recipe Dill & Caper Aïoli (see next page)
Vegetable oil as needed
Wild greens, washed
12 lemon wedges

    1. In a medium mixing bowl, combine the salmon, both bell peppers, cilantro, bread crumbs, mustard, eggs, vinegar, mayonnaise, Tabasco sauce, salt, and black pepper and mix well. The mixture should be compact but pliable.

    2. Using a 4" cake ring mold and a 1/2-cup scoop, form the mixture into cakes.

    3. Place the cornflake crumbs in a shallow bowl. Press each cake into the crumbs, coating all sides. Place all coated cakes on a baking sheet and put into the freezer for 15 minutes to firm the mixture and adhere the crumbs.

    4. Prepare the Dill & Caper Aïoli.

    5. In a medium nonstick skillet, heat 1/4" vegetable oil over medium heat. Gently add the cakes and cook until golden brown on both sides, making sure they are cooked through.

6. Place each cake on a small appetizer plate with some wild greens, 1 lemon wedge, and some aïoli. Makes 12 appetizers (cakes).

DILL & CAPER AÏOLI
1 ¹/₂ cups mayonnaise
¹/₄ cup minced capers
1 teaspoon minced fresh dill
1 tablespoon fresh lemon juice
¹/₄ teaspoon black pepper

In a small mixing bowl, combine all of the ingredients and mix well. Makes about 1 ³/₄ cups.

* See Food Sources in the Appendix.

Braised Adirondack Snowshoe Hare with Dates & Caramelized Pearl Onions

A perfect regional dish prepared with hare (wild rabbit) — you can substitute domestic rabbit if hare is unavailable.

½ cup vegetable oil
1 cup peeled baby pearl onions
All-purpose flour as needed
Salt and black pepper as needed
8 leg/thigh pieces hare or domestic rabbit, skinned and trimmed
½ cup finely diced onions
5 garlic cloves

2 cups Madeira wine
6 cups rabbit demi-glaze or veal or chicken stock
1 pound dates, pitted
10 allspice berries
¼ pound (1 stick) unsalted butter
Roux as needed*

1. In a heavy, deep ovenproof pot or Dutch oven, heat the vegetable oil over high heat. Add the pearl onions and quickly brown (caramelize). With a slotted spoon, remove the onions from the pot and set aside.

2. Retain the hot oil. In a shallow bowl, combine the flour, salt, and black pepper and dredge the hare pieces in the flour mixture. Place the floured pieces in the hot oil and brown on all sides. Remove from the pot and set aside.

3. Add the diced onions and garlic to the remaining oil in the pot and sauté until golden brown. Quickly add the wine and deglaze the pot. Reduce the wine by half.

4. Preheat the oven to 350º F. Add the demi-glaze to the pot and bring to a boil. Add the reserved hare and pearl onions, dates, allspice berries, and a pinch of salt and black pepper.

5. Bring all of the ingredients to a simmering boil. Place the pot, covered, into the oven and braise for 1 ½ hours.

6. Remove the pot from the oven. Carefully remove the hare with tongs or a meat fork. Keep warm.

7. Place the pot on the stove top and reduce the liquid by half. Whisk in the butter until smooth. Add a little roux if the sauce appears too thin.

8. Place the hare in the center of each plate and spoon the sauce over the top. If desire, serve with polenta or rice. Serves 4–8.

* See Cooking Basics in the Appendix.

A. P. Smith's
HOTEL SARANAC OF PAUL SMITH'S COLLEGE
101 Main Street
Saranac Lake, New York 12983
518-891-2200

INN AT SARATOGA

One of the most interesting places to stay on Broadway in Saratoga Springs is the Inn at Saratoga. Its Victorian-style rooms have the aura of the old Saratoga days of men in high hats and ladies in pretty coat dresses. Besides offering a comfortable stay, the inn has been consistently good at serving upscale gourmet dinners with a regional flare. The Sunday Jazz Brunch in the summer is always sold out. Running the kitchen these days is Todd deWolf, a capital region veteran, whose experience keeps it all together in the heat of Saratoga during the explosive days of August, high-tide track season!

Skillet-Seared Duck Breast with Apple & Orange Chutney

2 large boneless duck breasts
Vegetable oil as needed
¼ cup apple cider vinegar
½ cup firmly packed brown sugar
½ teaspoon chopped garlic
½ teaspoon chopped fresh gingerroot
Pinch chili powder
Pinch ground cinnamon

1 McIntosh apple, peeled, cored, and diced ½"
One 5-ounce can mandarin oranges, drained
1 tablespoon toasted almond slivers (see page 30)
1 tablespoon raisins
1 tablespoon diced red bell pepper

1. With a sharp knife, score the skin side of each duck breast. In a medium skillet, heat 1 tablespoon vegetable oil over medium heat. Place the duck breasts skin-side down in the skillet and render the skin until crisp. Turn the breasts over and cook until desired doneness. Remove from the pan and keep warm.

2. In a small saucepan, combine the vinegar, sugar, garlic, gingerroot, chili powder, and cinnamon and bring to a low simmer.

3. When the liquid begins to thicken, add the apple and oranges and simmer for 3 minutes. Stir in the almonds, raisins, and bell pepper and heat through.

4. Thinly slice the duck breasts and fan the slices onto each plate. Spoon the chutney over the duck. If desire, serve with wild rice. Serves 2.

THE INN AT SARATOGA
231 Broadway
Saratoga Springs, New York 12866
518-583-1890
www.theinnatsaratoga.com

LAKE PLACID LODGE

Another luxury lakeside mountain resort in the Adirondacks is the Lake Placid Lodge. Its beautiful dining room has views of Lake Placid and Whiteface Mountain and is under the supervision of a husband and wife team, Robert and Vicki Breqette. Executive Chef Robert's career has taken him to places all over the Northeast, including the Four Seasons Hotel and Todd Weiss at Stowe. Vicki hails from London, where she worked in various top restaurants, only to find herself ultimately at the Point, a sister resort of the Lake Placid Lodge. She held the Executive Chef position there between 1995 and 1996. The menu at the Lodge features sophisticated American cuisine with a natural Adirondack flare.

Pine Jelly & Citrus-Glazed Adirondack Trout over Potato Parmentier, Local Wild Mushrooms & Roasted Ramps with Apple Cider Reduction

GLAZE
1 cup fresh orange juice
1/2 cup fresh lemon juice
1 cup pine-scented jelly*

APPLE CIDER REDUCTION
4 cups chicken stock
2 cups apple cider
1 cup hard apple cider (alcohol)
2 tablespoons unsalted butter

POTATOES, MUSHROOMS & RAMPS
1 pound mixed fresh wild mushrooms (cèpes, trumpets, chanterelles)
4 tablespoons canola oil
4 medium potatoes, peeled and diced 1/2"
1 pound ramps (wild leeks) washed, trimmed, and cut into 1" pieces
1 tablespoon unsalted butter
Salt and black pepper to taste
1 tablespoon chopped fresh thyme
2 tablespoons chopped fresh parsley

TROUT
Four 6-ounce boneless trout fillets
Salt and black pepper as needed
All-purpose flour as needed
Clarified butter as needed
Chopped fresh parsley

1. Prepare the glaze by combining the orange and lemon juices in a small saucepan over high heat. Bring to a simmering boil and reduce the liquid by two-thirds. Add the pine jelly and stir to

mix. Remove from the heat and set aside.

2. Prepare the cider reduction by combining the stock and apple and hard ciders in a large saucepan over high heat. Bring to a simmering boil and reduce to a syrupy consistency. Whisk in the butter until smooth. Remove from the heat and set aside.

3. Prepare the mushrooms by washing and trimming. Tear the mushrooms into large pieces and set aside.

4. Prepare the potato mixture by heating the oil in a large heavy skillet over high heat until almost smoking (light haze). Add the potatoes and fry until almost golden brown. Add the ramps and stir for 1 minute. (Ramps or wild leeks are available in the spring.) Add the reserved mushrooms, butter, salt, black pepper, thyme, and parsley and gently mix. Reduce the heat and continue to sauté until the mushrooms and potatoes are cooked through. Remove the pan from the heat and keep warm.

5. Prepare the trout by seasoning the fillets with the salt and black pepper. Dust both sides with the flour. In a large skillet, heat $1/4$" clarified butter over medium heat. Pan sear and brown both sides of the fillets and sauté until cooked through. Drizzle the reserved glaze over the fillets and turn off the heat.

6. Divide the potato mixture and place in the center of each plate. Place 1 trout fillet on top and drizzle the reserved cider reduction around the plate. Sprinkle with the parsley. Serves 4.

* See Food Sources in the Appendix.

LAKE PLACID LODGE
Whiteface Inn Road
Lake Placid, New York 12946
518-523-2700
www.lakeplacidlodge.com

THE LAMPLIGHT INN BED & BREAKFAST

For those of you in search of the best breakfast home fries: look no further. The Lamplight Inn of Lake Luzerne, a gorgeous Victorian-style B&B, tastefully decorated with antiques and a unique doll collection, is famous for its elaborate breakfast of fresh fruit, homemade baked goods, omelettes, house granola, waffles, and best of all — "Gene's famous home fried potatoes!" This well-guarded recipe was finally made public by Innkeepers Gene and Linda Merlino after raves from yours truly. After preparing the home fries, crack some eggs into the skillet, whip up an omelette, and enjoy the simple pleasures of a good breakfast.

Gene's Famous Home Fried Potatoes

6 medium Idaho potatoes, washed
Corn oil as needed
1 green bell pepper, seeded, deveined, and diced $^1/_4$"
1 medium onion, diced $^1/_4$"
Lawry's seasoning salt to taste
Salt and black pepper to taste
$^1/_4$ cup Italian-flavored bread crumbs

1. In a large pot, cover the potatoes with cold water and bring to a boil. Cook the potatoes until they slowly slide off a fork when pierced and lifted. Drain the water and let the potatoes cool. Peel the potatoes and cut into 1" cubes.

2. In a large skillet, heat $^1/_4$" corn oil over high heat. Add the bell pepper and onion and sauté until the onion is golden. Add the potato cubes and gently toss with the vegetables.

3. Sprinkle the mixture with the Lawry's seasoning, salt, and black pepper. Add the bread crumbs and toss, turning the potatoes until golden brown. Reduce the heat and slowly cook for 5 minutes more or until hot and crispy. Serve hot. Serves 6.

THE LAMPLIGHT INN BED & BREAKFAST
2129 Lake Avenue
Lake Luzerne, New York 12846
518-696-5294; 800-262-4668
www.lamplightinn.com

LODGE AT LAKE CLEAR

Searching for great German food, like sauerbraten, rouladen, schnitzel, and strudel, can be like searching for a needle in a haystack until you take Route 30 up to the Lodge at Lake Clear. Upstairs in the beautiful restaurant, which serves a mix of rustic German and Adirondack cuisine, one can enjoy high-quality meals prepared by Innkeeper Cathy Hohmeyer. Downstairs in the Beer Keller, Innkeeper Ernest Hohmeyer can offer you many exclusive European beers in a cozy, old-world lounge atmosphere, especially in ski season with the open fireplace — it's a great place to be.

Rösti Trout

2 medium Idaho potatoes, peeled
1 egg, beaten
$^1/_8$ teaspoon salt
$^1/_4$ teaspoon black pepper
$^1/_4$ teaspoon hot Hungarian paprika*
Clarified butter as needed*
One 10-ounce boneless trout fillet

1. With a grater, shred the potatoes into a medium bowl. Add the egg, salt, black pepper, and paprika and mix well.

2. In a medium nonstick skillet, heat $^1/_4$" clarified butter over high heat. Quickly place half the potato mixture in the pan in the form of the trout fillet. Place the fillet on top of the potato mixture and cover with the remaining potato mixture.

3. The fish is now sealed inside the potato mixture. Sauté both sides until golden brown, about 3 minutes per side. The fish will be tender inside the crispy potato crust. If desired, drizzle a little basil pesto on the fish for extra flavor. Serve immediately. Serves 1.

* See Food Sources and Cooking Basics in the Appendix.

THE LODGE AT LAKE CLEAR
Routes 30 and 186
Lake Clear, New York 12945
518-891-1489
www.lodgeonlakeclear.com

MERRILL MAGEE HOUSE BED & BREAKFAST

Rolling into Warrensburg, you might be looking for a place that has it all: lodging, breakfast, lunch, dinner, and fireplace pub. Look for the town bandstand, and right across on Hudson Street you'll find the Merrill Magee House, an historic inn dating back to 1812 and now listed on the National Register of Historic Places. Exquisite food, combined with an extensive wine list and various imported beers, has made this establishment a popular dining spot. The choice of ingredients in this recipe reflects the kitchen's loyalty to Adirondack roots.

Warrensburg Pork Roast with Blackberry Sauce

3 cups favorite stuffing mix
1 Granny Smith apple, peeled, cored, and diced 1/4"
1/4 cup chopped walnuts
3–4 pounds boneless pork loin
Salt and black pepper as needed
1 recipe Blackberry Sauce (see below)

1. Prepare the stuffing according to package directions. Add the apple and walnuts.

2. Preheat the oven to 350º F. Butterfly the pork loin by inserting a boning knife following the side seam with a 1" incision. Spread the loin out flat. Cover with plastic wrap. With a meat mallet, flatten the pork loin 2"–3" wider, without tearing the meat.

3. Remove the plastic wrap. Place the stuffing in the center of the pork loin lengthwise. Roll the pork together and tie off with butcher twine.

4. Place the pork in a roasting pan and sprinkle with the salt and black pepper. Place in the oven and roast for 1 1/2 hours, or until the internal temperature reaches 165º.

5. Remove the port roast from the oven and let rest for 20 minutes to settle the juices before slicing and removing the twine.

6. Prepare the Blackberry Sauce.

7. Slice the pork into desired portions and ladle the sauce over the pork. If desire, serve with roasted potatoes and seasoned vegetables. Serves 4–6.

BLACKBERRY SAUCE

1 1/2 cups white wine
1 cup blackberry brandy
1/2 cup blackberry or black currant jam
1 1/2 cups granulated sugar

1 tablespoon fresh lemon juice
3–4 tablespoons cornstarch
1 cup water
2 cups frozen (not fresh) blackberries, thawed

1. In a large saucepan, combine the wine, brandy, jam, sugar, and lemon juice over low-medium heat. Stir constantly until the sugar dissolves completely.

2. In a small bowl, mix the cornstarch with the water, forming a smooth paste. Whisk the cornstarch mixture into the saucepan. Cook, stirring constantly, over low-medium heat. The mixture will change in color from light purple to deep, dark (almost black) rich purple.

3. Add the blackberries and their juice. (Do not stir to avoid breaking the berries.) Keep warm.

MERRILL MAGEE HOUSE BED & BREAKFAST
2 Hudson Street
Warrensburg, New York 12885
518-623-2449
www.webny.com/merrillmageehouse

MIRROR LAKE INN

Overlooking Mirror Lake, in the heart of the former winter Olympics town, is the luxurious resort hotel Mirror Lake Inn. In winter or summer, the four-diamond, award-winning hotel is buzzing with guests looking for relaxation at the on-premise spa or a wonderful dinner by candle-light in the restaurant, which serves superb cuisine under the watchful eye of Executive Chef Matt Baldwin. At the Inn since 1994, Matt, a graduate of the Cobleskill Culinary University Program, had sharpened his skills at various prestigious resorts throughout the Northeast until finding a permanent home here in Lake Placid. His culinary gifts have not gone unnoticed, as witnessed in write-ups and feature articles in such national magazines as *Food Arts, Town & Country, Gourmet, Condé Nast Traveler,* and many more. Matt shares some of his Adirondack-inspired recipes with us, such as this terrine de foie gras and the following dessert recipe.

Foie gras, a gourmet favorite, is the goose or duck liver from geese or ducks fed a special diet of corn. Its silky, buttery flavor makes it a delicacy, either sautéed or slowly cooked in a terrine.

Terrine of Foie Gras

1 pound uncooked boneless duck meat
1 shallot, finely chopped
¼ cup rendered duck fat
3 tablespoons Dijon mustard
¼ cup heavy cream
Salt and black pepper as needed

12 strips uncooked bacon
6 ounces Grade B foie gras*, sliced
½ cup sun-dried cranberries
1 whole black truffle, thinly sliced*
6 ounces pâté de foie gras, sliced

1. Preheat the oven to 350º F. In a food processor, combine the duck meat, shallot, and duck fat and process until smooth. Add the mustard, cream, and a dash of the salt and black pepper and process until smooth.

2. In a porcelain terrine mold, line the bottom with the bacon. In successive layers, place a layer of the pureed duck meat mixture, a layer of the sliced foie gras, a sprinkle of the cranberries and truffle slices, and finally a layer of the pâté de foie gras. Top with a layer of the duck meat mixture.

3. Cover the terrine with a lid or aluminum foil and bake in a water bath for 2 ½ hours, or until an internal temperature of 130º F has been reached. Remove from the oven and place in the refrigerator overnight.

4. To remove the terrine, carefully insert a knife dipped in hot water on the side of the mold and slide the knife along the sides to loosen. Turn the mold upside down and tap the bottom of the mold.

5. Slice the cold terrine onto each plate and if desire, arrange with toast points, blackberry jam, and fresh blackberries. Serves 6 – 8.

* See Food Sources in the Appendix.

Mascarpone-Stuffed Poached Pears

Local pears from the eastern Adirondack border, near Lake Champlain and Vermont, are used in this scrumptious dessert — a smooth ending to a delicious dinner at the Mirror Lake Inn.

2 cups water
1 cup granulated sugar
1 cup port wine
2 cinnamon sticks
6 Bosc pears
2 cups mascarpone cheese*

1. In a large saucepan, combine the water and sugar and bring to a boil. Reduce the liquid until syrupy. Add the wine and cinnamon sticks.

2. Peel the pears, leaving the stem on. Place the pears in the saucepan and poach for about 1 hour or until semisoft. Let cool.

3. Place the pears stems up. Cut off the caps about three-fourths of the way up. With a teaspoon, scoop out the seeds in the centers. Carefully fill the centers with the cheese. Place the stem cap lid on top of each pear and drizzle with the poaching liquid. Serve immediately. Serves 6.

* See the Cheese Glossary in the Appendix.

MIRROR LAKE INN
5 Mirror Lake Drive
Lake Placid, New York 12946
518-523-2544
www.mirrorlakeinn.com

THE POINT

One of the world's most exclusive resorts can be found (by secret directions only) on Saranac Lake on the Upper Saranac Lake Peninsula. This former William Avery Rockefeller camp displays the Adirondacks' charm and beauty at its highest level, according to many travel magazines, such as *Condé Nast Traveler* and *Harpers Hideaway Report*. Executive Chef Kevin A. McCarthy, a Culinary Institute of America graduate, has seen most of the world as a chef in different settings, before running the show at The Point. The ever-changing daily menu provides Chef Kevin with the freedom to use local fresh ingredients for his superb cuisine. Local mushrooms from foragers are a favorite ingredient used in many of his recipes. Try this delicious ragout.

Adirondack Mushroom Ragout

Olive oil as needed
1 pound fresh morels, cleaned and trimmed
1 pound fresh porcini, cleaned and trimmed
1 pound fresh chanterelles, cleaned and trimmed
4 garlic cloves, minced
2 shallots, minced
1 cup heavy cream
Salt and black pepper to taste
1 bunch fresh chives, finely chopped
1 large tomato, peeled, seeded, and diced ¹/₄"
Baked puff pastry or bruchetta toast

1. In a large skillet, heat ¹/₄" olive oil over high heat. Add all of the mushrooms and sauté until begin to wilt. Add the garlic and shallots and sauté for 5 minutes or until lightly browned and soft.

2. Add the cream and bring to a simmering boil. Add the salt and black pepper. Stir in the chives and tomato and heat through. Serve over the puff pastry or bruchetta toast. Serves 6.

THE POINT
518-891-5674
www.pointny.com

THE SAGAMORE HOTEL

Overlooking Lake George in the beautiful town of Bolton Landing, The Sagamore Hotel is a part of Adirondack history. Since 1883, it has been standing proudly through turbulent times, but in 1983, it received a major renovation. Today, it is a luxury resort boasting 350 lodging options from suites to lofts. In the food service, the resort offers options from the casual Mister Brown's Pub to the exclusive Trillium Restaurant. Executive Chef Thomas J. Guay, also Director of Operations for the Sagamore's dining venues, carries through the tradition of the Sagamore's creative, regional American cuisine. As a Culinary Institute of America graduate, Chef Thomas crisscrossed the U.S. and worked at various prestigious venues, such as the Woodstock Inn in Vermont, before returning to the Sagamore, where he had started his career in 1986 as a sous chef. Judging from the following recipe, we are happy to have him back!

Apple-Dusted Landlocked Salmon with Apple & Jícama Slaw with Cider Butter Sauce

1 recipe Apple & Jícama Slaw (see next page)
Six 5-ounce salmon fillets, skin on
4 tablespoons apple powder*
1 tablespoon fresh herb blend (parsley, chives, thyme, chervil)
Olive oil as needed
1/4 cup white wine
1/4 cup apple cider
1 recipe Cider Butter Sauce (see next page)
Salt and black pepper as needed
1 teaspoon chili powder

1. Prepare the Apple & Jícama Slaw.
2. Lightly dust the fillet sides of the salmon with some apple powder and the herb blend. In a large sauté pan, heat 1 tablespoon olive oil over high heat. Place the salmon skin-side down and sauté until the skin is crisp. Turn the salmon over and continue to sauté until the fillets are golden brown.
3. Remove the salmon from the pan and place skin-side up on a cutting board. Carefully remove the salmon skin with a knife and peel away the brown fatty tissue from both the fillet and the skin. Set aside the skin.
4. Preheat the oven to 350° F. Place the salmon fillet-side up on a sizzle platter and pour the wine and cider around the fillets. Place in the oven for 5–7 minutes or until cooked through. Keep warm. Set aside all cooking juices (to be used in the sauce).
5. Prepare the Cider Butter Sauce.
6. Season the reserved skin with the salt and black pepper and a light dusting of the chili

powder and some apple powder. Rub each side with a little olive oil and place on a greased baking sheet. Place in the oven (350º) for 6–8 minutes or until crispy.

7. On each plate, pour a little cider butter sauce. Top with the slaw. Place 1 fillet on top of the slaw and garnish with the crisp skin. Lightly sprinkle the remaining apple powder over the top and serve immediately. Serves 6.

APPLE & JÍCAMA SLAW

2 McIntosh apples, peeled, cored, and thinly sliced
1 jícama root, peeled and thinly sliced
1 bunch fresh cilantro, finely chopped
4 tablespoons cider vinegar
Salt and black pepper to taste

In a medium mixing bowl, combine the apple and jícama slices, cilantro, and vinegar. Lightly toss and season with the salt and black pepper. Set aside.

CIDER BUTTER SAUCE

³/₄ cup apple cider
³/₄ cup white wine
1 bunch fresh thyme
2 shallots, minced
2 bay leaves
1 teaspoon white peppercorns
¹/₂ pound (2 sticks) unsalted butter
Pinch ground cinnamon
Salt and black pepper to taste

1. In a small saucepan, combine the cider, wine, and reserved cooking juices (see step 4. on page 186). Add the thyme, shallots, bay leaves, and white peppercorns and bring to a simmering boil. Reduce the liquid until almost dry.

2. Whisk in the butter to create a smooth, silky sauce. Add the cinnamon, salt, and black pepper. Keep warm.

THE SAGAMORE HOTEL
Sagamore Road
Bolton Landing, New York 12814
518-644-9400
www.thesagamore.com

To make apple powder: *Preheat the oven to 150º F. Place peeled apple slices on a baking sheet and bake until dried and crispy. Place the dried apple slices in a coffee bean grinder and grind to a fine powder.*

WAWBEEK RESORT

For delicious Adirondack cuisine coupled with a unique setting and view, head over to the Wawbeek Resort. You'll find their two-story restaurant and lounge situated on the large property overlooking Upper Saranac Lake. In a true Adirondack-style setting, designed by Proprietors Norman and Nancy Howard, dinner guests can enjoy the exquisite regional menu items prepared by Chef Eric Rottner. As a native of the Adirondack region, Chef Eric has worked at various regional restaurants and can be considered one of the new breed of innovative Adirondack chefs infusing local ingredients into their menus. After a hearty dinner, walk down to the boat launch and enjoy a canoe excursion on gorgeous Upper Saranac Lake! Here are some of the Chef's specialties.

Wild Mushroom Strudel

2 tablespoons unsalted butter
2 pounds fresh mushroom blend (oyster, portobello, shiitake)
Salt and black pepper
1 cup thinly sliced sun-dried tomatoes
1 cup crumbled Feta cheese
3 tablespoons finely chopped fresh herb blend (parsley, thyme, basil)
6 sheets phyllo pastry
Melted butter as needed

1. In a large skillet, melt the 2 tablespoons butter over medium heat. Add the mushrooms and sauté until soft. Add the salt and black pepper to taste. Add the sun-dried tomatoes and let the mixture cool. Stir in the cheese and herbs.

2. Brush each phyllo sheet with the melted butter and layer all 6 sheets on top of each other. Spoon the mushroom filling lengthwise on the layered sheets. Roll the sheets around the mushroom filling and brush the outside with butter. Place in the refrigerator for 1 hour to set.

3. Preheat the oven to 350º–375º F. Place the strudel in the oven and bake for 10 minutes or until crispy. Let the strudel stand for 5 minutes to set. With a sharp knife, cut the strudel into desired portions. Makes about 10 appetizer portions.

Port Bay Chop

Two 16-ounce French-cut pork loin chops
Salt and black pepper as needed
¼ cup port wine
¼ cup Grade A Adirondack maple syrup
1 teaspoon minced shallots
¼ cup demi-glaze or brown sauce*
1 tablespoon sun-dried cranberries

1. Preheat the grill or broiler to very hot. Sprinkle the chops with the salt and black pepper. Mark and sear both sides of the chops over high heat. Reduce the heat and cook the chops until the internal temperature reaches 160º F or finish in the oven until firm.

2. In a small saucepan, combine the wine, syrup, and shallots and bring to a boil over high heat. Reduce the liquid to one-half. Add the demi-glaze and mix well. Spoon the sauce over the chops and sprinkle with the cranberries. Serve immediately. Serves 2.

* See Cooking Basics in the Appendix.

THE WAWBEEK RESORT
553 Panther Mountain Road (off Route 30)
Tupper Lake, New York 12986
518-359-2656
www.wawbeek.com

CHAPTER 7

RECIPES FROM RESTAURANTS & CHEFS

The majority of restaurants serving Adirondack-style cuisine are within the compounds of inns, hotels, and resorts. Most of the restaurants, in and out of the Adirondack State Park, have menus geared to travelers seeking simple Continental cuisine, catering to the families crowding the streets in the summer. As time goes by, this will slowly change as the regional cuisine grows, and more local, creative chefs open their own little places.

We have selected a handful of establishments known for their uniqueness and regional approach to foods. Their varied offerings range from gourmet-style dinners to simple diner fare, all prepared in good taste!

You may find, however, that many of the region's restaurants feature different cuisines, such as Italian, Continental, Chinese, or German — all serving delicious foods throughout the North Country. Remember, variety is an essential stimulus for our taste buds.

EDISON CLUB

The Edison Club is located south of Saratoga, New York, in the town of Rexford. Formerly a private country club for executives of General Electric, it is now open for membership, and its two dining rooms are open to the public. Spearheading the direction of the kitchen is Chef Dave Martin, known as one of the top innovators of Adirondack cuisine, dating back to his days as chef at the prestigious Friend's Lake Inn, where he had already started experimenting with ingredients native to the Adirondacks. Attached to his illustrious résumé are two awards from The James Beard House; in addition, he has been featured chef in *Country Inns* magazine and is the noon-time chef each Friday on Channel 10 Albany, an ABC affiliate.

To bring out the creative, adventurous, and daring pastry chef in you, try this fabulous dessert by Chef Martin. You will need an ice-cream maker, or you can simply purchase pumpkin ice cream at a specialty ice-cream shop.

Pumpkin Ice Cream with Chipotle-Maple Syrup, Corn Cakes & Pecans

PUMPKIN ICE CREAM
One 16-ounce can pumpkin puree
1 cup firmly packed light brown sugar
$1/4$ teaspoon ground cinnamon
$1/8$ teaspoon ground nutmeg
$1/4$ teaspoon ground ginger
1 cup half-and-half
$1/2$ teaspoon orange zest
$1/4$ cup fresh orange juice
2 cups heavy whipping cream

CHIPOTLE MAPLE SYRUP
1 cup Grade A Adirondack maple syrup
1 teaspoon crushed chipotle pepper (dried, smoked jalapeño pepper)*
2 tablespoons water

CORN CAKES
1 cup all-purpose flour
$1/2$ cup yellow cornmeal
$1/4$ teaspoon salt
2 tablespoons granulated sugar
$1/4$ teaspoon baking soda
1 tablespoon baking powder
$1 1/4$ cups buttermilk or milk
2 large eggs, slightly beaten
2 tablespoons unsalted butter, melted
Vegetable oil as needed
1 cup chopped pecans for garnish

1. Prepare the ice cream by combining all of the ingredients in a large bowl. Pour the mixture into the canister of an ice-cream maker and freeze according to the manufacturer's directions. Makes about 2 quarts.

2. Prepare the syrup by combining all of the ingredients in a small saucepan on medium heat. Slowly simmer for about 15 minutes. Strain through a fine sieve or cheesecloth. Let cool to room temperature. Makes about 1 cup.

3. Prepare the corn cakes by sifting together the flour, cornmeal, salt, sugar, baking soda, and baking powder in a large mixing bowl. In a separate bowl, whisk together the buttermilk, eggs, and melted butter. Add the wet ingredients to the dry ingredients and stir with a wooden spoon to combine (the batter will be lumpy).

4. Brush a griddle or skillet lightly with vegetable oil and heat the oil until moderately hot. Drop 1 tablespoon of the batter onto the griddle, leaving a small space between the corn cakes. Cook the cakes until the undersides are golden brown, and the edges begin to dry. Flip the cakes and cook until the second side is brown. Repeat the procedure using the remaining batter. Keep warm in the oven. Makes about 32 cakes.

5. On each dessert plate, place 4 corn cakes, overlapping each other. Place 2 ($^1/_2$-cup) scoops of the ice cream over the cakes. Drizzle 2 tablespoons of the syrup over the ice cream. Sprinkle 1 tablespoon or more chopped pecans over the ice cream and cakes. Serve immediately. Serves 8.

* See Food Sources in the Appendix.

EDISON CLUB
891 Riverview Road
Rexford, New York 12148
The Grill — Casual Dining
The Edison Room — Fine Dining
518-399-2393
www.edisonclub.com

HOT BISCUIT DINER

For the best biscuits in the Northeast, head over to the Hot Biscuit Diner in Ticonderoga, New York. Orley and Bonnie Dixon, along with son Craig, are known for their large, flaky, airy biscuits with sawmill gravy — a real Adirondack breakfast treat. They are also famous for their soups, pies, muffins, and good ole country dinners at very reasonable prices. The restaurant's entrance showcases a United States map, with flags pinpointing visitors' origins from all over the country. Even Art Carney of "The Honeymooners" donated his fishing pole to this popular restaurant.

Famous Hot Biscuits with Sawmill Gravy

4 cups all-purpose flour
2 ¹/₂ teaspoons salt
3 tablespoons plus 1 teaspoon baking powder

¹/₄ cup plus 3 tablespoons vegetable shortening
1 ³/₄ cups plus 2 tablespoons buttermilk
1 recipe Sawmill Gravy (see below)

1. Preheat the oven to 425º F. In a large bowl, sift and mix together the flour, salt, and baking powder. Cut in the shortening with a pantry blender or a fork until the mixture resembles course crumbs. Gradually add the buttermilk and mix until you have a soft dough. (Do not handle the dough too much.)

2. On a floured work surface, roll out the dough with a rolling pin to ³/₄" thick. With a biscuit cutter or glass, cut out rounds of dough and place on a greased baking sheet close to each other (this will make them fluffy and rise more) and bake for about 15 minutes. Remove the biscuits from the oven and keep warm.

3. Prepare the Sawmill Gravy.

4. Place 2 hot biscuits on each plate, ladle the hot sausage gravy over the biscuits, and enjoy a great breakfast. Serves 12 hungry Adirondack campers! Makes about 24 biscuits.

SAWMILL GRAVY
Vegetable oil as needed
1 pound high-quality fresh sausage

2 cups all-purpose flour
¹/₂ gallon milk
Black pepper as needed

1. In a large heavy skillet, heat ¹/₄" vegetable oil. Add the sausage and brown and break up until cooked. Turn off the heat. Stir in the flour until incorporated, having absorbed all of the grease.

2. Slowly add the milk, stirring constantly. Turn the heat to medium and slowly simmer, stirring constantly, until thickened. Add the black pepper. Keep warm.

HOT BISCUIT DINER
428 Montcalm Street
Ticonderoga, New York 12883
518-585-3483

NOONMARK DINER

Heading for Lake Placid, you just turned off I-87 onto Route 73, and you are rather tired from the long but anticipated drive from the South. We recommend that you remain calm and patient, because Route 73 will lead you to Keene Valley, and rather soon, you'll pull into the crowded parking lot of the Noonmark Diner. It's known as a safe haven for locals, campers, hikers, and tourists looking for a good old-fashioned, homemade meal, accompanied by fabulous on-premise-made pies, doughnuts, muffins, and other goodies. Some folks just stop in to pick up a loaf of the superb bread for a picnic basket or lunch box, but they frequently end up taking a fresh pie for the good ole sweet tooth! Check out the following pie creation, submitted by Lola Porter, owner of this landmark oasis!

Apple & Cheese Crumb Pie

1 recipe Cheese Filling (see below)
1 recipe Crumb Topping (see next page)
4 cups sliced apples (preferably Granny Smith)
1 cup granulated sugar
2 tablespoons bread flour
$^1/_2$ teaspoon ground cinnamon
$^1/_4$ teaspoon ground nutmeg
$^1/_4$ teaspoon fresh lemon juice
One 9" unbaked pie shell*
1/8 cup finely chopped walnuts

1. Prepare the Cheese Filling.
2. Prepare the Crumb Topping.
3. Preheat the oven to 325º F. In a medium mixing bowl, combine the apples, sugar, flour, cinnamon, nutmeg, and lemon juice and mix well.
4. Place the pie shell in a pie plate. Pour the apple mixture into the pie shell and sprinkle the walnuts over the mixture.
5. With a rubber spatula, spread the cheese filling evenly over the pie mixture. With your hand, sprinkle the crumb topping evenly over the cheese mixture. Place in the oven and bake for 45–60 minutes. Serve hot. Serves 6.

CHEESE FILLING
Two 8-ounce packages cream cheese at room temperature
1 large egg
$^3/_4$ cup granulated sugar
$^1/_4$ teaspoon vanilla extract

In a medium mixing bowl, combine all of the ingredients and mix well. Makes enough filling for 2 pies.

CRUMB TOPPING
1 cup bread flour
$^1/_2$ cup firmly packed light brown sugar
$^1/_2$ cup butter at room temperature

In a medium mixing bowl, combine all of the ingredients and mix well until pliable.

* See Cooking Basics in the Appendix.

NOONMARK DINER
Main Street (Route 73)
Keene Valley, New York 12943
518-576-4499

PAPA'S ICE CREAM PARLOR AND RESTAURANT

Those who are looking for nostalgia in the Adirondacks better stop at Papa's in Lake Luzerne. Since 1977, Papa (Fred Gardner) and Nana (Edie Cimler Gardner) have been serving old-fashioned ice-cream sundaes, breakfast, lunch, and home-style dinners in a charming setting full of memorabilia: hundreds of photographs, milk bottles, milk crates, and soda bottles. An outside deck overlooks the Hudson River — great in the summer. A truly charming establishment to visit in search of a simple quality meal or a sweet.

Adirondack Burger

1 recipe Hollandaise Sauce (see below)
One 4-ounce hand-packed burger
2 slices Canadian bacon
One 3-ounce butter croissant

1. Prepare the Hollandaise Sauce.
2. Cook the burger to order, as you fry the bacon.
3. Toast the croissant. Place the cooked bacon on the bottom piece of croissant, place the burger on top, and cover with the hollandaise sauce. Place the top of the croissant over the sauce. Serves 1.

HOLLANDAISE SAUCE
5 egg yolks
$1/8$ cup water
$1/2$ pound (2 sticks) butter, clarified*
Juice of 1 lemon
Dash cayenne pepper

1. In a large saucepan, combine the egg yolks and water and whip over high heat, beating constantly. Whip as much air as possible into the egg yolks. (Be careful not to make scrambled eggs.)
2. Cook until you can make peaks, beating constantly. Remove from the heat and slowly add the butter and continue to whip. Add the lemon and cayenne pepper. Keep warm, stirring frequently.

* See Cooking Basics in the Appendix.

PAPA'S ICE CREAM PARLOR AND RESTAURANT
35 Main Street
Lake Luzerne, New York 12846
518-696-3667

PITKINS RESTAURANT

Established in 1907 and currently operated by Ernest and Marie Rice, Pitkins Restaurant is the place to be for down-home, country-style cooking, and best of all for authentic Texas-style BBQ. Besides fork-tender ribs, brisket, and chicken, served in a simple but Adirondack setting, you will love the homemade pies and desserts.

Hot Summer Peach Cobbler

One 13-ounce can sliced peaches in syrup
$^1/_2$ teaspoon ground cinnamon
3 tablespoons cornstarch
2 tablespoons unsalted butter
1 cup all-purpose flour
1 tablespoon granulated sugar
1 $^1/_2$ teaspoons baking powder
$^1/_2$ teaspoon salt
3 tablespoons vegetable shortening (preferably Crisco)
$^1/_2$ cup whole milk

1. Preheat the oven to 400° F. In a medium saucepan, combine the peaches in syrup, cinnamon, and cornstarch and carefully mix without breaking the peaches. Bring to a simmering boil and simmer for 1 minute. Add the butter and stir to melt. Pour the mixture into a 1 $^1/_2$-quart 9" x 13" baking dish.

2. In a medium mixing bowl, combine the flour, sugar, baking powder, and salt and mix well. Add the shortening and milk and mix until the mixture is a thick batter.

3. Drop 6 spoonfuls of the batter onto the hot peaches, creating 6 islands among the peaches. Place in the oven and bake for 25 – 30 minutes. Serve hot. Serves 8.

PITKINS RESTAURANT
1085 Main Street
Schroon Lake, New York 12870
518-532-7918

RAQUETTE LAKE NAVIGATION CO.

Whereas most boat cruises or tours fail in the food department, we are happy to report that excellent gourmet fare is available aboard the *W. W. Durant,* operated by the Pohl family. Beautiful Raquette Lake, with its many islands and classic waterfront Adirondack camps, offers a perfect setting for enjoying great food while admiring the scenery, whether for a brunch, a dinner, a moonlight cruise, a foliage tour, or a winter carnival special. For a very reasonable fixed price, dinners are offered with a choice of freshly prepared entrées, desserts, and starters like this typical Adirondack-style butter bean soup. The chef even smokes his own bacon!

Butter Bean Soup

1 pound dried butter beans
Vegetable oil as needed
¹/₄ pound good-quality smoked bacon, diced ¹/₄"
2 large onions, finely diced
All-purpose flour as needed
2 quarts warm chicken stock
3 bay leaves
Salt and black pepper to taste
1 pint heavy cream

1. In a large plastic bowl, soak the butter beans overnight with plenty of water to cover. Drain and rinse just before use.

2. In a large, heavy soup pot or kettle, heat ¹/₄" vegetable oil over high heat. Add the bacon and fry some of the fat. Add the onions and lightly brown.

3. Once the bacon and onions are fully browned, add enough flour to bind, creating a rouxlike substance. Slowly add the warm stock and bay leaves, stirring constantly and mixing with a wooden spoon.

4. Once the mixture is smooth, add the rinsed beans and mix well. Bring to a boil over high heat, stirring frequently. Once the mixture starts to bubble, reduce the heat to a very slow simmer.

5. Simmer the soup, stirring occasionally, for 2 hours, or until the soup is smooth (the beans have broken up). Add the salt and black pepper. Stir in the cream just before serving. If the soup is too thick, add hot chicken stock. Makes 8–10 bowls.

RAQUETTE LAKE NAVIGATION CO.
(Route 28) Main Street, Pier 1
Raquette Lake, New York 13436
315-354-5532
www.raquettelakenavigation.com

RICHARD'S FREESTYLE

After being at the Wawbeek Resort since 1997, Chef Richard Brosseau decided it was time to start a place of his own, to showcase his creative cuisine infused with local ingredients. Located under the EMS Store, overlooking Lake Placid, this charming new restaurant is a breath of fresh air on Main Street. Chef Richard follows the season, typical in this winter-style recipe.

Maple-Glazed Venison Loin with Potato Rösti

VENISON

Four 6-ounce venison loins
Salt and black pepper as needed
Vegetable oil as needed
Red wine as needed
6 tablespoons Grade A Adirondack maple syrup
3 tablespoons red wine vinegar
1 tablespoon butter
2 tablespoons veal or venison demi-glaze

RÖSTI

2 large Yukon Gold potatoes, peeled
Salt and black pepper to taste
4 teaspoons olive oil

1. Prepare the rösti by shredding the potatoes with a grater into a bowl. Add the salt and black pepper.

2. In a large nonstick skillet, heat the olive oil over medium heat. Cook the potatoes, slowly raising the heat, until the potatoes are golden brown. Flip the rösti and brown the other side. Keep warm.

3. Prepare the venison by seasoning with the salt and black pepper. In a sauté pan, heat 2 tablespoons vegetable oil over high heat. Sear the loins on all sides to a golden brown (the venison should be cooked rare-to-medium rare). Remove the loins from the pan and keep warm.

4. Deglaze the pan with the wine. Add the syrup, vinegar, butter, and demi-glaze and reduce to a glaze.

5. Cut the rösti pancake into 4 equal wedges. Place 1 wedge on each plate. Slice each loin and fan around the rösti. Drizzle with the glaze. Serves 4.

RICHARD'S FREESTYLE
51 Main Street
Lake Placid, New York 12946
518-523-5900

APPENDIX

COOKING BASICS

In this section, we try to clarify definitions and answer frequently asked questions related to food. While you are mastering your food basics, remember, you are on the road to being an even better cook. Cookbooks should be fun and realistic for the home cook. Referring to this section while preparing the recipes will make your cooking educational and fun!

Ingredient Definitions, Cooking Methods, Culinary Terms

Aïoli: A flavored, infused mayonnaise, mostly infused with garlic, currently very trendy in haute cuisine.

Al dente: Cooked until almost tender, but still chewy, crunchy with a bite. Used to describe vegetables or pasta.

Allspice: A ground evergreen berry, resembling the taste of a combination of cinnamon, nutmeg, and cloves. Great for baking and pickling.

Barding: A traditional French technique where bacon or fat is inserted over or in lean meats to obtain juiciness in the meat.

Basting: Coating with sauce, pan juices, or marinade during the cooking process to prevent food from drying out.

Blanching: Submerging food very briefly in boiling water for a few minutes, then plunging into cold water to shock. Necessary before freezing certain vegetables or to brighten food.

Braising: Simmering food slowly in liquid, resulting in tender, flavorful dishes. Mostly applied to tough cuts of meat.

Brine: An herb, spice, and sugar saltwater solution to preserve or flavor food.

Browning: Searing meat, fish, or poultry in a very hot pan to color and seal in juices.

Capers: Small, unopened Mediterranean flower buds dried and brined. Add a pungent essence to food.

Caramelizing: Heating sugar until it turns light or dark brown. Also to cook foods to release natural sugars, resulting in flavoring or browning.

Chocolate:
>   **Milk chocolate**: Contains milk solids, cocoa, butter, and sugar.
>   **Semisweet chocolate**: Made with chocolate liquor (35%), sugar, and cocoa butter. Also known as bittersweet.
>   **Unsweetened chocolate**: Refined with chocolate liquor but not sweetened. Also called baking chocolate.
>   **White Chocolate**: Mixture of cocoa butter, sugar, and milk solids, excluding chocolate liquor.

Chutney: A raw or cooked mixture of fruit, herbs, and vegetables, including vinegar and sugar. Used as a condiment or dip.

Cilantro: The leaves of the coriander plant, with a distinctive flavor hinting at citrus, mint, sage, and parsley. Coriander is dried and ground and used as a spice.

Clarifying: Removing impurities from butter or stocks, particularly butter. Milk solids are removed by pouring off the clear butter once melted.

Confit: Slowly cooked meat or poultry in its own fat until very tender. Stored in a pot covered completely with its own fat.

Coring: Removing the central core of fruits or vegetables.

Cornish hen: Small hybrid bird, delicate in flavor.

Creaming: Mixing a softened ingredient, like butter or cream cheese, with other ingredients until well blended.

Crème fraîche: A soured, cultured cream product excellent with desserts or smoked products.

Crêpe: A very thin pancake, often filled and rolled with various ingredients, such as fruit compotes or ragouts.

Curing: Smoking, brining, or salting meat or fish to preserve and flavor.

Deglazing: Adding liquid to a hot roasting pan or skillet to loosen particles that adhere to the bottom of the pan. This is usually the base for gravies or sauces, especially when wine is added.

Deveining: Removing the black intestinal vein in a shrimp or lobster, which is bitter and unattractive; also, removing the interior ribs of peppers.

Double boiler: A set of two pans nestled on top of each other with boiling water simmering in the bottom pan. A technique used to cook or melt delicate foods (heavy cream, chocolate).

Dredging: Coating food with a dry ingredient.

Drippings: Liquid collected when meats and poultry are roasted, often used to make gravies.

Drizzling: Dribbling a liquid lightly over foods without overpowering or covering the food.

Dry rub: A mixture of spices or herbs rubbed onto meats or poultry for flavor enhancement.

Dusting: Sprinkling a light layer of powdery ingredients, such as cocoa, flour, or confectioners' sugar. Dusting greased cake pans prevents cake from sticking.

Egg wash: Beaten eggs, yolks, or whites mixed with a liquid to glaze baked goods.

Emulsion: By vigorous blending or whisking, two or more liquids are stabilized temporarily (vinaigrette) or more stable (mayonnaise). Stable emulsions require an emulsifying agent, such as egg yolks or mustard, which helps hold ingredients together.

Flour:

  All-purpose flour: General use flour consisting of mixed soft and hard wheats, used in a wide range of foods.

  Buckwheat flour: Dark, nutty, slightly sweet flour used primarily in pancakes, crêpes, and blinis.

  Bread flour: High-protein, unbleached, hard wheat flour resulting in higher rise, structure, and elastic dough in breads and pizza crusts.

  Cake flour: Low-protein, high in starch, bleached soft wheat flour containing cornstarch. Its ability to hold water and sugar prevents cakes from falling.

  Corn flour: Finely ground white or yellow cornmeal.

  High-gluten flour: High-protein flour, milled from hard wheat, commonly mixed with low-protein flours such as rye.

  Rye flour: Slightly bitter, tangy flour resulting in heavy, dense breads.

  Whole wheat flour: Milled from whole grains of wheat, containing bran and germ. Very dense baking results.

Focàccia: Flat, rustic flatbread, made with soft yeast dough.

Folding: Incorporating one ingredient into another without beating by gently lifting from underneath with a rubber spatula.

Frittata: Italian egg preparation technique, resembling a crustless quiche, where various ingredients are added; or the raw egg product rather than a filling.

Ganache: A filling or spread for cakes and tortes, consisting of melted chocolate and cream.

Glaze: To coat hot or cold foods with a thin liquid mixture to create a smooth and shiny appearance.

Honey: Honey ranges from white to dark brown. The lighter the honey, the more delicate its flavor.
Light, mild honey: Acacia, alfalfa, clover, lavender, orange blossom, rosemary.
Dark, strong honey: Buckwheat, chestnut, tupelo, wild flower.

Julienne: To cut into thin match-sized strips.

Juniper berries: Blue-black berries, sold dried and used to flavor meats, sauces, and marinades. Very bitter and pungent flavor. Also used to flavor gin.

Leek: Related to garlic and onion, it has the appearance of a large scallion, but it has a milder flavor. Perfect for soups and stews.

Macerating: A flavor infusion technique of soaking food in a liquid.

Maple syrup: Obtained by tapping maple trees. The sap is boiled down to a syrup during early spring. There are three grades.

  Grade A: Clear, gold, delicate flavor.

  Grade B: Vermont produced, strong dark flavor.

  Grade C: Robust, molasseslike flavor.

Marinade: A seasoned, acid-based liquid in which foods are soaked to acquire flavor and/or tenderness.

Medallion: A coin-shaped cut of meat for grilling and sautéing.

Meringue: A mixture of stiffly beaten cold egg whites and sugar, used for baking, especially for topping pies.

Mincing: Chopping into extremely fine pieces.

Mirepoix: A mixture of diced carrots, onions, and celery, used to season sauces, soups, and stews and a foundation for roasting meats.

Molasses: A by-product of sugar refinement, resulting in syrup used to sweeten baked goods and sauces.

  Light Molasses: Lighter in color and flavor.

  Dark Molasses: Darker, thicker, and less sweet.

Molding: Forming foods in various shapes using rings, terrines, and timbales.

Mousse: Foamy, frothy, airy, rich concoction of sweet or savory ingredients usually made from cream and egg whites.

Mulling: Infusion of spices and fruits in a liquid.

Mustard: Mixture of ground mustard seed and water.

American mustard: Bright yellow, mild but pungent.

Chinese mustard: Hot, pale, and yellow.

Dijon mustard: Smooth, tangy, containing wine, herbs, and brown and black seeds.

English mustard: Very hot.

German mustard: Mild to hot, sweet undertone, dark.

Ground mustard: Finely ground mustard seed.

Okra: A ridged-skinned, oblong-shaped pod, used in stews and gumbos. Very popular in the South where it is also fried as a side dish.

Pancetta: A flavorful Italian bacon that is rubbed with spices and rolled into a roulade. From the pork belly, it is cured not smoked.

Parboiling: Cooking food partially in boiling water as a preparatory step.

Parchment paper: Used as a nonstick surface for lining cake pans and baking sheets.

Parsnip: Related to the carrot, the creamy, white root vegetable has a pleasantly sweet flavor, perfect for soups and stews.

Pectin: A flawless, gelatinlike substance found generally in the skins and seeds of certain fruits. This causes them to gel when boiled with sugar and forms of acid. Some fruits, such as red currants, are higher in pectin than others with a lower amount, such as strawberries. Liquid or powdered pectin is available when making preserves to compensate for any low pectin levels.

Pesto: An emulsified mix or paste of herbs, garlic, cheese, and olive oil often augmented with nuts.

Phyllo dough: Light-textured, paper-thin sheets of dough, used for strudels and flaky pastries.

Pickling: Flavoring and preserving food in a brine or vinegar or both (pickles, corned beef, sauerbraten).

Pickling spice: A mélange of allspice, bay leaves, black pepper, cardamom, celery seed, chili pepper, cloves, coriander, dill seed, garlic, ginger, mace, mustard, and red pepper. In combination with liquids, it is use to pickle foods.

Pilsner: A common light beer originally developed in Czechoslovakia.

Pinch: An inexact measuring term in cooking when less than a $1/8$ teaspoon is needed. A casual finishing touch.

Piping: Placing soft food of various types (whipped cream, frosting, mashed potatoes) in the wide end of a pastry bag and forcing it out of the narrow-ended tip to create various decorations on foods.

Planking: A special technique where food is cooked on a well-oiled, heated wood plank, with succulent results.

Poaching: Gently cooking foods in an almost simmering seasoned liquid to acquire a full delicate flavor.

Poultry seasoning: A blend of herbs and spices, usually parsley, sage, thyme, and marjoram. Used generally in stuffings.

Pounding: Tenderizing or flattening foods with a heavy object; also a technique to cook foods quickly or for rolling the food around a filling (roulade of veal).

Preheating: Bringing the oven, grill, or pan to a desired temperature according to recipe, before adding the food.

Preserve: Chunks of fruit cooked with sugar and often pectin to create a spread. Preservation techniques date back centuries when seasonal fruits were preserved for the winter months.

Proofing:
1. Testing yeast if it is active enough for baking.
2. The second rise or fermentation period of a yeast dough after it has been shaped.

Prosciutto: The rear leg of pork is seasoned, salt-cured, and air-dried for 10 months to 2 years, resulting in a distinctive fragrance and mellow flavor. This Italian original is served best sliced paper-thin.

Puff pastry: A labor-intensive method of creating a rich, buttery, and flaky pastry by repeatedly rolling chilled pieces of butter between layers of pastry.

Pumpernickel: A dense, dark German bread made with rye flour, enhanced with molasses, flavored often with caraway seeds.

Punching down: A technique in baking yeast breads — to punch down the dough's first rise to redistribute the yeast for its second rise, resulting in a more even crumb in the bread.

Quail: Prized for its delicate, sweet, and nutty flavor, this American bird is now farm-raised and appears on many restaurant menus in various forms of preparation.

Quenelle: Oval-shaped dumpling of ground meats mixed with eggs.

Quick breads: Baked goods not requiring rising time

or yeast. Instead leavening agents, such as baking powder, baking soda, or just eggs are used (biscuits, muffins).

Ragout: A mixture of uniform pieces of meat, poultry, fish, or vegetables braised in liquid for a stew or a topping.

Ramekin: A small, round, ceramic baking dish used for individual portions of sweet or savory dishes.

Ramp: A wild leek, a variety of wild onion, now popular among chefs. Available at most farmers' markets.

Ratatouille: A French-derived vegetable stew simmered in olive oil.

Reconstituting: Adding liquid to dehydrated foods to return them to their original consistency (sun-dried cranberries).

Reducing: Simmering or boiling liquids to thicken and concentrate.

Relaxing: Dough must rest after it has been punched down so that the elastic gluten strands can relax, resulting in an easier shaped and well-risen loaf.

Rendering: Straining the pan drippings to capture rendered fat, such as bacon, duck, or chicken fat, to use in recipes.

Reserving: Setting an ingredient or recipe component aside for later use.

Resting:
1. See Relaxing (above).
2. Pie dough is refrigerated for 30 minutes to chill and firm fat and distribute moisture.
3. Batter for crêpes, when refrigerated a period of time, will result in a more tender crêpe from expansion of flour particles in the liquid.
4. Roasted meats should rest after removed from the oven. During the roasting process, juices have been drawn to the center of the meat, resulting in a dry edge. The slow redistribution of the juices during resting will return the meat to its full juiciness.

Rhubarb: Also known as "pieplant," a reputation earned for its use in pies and cobblers, rhubarb is a field-grown spring crop and a hothouse-grown crop year-round. This red celery like vegetable is cooked with sugar to counter its tartness.

Risotto: A creamy-flavored rice dish made from medium-grain Arborio rice. Its delicious earthy flavor and hands-on preparation has made it into a popular restaurant dish.

Rolled oats: A cereal grain of central European origin, which has been steamed and flattened, cut into flakes, and processed for quick cooking. A popular breakfast cereal, oats also are often used as an additive to various baking products, such as breads and cookies.

Rösti: A famous Swiss concoction of grated potatoes sautéed and pressed into pancake form.

Roulade: Tied, rolled-up meat, poultry, or fish, usually stuffed.

Roux: A thickening agent for soups and sauces (see individual recipe).

Rutabaga: A large turniplike vegetable with a sweet mustardlike flavor that mellows out when cooked. Excellent roasted and stewed or pureed with butter.

Salsa: A combination of compatible smooth or chunky vegetables and/or fruits accordingly seasoned. Used as a topping or a condiment.

Salt:
Celery salt: Table salt flavored with ground celery seed.
Iodized salt: Table salt with iodine additive as preservative.
Kosher salt: Coarse-grained salt, great for roasting.
Pickling salt: Finely ground table salt without additives, used for curing and pickling.
Sea salt: Evaporated from seawater.
Table salt: Regular, fine-grained salt with some additives.

Salting: Preserving meat or fish with salt or a salt solution.

Salt pork: Salted pork fat from the belly. It is great to use for winter soups. Heavy usage in New England cooking.

Sautéing: Cooking foods quickly in a small amount of fat.

Schnitzel: Thin veal, pork, or chicken cutlet sautéed in butter.

Scone: A small, crusty quick bread generally served with tea, butter, and preserves.

Scoring: Making shallow incisions in meats to tenderize and for flavor penetration when marinating.

Searing: Crusting and browning food quickly over high heat to seal in juices and flavors.

Shallot: A small, mild-flavored member of the onion family, used for sauces, soups, and reductions.

Sifting: Separating ingredients through a sifter and removing large particles.

Simmering: Maintaining a liquid's temperature just below the boiling point (185º F).

Smoking point: Oils have different smoking points. This is the point where a fat begins to break down by emitting smoke. Beyond this point, the oil reaches its flash point and catches fire. Peanut, canola, and corn oil are used for frying and sautéing because of their higher smoking point, opposed to virgin olive oil, which is more suitable for flavoring uses.

Spätzle: German-style noodles consisting of egg, milk, and flour, pressed through a large-holed colander into boiling water. Generally served with heavy, gravy and meat dishes.

Steep: To soak dry ingredients in wet ingredients in order to extract flavor from the dry ingredient.

Stock: A homemade broth extracting flavor from meat, bones, fish, poultry, or vegetables by simmering for hours.

Streusel: A crumbly topping composed of butter, flour, and sugar combined with various dry ingredients. Used for breads, coffee cakes, muffins, and pies.

Strudel: A crispy, European-style pastry generally stuffed with fruits or meats.

Studding: Inserting flavoring ingredients, such as cloves or garlic, into meats before roasting.

Sugar:

Brown sugar: Granulated sugar colored with molasses. Light brown sugar has a lighter flavor than the stronger dark brown.

Castor sugar: Slightly finer than granulated.

Confectioners' sugar: Very powdery, mixed with a little cornstarch. Used for dusting and decorating.

Granulated sugar: Most common sugar extracted from sugarcane or beets. Superfine sugar is made from finely ground granulated sugar.

Maple sugar: Made from boiling maple sap almost dry. Commonly used to mold into candy.

Raw sugar: A partially refined sugar.

Sweating: Cooking foods over low heat to release juices without browning.

Tapenade: A classic provincial dish of mashing ingredients into a spreadable paste, usually garlic, olives, anchovies, and capers.

Teflon: Synthetically coated cookware. Food does not stick to the cookware.

Terrine: A rectangular or oval earthenware cooking and serving dish. Usually used for terrines.

Tenderizing: See Pounding (above).

Thawing: A process of restoring food to room temperature. Thaw frozen foods overnight in the refrigerator as a safety precaution.

Thickening agents:

Arrowroot: Used as a substitute for cornstarch. Being less chalky tasting and creating a beautiful sheen, it is frequently used by gourmet chefs.

Butter: Stirred into a sauce before serving creates a gloss and lightly thickens.

Cornstarch: Used for pie fillings, fruit sauces, and Asian cooking, it is known for its shiny appearance but chalky taste. Mix with cold water before use.

Cream: Heavy cream added to a sauce will lightly thicken it.

Egg yolks: To thicken hollandaise, sabayons, or custards.

Flour: Used with butter to create a roux.

Gelatin: Animal protein dissolved in liquid for a gelatin dessert or a mousse.

Reduction: Cooking down liquid until thickened.

Tomato paste: Thickens tomato-based sauces.

Vegetable puree: Soups or sauces can be pureed and thickened with vegetables, such as beans or potatoes.

Truffle: Underground aromatic fungus primarily found in Italy, France, England, and the Northwest in the United States. Growing around roots of oak trees, the truffles are sniffed out by trained dogs or pigs. The two most valuable truffles are the black truffle of France and the white truffle of Piedmont, Italy.

Trussing: Tying up, usually poultry or meats, to avoid the stuffing from leaking out or to create a uniform shape when presented whole at the table.

Turnip: A root vegetable, part of the cabbage family. Its mild, sweet flavor makes it perfect roasted, pureed, or cooked in stews and soups. In recent years, it has gained popularity among chefs looking for new vegetables to experiment with. Turnips used to be considered a poor man's crop.

Vegetable shortening: This solid white fat made by hydrogenating vegetable oils, such as soybean, is often used in recipes to create flakier pie crusts and cookies. Where butter has a percentage of water, vegetable shortening is 100 percent fat. It also requires less creaming than butter. Sometimes both are combined to create flavor and flakiness.

Water bath: A pan of boiling water that provides a moist environment for baking delicate foods, such as custards, mousse, terrines, cheesecakes, and puddings. It also can function as a double boiler to keep soups or sauces hot without scorching or burning.

Weisswurst: A German white sausage made from pork, veal, and spices.

Worcestershire sauce: A dark, commonly available sauce containing anchovies, chili peppers, cloves, corn sweeteners, molasses, tamarind, and vinegar.

Yam: In the United States, the orange-fleshed sweet potato is often referred to as a yam. The true yam, originating in the tropics with 600 varieties, is a tuber produced from a tropical vine and has a higher sugar content than a sweet potato.

Yeast: A microorganism leavening agent used for making breads and for transforming fruits and barley into alcohol.

Brewer's yeast: Grown on hops and used to make beer.

Baker's yeast: Available as active or compressed yeast.

Active dry yeast: Available in $1/2$-ounce envelops as regular or quick-rise, which cuts rising time in half.

Compressed yeast: Compressed yeast (mixed with cornstarch) comes in $1/3$-ounce packages and must be kept refrigerated.

Zabaglione: A light, custardlike, frothy dessert that consists of egg yolks, sugar, and wine or brandy and is prepared over simmering water similar to hollandaise sauce.

Zest: The colored peel/rind of citrus fruits, such as lemons, limes, or oranges, used to perk up or accent foods. Zest is removed by using a zester or the fine part of a grater.

Butter Basics

Butter is the ultimate ingredient in cooking, be it for flavor or versatility. Used in a roux, in finishing sauces, or in baking and flavoring, it is important to know how best to work with it. Here is a list of techniques and generally used methods in using butter. When purchasing domestic butter, you will find salted and unsalted butter. Most chefs and cooks prefer unsalted or sweet butter. It has a more rounded and neutral flavor, and the absence of salt prevents foods from being too salty — remember, you can always add salt, but not take it away! In gourmet shops, European and farm butters are sold for higher prices, but these are great butters because of the higher fat content — creamier, smoother, richer, truly worth the extra money.

Melted Butter: Butter is simply slowly melted and used to flavor vegetables or to brush on baked goods. Use unsalted or sweet butter for the freshest taste.

Clarified Butter: Chefs prefer clarified butter for many reasons and always have a batch handy in everyday preparations. The milk solids in the butter are removed, which prevents the butter from burning when sautéing. Water is also removed. In other words, clarified butter is purified butterfat, with water and milk solids removed.

CLARIFIED BUTTER
1 $1/4$ pounds butter

1. In a heavy saucepan, melt the butter over medium heat. Remove and skim the froth from the surface.

2. Carefully pour or ladle the clear, melted butter into a separate container, leaving the milky water at the bottom of the pan. The clear butter is your clarified butter. Makes about 1 pound.

Brown Butter: This is whole melted butter that is heated until it turns light brown, with a goal to create a nutty flavor to enhance white meats, fish, and vegetables before serving. This is a tricky method, where you cannot overbrown the butter. Remove the pan quickly from the heat and transfer the butter to a nonheated pan.

Compound Butter: Butter is softened to room temperature, then flavor-making ingredients are added to enhance the butter. The butter is rolled into a cylinder in wax or parchment paper and refrigerated. Slices are then cut off and placed on grilled items just before serving for flavor, presentation, and saucing. Popular examples are herb, citrus, or garlic butter. Some chefs even use pieces of these butters to finish sauces. A very typical, basic compound butter is Maître d' Hotel butter.

MAÎTRE D' HOTEL BUTTER
1 pound unsalted butter at room temperature
$1/4$ cup chopped fresh parsley
$1 1/2$ tablespoons fresh lemon juice
Pinch white pepper

1. Using a mixer with a paddle attachment, whip the butter at low speed until creamy and smooth. Add

the parsley, lemon juice, and white pepper and blend slowly until well mixed.

2. Roll the butter into a cylinder on a sheet of parchment paper until 1" thick. Chill in the refrigerator.

3. Place ¼" thick slices on grilled or broiled meats just before serving. Makes 1 pound.

Beef Stock

Even though beef base, bouillon, or canned beef stock are available at your fingertips, it is always tastier to make a stock from scratch. The most important thing in this recipe is the browning of the bones. If you burn the bones, you will have a bitter stock.

BEEF STOCK
5 pounds beef bones, cut into 3" pieces
2 medium onions, coarsely chopped
4 medium carrots, coarsely chopped
4 celery stalks, coarsely chopped
5 quarts cold water
1 cup tomato paste
1 bay leaf
2 fresh thyme sprigs
4 fresh parsley sprigs
2 whole cloves

1. Preheat the oven to 400° F. Put the beef bones into a large roasting pan and place in the oven. When the bones are halfway browned, add the onions, carrots, and celery and continue roasting until the bones and vegetables are nicely browned.

2. Remove the bones and vegetables from the roasting pan and place in a stockpot. Cover the bones with the water and bring to a boil over high heat. Reduce the heat and let the stock simmer, skimming off the fat.

3. Remove the fat from the roasting pan and deglaze the pan by adding hot water to the pan and scraping the bottom with a metal spatula, loosening the brown drippings and flavor-making particles.

4. Add the deglazed liquid, tomato paste, bay leaf, thyme, parsley, and cloves to the stockpot and simmer for 6 hours, skimming fat from the surface if necessary. Add water as needed to keep the bones covered.

5. Strain the stock through a strainer or cheesecloth and let cool before refrigerating. The stock can be refrigerated for 5 days or frozen until needed. Basic beef

stock is the foundation of many sauces, especially brown sauce (see below). Makes 4 quarts.

BROWN SAUCE
¼ pound (1 stick) unsalted butter
2 medium onions, diced ½"
2 celery stalks, diced ½"
3 medium carrots, diced ½"
¾ cup all-purpose flour
3 quarts Beef Stock (see above)
½ cup tomato paste
1 bay leaf
1 fresh thyme sprig
5 fresh parsley sprigs

1. In a large heavy stockpot, melt the butter and sauté the onions, celery, and carrots until browned. Add the flour to bind and make a roux (thickening agent method). With a wooden spoon, stir the roux over medium heat until lightly browned.

2. Slowly add the stock and tomato paste to the roux and bring the mixture to a boil, stirring constantly. Reduce the heat to simmer, give the sauce a good whisk, and skim the surface for any fat. Add the bay leaf, thyme, and parsley and let the sauce simmer over low heat for 1½ hours, or until the sauce is reduced to 2 quarts.

3. Strain the sauce through a strainer, pressing lightly with a spoon to extract juices from the cooked vegetables. Let cool. Refrigerate or serve immediately. Makes 2 quarts.

Brown sauce is an important basic sauce, which can be used by itself or as a base for new sauces by simply adding ingredients:

Bordelaise: Brown sauce with red wine, shallots, peppercorns, herbs, and butter.
Chasseur: Brown sauce with white wine, tomatoes, mushrooms, shallots, and tarragon.

For a very basic, but less flavorful, quick brown sauce, mix desired quantity of Beef Stock (see above) or store-bought beef stock with a roux or cornstarch over medium heat. Bring to a simmer and add additional thickening agents until desired thickness has been reached. It is very handy to have a container of brown sauce, either long-cooking or quick, in the refrigerator, even if it is just to smother French fries in gravy!

Chicken Stock

Nothing beats a great chicken stock (Adirondack penicillin) for any sauce preparation. In the supermarket or butcher shop, chicken stock packets are offered, featuring stock-producing parts, such as the back, carcass, legs, or wings — the more bone, the better stock. You will find that these parts are inexpensive, and therefore, it is worth a try to make your own stock. Besides, your house will be filled with the pleasant aroma of a lingering stock, creating a mouthwatering anticipation of good food to come or maybe a sales tactic if conducting an open house for real estate transactions!

2 tablespoons vegetable oil
4 pounds chicken parts, rinsed under cold water and
   cut into small pieces
4 medium onions, cut into quarters
1 pound carrots, cut into chunks
4 celery stalks, cut into chunks
1 pound leeks, washed, trimmed, and cut into chunks
2 gallons cold water
4 whole plum tomatoes (do not cut)
2 teaspoons white peppercorns
5 bay leaves
8 fresh parsley sprigs

1. In a large heavy stockpot, heat the vegetable oil over high heat. Add the chicken, onions, carrots, celery, and leeks and sauté until lightly browned.

2. Add the cold water and bring to a boil. Remove the scum with a ladle. Add the tomatoes, white peppercorns, bay leaves, and parsley and return the liquid to a boil. Reduce the heat and gently simmer for about 6 hours.

3. Strain the liquid. Return the strained stock to a boil and reduce the quantity to 2 quarts, which is about one-fourth of its original quantity. This procedure will intensify the flavor by concentration.

4. Let the stock cool and skim off any fat. The stock can be refrigerated for about 4 days or frozen until needed. Makes 2 quarts.

Veal Stock

Here is another stock not carried in common markets, but ooh so delicious and helpful in creating scrumptious recipes and dishes at home. Most home cooks turn to beef stock instead, but for the patient among you, try this veal stock. Veal bones are available at most meat markets.

10 pounds veal bones, rinsed under cold water
1 pound leeks, washed, trimmed, and cut into chunks
2 medium onions, cut into chunks
1 1/2 pounds carrots, cut into chunks
3 celery stalks, cut into chunks
3 1/2 pounds plum tomatoes, cut into chunks
2 gallons cold water
1 teaspoon white peppercorns
4 fresh thyme sprigs
8 fresh parsley sprigs
5 bay leaves

1. In a large heavy stockpot, combine the veal bones, all of the vegetables, and cold water and bring to a boil over high heat. Remove any scum off the surface.

2. Add the peppercorns, thyme, parsley, and bay leaves and simmer very gently for 8 hours over low heat.

3. Strain the stock through cheesecloth or a very fine strainer. Return to a boil and reduce to 2 quarts. Let cool.

4. Refrigerate the stock overnight, then remove the fat from the top. The stock will have a gelatinous consistency due to the extraction of marrow from the veal bones. The stock can be refrigerated for 3 days or can be frozen until needed. Makes 2 quarts.

For a dark veal stock or demi-glaze, roast the veal bones and vegetables in a 350° F oven until golden brown to develop the caramelization for browning the stock. Follow the same procedure as above, by combining the roasted veal bones, vegetables, water, herbs, and spices and simmering for 8 hours.

Fish Stock

Have you ever noticed that supermarkets carry cans of beef or chicken stock, but never a true fish stock. Here is a great recipe — quite simple and fairly quick to make. Fish bones are available at most fish stores, or perhaps some anglers in the family are willing to save their fish bones after filleting their catch. Recommended fish bones are ones with a neutral flavor, such as flounder, sea bass, cod, or snapper. If using freshwater fish bones, stick to pike, bass, or trout bones.

2 tablespoons vegetable oil
4 pounds fish bones, rinsed under cold water
2 medium onions, cut into chunks
6 celery stalks, cut into chunks
1 pound leeks, washed, trimmed, and cut into chunks
2 cups white wine
5 quarts cold water
2 teaspoons white peppercorns
4 fresh thyme sprigs
5 bay leaves

1. In a large heavy stockpot, heat the vegetable oil over high heat. Add the fish bones and all of the vegetables and lightly sauté but do not discolor. Add the wine and cold water and bring the stock to a boil. Remove any scum from the surface.

2. Add the peppercorns, thyme, and bay leaves and simmer very slowly over low heat for 25 minutes.

3. Strain the stock through cheesecloth or a very fine strainer. Return the stock to a boil and reduce to 2 quarts. The stock can be refrigerated for 4 days or frozen until needed. Makes 2 quarts.

CHEESE GLOSSARY

The world of cheese is a big one. There are many varieties in the refrigerator case of your local cheese seller. The following information will hopefully clear up some of the mysteries of cheese. Flavors of cheese depend on many elements: how long it was aged, its storage, and the diet staple of the producing animal. Cheeses are divided into fresh and ripened (aged): fresh cheeses are curds separated and drained from excess watery whey; ripened cheeses undergo an aging process to develop a distinctive, often strong flavor. The longer a cheese ages, the drier and more flavorful it becomes.

Categories of Cheese

FRESH CHEESE

These unripened cheeses are mostly used in desserts, sandwiches, and breakfast items.

Cottage cheese: A mild cheese consisting of large or small curds mixed with cream or milk.
Cream cheese: A mild cheese made from whole milk and cream. Great for fillings, hors d'oeuvres, and baking.

Dry-Curd cottage cheese: Like cottage cheese, but without the cream or milk. Used for baking.
Farmer cheese: Similar to cottage cheese, but with no curds. It is pressed into a block. Great for salads.
Mascarpone: A very smooth, rich, Italian-style cheese. Used in desserts, such as tiramisù.
Mozzarella: A stretch, curd-style cheese produced by immersing cow's or buffalo's milk curds in hot water, where they are kneaded and stretched to the desired shape. Good for baked dishes.
Provolone: A southern Italian-style cheese, mild and smoky flavored, aged 2-3 months. More tangy and sharper when aged 6-12 months for gourmet snacking. Often smoked. Great in sandwiches.
Ricotta: A whey-based cheese made from heating the whey drained from mozzarella and provolone production. Milk is added, mostly cow's stateside, but sheep's or goat's overseas. Great for desserts or pasta dishes.

SOFT-RIPENED CHEESE

Uncooked and molded, the curds of these cheeses are left to firm naturally and aged for a short period. With a soft texture and a firm, edible rind, which is often flavored with herbs, brine, or alcohol, they are great for spreading, or on bread and cheese plates, or sometimes baked in a crust, such as Brie in puff pastry.

Brie: A creamy, buttery soft cheese made from raw (Europe) or pasteurized milk (U.S.). Brie is best served when ripe.
Camembert: This cheese, similar to Brie, originated in France. It has a yellow interior and an edible rind, and when ripe, it oozes thickly. Perfect with crusty bread.
Limburger: A strong, pungent cow's milk cheese, which is washed in brine during ripening, contributing to the strong smell. A real "cheese board" cheese. Perfect with beer and dark breads.

SEMISOFT CHEESE

These cheeses are cooked and pressed in various shapes. They are great for cheese boards, sandwiches, or melting.

Havarti: Originally a Danish cheese, now U.S. produced, often infused with dill. Extremely mild, made from cow's milk. All-purpose use.

Monterey Jack: Originally from California, a mild, bland cow's milk cheese often infused with hot pepper (Pepper Jack). All-purpose use.

Muenster:
1. **American**: Orange rind, bland.
2. **European**: Red/orange rind, fuller flavored.

Port du Salut: A French (Brittany region), creamy, smooth, and savory-flavored cheese with an orange rind. Perfect with fruit.

SEMIFIRM/SEMIHARD CHEESE

These are popular uncooked cheeses, pressed in various forms and aged accordingly. They are often sold smoked.

Cheddar: A white to yellow, mild to sharp, salty cheese from cow's milk.

Edam: A red wax-covered Dutch import is a smooth and tangy cow's milk cheese. Perfect for a cheese board.

Emmenthaler: A nutty-flavored, Swiss-made cheese with large holes made from cow's milk. Often confused with Swiss cheese.

Fontina: A mild, fruity, Italian cow's milk cheese now produced in the U.S. as well. Great for melting and all-purpose use.

Gouda: A cheese similar to Edam, but milder. Often smoked and now made with goat's milk (easier to slice than other goat's milk cheeses).

Gruyère: A creamy, European cow's milk cheese with great nutty flavor. Good for fondues or au gratin.

Jarlsberg: A lighter cheese, but similar to Gruyère. All-purpose use.

Swiss: A mild, nutlike-flavored cow's milk cheese with smaller holes than Emmenthaler. All-purpose use.

FIRM/HARD CHEESE

These popular cheeses are cooked, pressed, and aged extensively for a firm texture.

Parmesan: A hard, dry cheese made from skimmed cow's milk and aged about 14 months. The sharp flavor makes it great for grating over pasta.

Parmesan-Reggiano: The Italian Parmesan version, aged a whopping 2 years. Some (Stravècchio) are aged 3-4 years, creating a complex flavor.

Pecorino-Romano: Another hard, dry cheese (in Italy made from sheep's milk) aged for various times to create a sharp-to- extra-sharp pungent flavor. Like Parmesan, great for pasta, risotto, or shaved over salads.

BLUE-VEINED CHEESE

These cheeses are infused with mold spores to develop a characteristic flavor and a fine streak of blue veins. Crumbled onto salads or mixed in dressings for dips, it is a delicious cheese type.

Danish Blue: A mild cow's milk cheese, smooth and creamy. Great with fruit.

Gorgonzola: A rich, savory, slightly pungent cow's milk cheese from Italy. Sold from mild to aged. Great with fruit salads and in sauces.

Maytag Blue: An American cow's milk, creamy-textured blue cheese.

Roquefort: One of the oldest cheeses in the world, dates back to Roman times. This blue cheese is exposed to a mold called *Penicillium roqueforti* and aged exclusively in limestone caverns in France. This rich, pungent, piquant cheese is great with salads or bread.

Stilton: Similar to Roquefort, this English cheese has a more cheddarlike flavor with a pale yellow interior with blue-green veins. This cheese stands by itself, plainly eaten with a glass of robust red wine or port.

GOAT/SHEEP CHEESE

Made from pure goat's or sheep's milk, or a blend with cow's milk, these cheeses have a very creamy, mild, earthy flavor when fresh, but become more tangy when aged. Molded in various shapes and often coated with herbs and nuts.

Bûcheron: A French goat's milk cheese that is tangy, mild, and spreadable and sold in log form.

Feta: Traditionally from Greece or Bulgaria, where it is made with sheep's milk, the cheese is cured and stored in a salty whey. Commercially produced, especially stateside, it is made with cow's milk, a milder version. Great for salads.

Montrachet: A mild, young goat's milk cheese with a soft, moist, creamy texture, mildly tangy. Sold in logs. Very popular. Great for salads and spreads.

DOUBLE/TRIPLE CREAM CHEESES

These cow's milk cheeses have extra cream added to them to extend the fat content, resulting in an extremely smooth, rich texture.

Boursin: A popular and easily available creamy cheese infused with garlic and herbs. All-purpose use.

Brillat-Savarin: A very buttery, rich, young French cheese.

L'Explorateur: A full-flavored, buttery, creamy, delicious Brielike cheese. Highly recommended, with crusty bread and a bottle of wine.

Cheese Tips

• Store cheese in the refrigerator, wrapped in wax paper first, then covered in aluminum foil.

• Store in a separate container to avoid flavor intrusion from other foods in the storage area.

FRUIT GLOSSARY

Apple Chart

NAME	COLOR/TEXTURE	USE
Cortland	Red, tart, firm	Applesauce, hand
Empire	Red or green, tart, sweet	Applesauce, hand
Fuji	Yellowish green, sweet, spicy	Hand
Gala	Gold with rosy overtone, sweet	Slow baking, hand
Golden Delicious	Yellow, sweet, juicy, mild	Frying, baking, pies, hand
Granny Smith	Green, sweet, tart, firm	Baking, hand
Honey Crisp	Red-green, juicy, crisp	All purpose
Ida Red	Red, hint of green, mildly tart	Baking, cooking
Jonagold	Red streaked yellow, firm, sweet	All purpose
McIntosh	Red, crisp, juicy	Applesauce
Northern Spy	Red blush, green, sweet, juicy	All purpose
Pippin	Pale green-yellow, creamy, tart	Pies
Red Delicious	Red, mushy	Applesauce, hand
Rhode Island Greening	Green, crisp, tart	All purpose
Rome Beauty	Red, sweet, tart	Baking, stuffed
Winesap	Dark red, sweet wine flavor	All purpose
York	Deep red-green strips	Applesauce, baking

Berry Chart

NAME	COLOR/TEXTURE	SEASON	USE
Blackberry	Black, sweet, tart	Spring–Fall	Pies, sauces, jams
Blueberry	Dark blue, sweet	Spring–Fall	Pies, sauces, jams
Boysenberry	Purple to red, blackberry hybrid, sweet, tart, large	Spring–Fall	Pies, sauces, jams
Cranberry	Red, tart, plump, firm	Fall	Pies, sauces, desserts, juice
Currant	Red or black, tart, sweet	Midsummer	Preserves, jams, dried
Gooseberry	Pale green, white striped, tart	Summer	Preserves, jams
Raspberry	Red, black, golden, fragrant, sweet	Summer–Fall	Preserves, jams, pies, sauces
Strawberry	Bright red, sweet	Spring–Early Summer	All purpose

Melon Chart

NAME	COLOR/TEXTURE	SEASON	USE
Cantaloupe	Beige-green, moist, wet	Midsummer	Salads, cold soups, hand
Casaba	Golden yellow, creamy, sweet	Fall	Salads, hand
Christmas	Dark green, creamy, white flesh	December	Salads, hand
Crenshaw	Bright yellow-green spots, fragrant	Early Fall	Salads, hand
Honeydew	Pale green, sweet, juicy	Summer-Fall	Salads, cold soups, hand
Persian	Brown netting over dark green, sweet	Late Summer	Salads, hand
Watermelon	Dark green, sweet, seed or seedless, red, orange, or yellow flesh	Summer	Salads, juices, pickling, hand

Pear Chart

NAME	COLOR/TEXTURE	SEASON	USE
Anjou	Green, egg shape, juicy	Oct.–May	Salads, desserts, baked
Asian/Chinese/ Japanese/Apple	Pale yellow, flowery fragrance	Aug.–Sept.	Salads, hand
Bartlett	Light green-yellow, aromatic	Aug.–Nov.	All purpose
Bosc	Green, long, tapered neck, sweet	Sept.–May	Baking, poached, hand
Comice	greenish yellow, blush of red, sweet, buttery, hint of spice	Oct.–Jan.	Hand
Red Bartlett	Red, sturdy, aromatic	Aug.–Nov.	All purpose, cooking
Secke	Dark green, reddish, smaller pear	Aug.–Jan.	Preserves
Winter Nellis	Brown-green, short pear, spicy	Nov.–May	Baking, poached, hand

VEGETABLE GLOSSARY

Bean Chart

NAME	COLOR/TEXTURE	AVAILABLE	USE
Appaloosa	Light beige with dark spots	Dried	All purpose
Black	Black, small	Dried	Soups, salsa, dips
Cannellini	Ivory white, oval	Dried	Soups, stews
Chickpeas/ Garbanzos	Beige, round, nutty	Dried	Hummus, soups, stews
Cranberry	Mottled red, oval, mild	Dried, fresh	All purpose
Fava/Broad	Light brown, pale green, oval, slightly bitter, grainy	Dried, fresh	Stews, side dishes
Flageolet	White or pale green, small, flavorful	Dried, fresh	Lamb dishes
Green/String	Green, long, crisp	Fresh	Side dishes, salads
Great Northern	White, oval, small	Dried	Soups, salads, baked beans
Haricot/French	Green, slender, small delicate	Fresh	Side dishes
Kidney	Dark red, pinkish, or white, kidney shaped	Dried	Stews, salads
Lentil	Green, brown, yellow, or red, flat, small	Dried	Soups, salads
Lima/Butter	White, pale green, wide, flat	Dried, fresh	Soups, side dishes

Navy	White, small, mild	Dried	Soups
Pink	Pale red, kidney shaped, smooth, sweet, meaty	Dried	Soups, side dishes
Pinto	Pale brown, oval, earthy	Dried	Soups, side dishes
Romano/Italian	Green, long, broad, robust	Fresh	Side dishes
Soy	Ivory, green, brown, black, mild	Dried	Soy milk, soy sauce, tofu
Split Pea	Pale green, yellow, meaty	Dried	Soups
Wax	Yellow, long, crisp (string)	Fresh	Side dishes, salads

Greens Chart

NAME	COLOR/TEXTURE	USE
Arugula	Dark green, notched leaves, nutty, peppery	Salads
Beet Greens	Red, green, smooth, thin, earthy	Salads, sauté
Bibb Lettuce	Pale green, loose leaves, tender	Salads
Boston Lettuce	Light green, loose leaves, tender	Salads
Broccoli Rabe	Dark green, yellow flowers, rippled, pungent	Sauté
Collard Greens	Dark green, large thick leaves, mild	Braised, boiled
Green/Red Leaf Lettuce	Ruffled leaves, delicate, mild	Salads, garnish
Iceberg Lettuce	Pale yellow, green, sturdy, crisp, bland	Salads, garnish, sandwiches
Kale	Dark green, crinkled leaves, earthy	Sauté, garnish
Mâche (field greens)	Green, oval leaves, delicate, mild	Salads
Mesclun	Variety of young tender greens	Salads
Mustard Greens	Light green, yellow, sharp-edged leaves, pungent	Sauté
Romaine	Green, crisp, sturdy, sweet	Salads
Sorrel	Pale green, triangular leaves, delicate, sour	Salads, soups
Spinach	Many varieties, crinkled leaves, flat or baby	All purpose
Swiss Chard	Red, green, crinkled leaves, earthy	Sauté
Turnip Greens	Green, leafy, pungent, spicy	Sauté
Watercress	Dark green, small round leaves, peppery	Salads, soups

Bitter Greens Chart

NAME	COLOR/TEXTURE	USE
Belgian Endive	White, torpedo shaped, crisp, bitter	Salads, braised
Chicory	Green, curled spiky leaves, crisp, bitter	Salads, sauté
Escarole	Green, broad leaves, crisp, bitter	Salads, sauté
Frisée	Light green, curly, tender, delicate, mild, bitter	Salads
Radicchio	Red, white streaks, delicate, mild, bitter	Salads, sauté, garnish

COOKING EQUIPMENT GLOSSARY

As a mechanic needs proper and updated tools to perform his or her job with ease and precision, today's chefs, cooks, and home cooks rely on the proper tools to achieve culinary excellence. In this section, we would like to help you sort out and understand your cooking equipment needs, which sometimes seems confusing with all of the choices offered today through cooking catalogs, stores, and even TV. As a chef, I believe that quality supersedes quantity. Often I find students in my cooking classes carrying around inexpensive knives that quickly turn dull and need replacement after a few months.

Invest in a good knife, quality cookware, and a good heavy butcher block or wooden chopping board. Look in your local or regional Yellow Pages and seek out restaurant supply companies open to the public. For the same or even less money, you can purchase professional equipment that is made to take abuse and last for many years. This is the best tip that you will receive from a chef. The glossary defines materials and sizes and gives the answers to those questions that you have always wanted to ask. Happy cooking!

Bakeware Materials

Aluminum: Being a great conductor of heat, baked goods brown evenly. Once removed from the oven, it cools quickly, which avoids burning the bottom of baked goods. Good for cookies.

Cast iron: Cast iron absorbs and releases heat relatively slower than other metals, resulting in delicate baked goods with fine thin crusts and moist interiors. Perfect for muffins and corn bread.

Ceramic/Glass: Radiant heat is conducted well, encouraging browning. Foods cook faster using these materials, which might require temperature adjustments in recipes. Perfect for pies and casseroles.

Nonstick:
  The good: Often foolproof, easy release of baked goods. Easy cleanup, less grease.
  The bad: Lightweight material, not sturdy, easy to scratch, requires use of wooden or rubber materials.

Steel: Strong and easy to clean, used by professionals. Excellent absorbers and distributors of heat. Find them in restaurant supply stores.

Baking Pans

Baking dish: All-purpose 9" x 13" x 2" rectangular dish. Used for au gratins, lasagnas, or brownies.

Baking sheet: Rectangular metal or nonstick 12" x 17" sheet pan with slightly sloping rims. Used for rolls, croutons, croissants, small cuts of meat, or reheating food. All-purpose use.

Cake/Springform pan: Cake pans are usually 1 $\frac{1}{2}$"-2" deep, 9" in diameter. A good-quality metal pan is recommended. Cake pans also come as springform pans, with removable clamp-secured sides, making it easy to remove the cake. Perfect for cheesecakes.

Cookie sheet: A low, rimmed, flat metal sheet designed to slide cookies onto a cooling rack. Also available in nonstick.

Loaf pan: A metal or glass 5" x 9" x 3" pan used for loaf cakes, quick breads, or meat loaf. Also available in smaller sizes or nonstick.

Muffin pan: Available in metal, aluminum, or nonstick and in various sizes from mini to jumbo. If available, cast-iron pans with a nonstick surface are preferred.

Pie pan: A conventional size in glass or metal is 9"-10" in diameter. Look for a wide rim to hold the fluted edge of the crust.

Tart pan: A shallow, fluted pan, sometimes with a removable bottom, with a 10" diameter.

Tube/Bundt pan: A baking favorite with a central tube, which allows the center of the cake to rise and bake evenly. Also for decorative uses. A 10" tube pan is a common size.

Basic Baking Tools

Baker's peel: A wooden board or tool to slide bread loaves or pizza in and out of the oven or onto a baking stone.

Breadboard: Wooden board used for kneading bread.

Cookie/Biscuit cutter: Made from plastic or preferably metal in different sizes and shapes. If unavailable, use a water glass or shot glass to cut out dough.

Cooling rack: A square, round, or rectangular wire rack with feet, to circulate air on all sides of baked goods. Available in chrome-plated metal, stainless steel, or nonstick aluminum.

Dough scraper: Used to lift and scrape dough as you work it.

Pastry bag: Made from different materials, these 8"–12" conical bags are designed to decorate cakes and pastry or to pipe out mousses or batters.

Pastry blender: A row of U-shaped wires attached to a wooden or plastic handle transforms fat and flour to a consistency suitable for dough. A very useful baking tool.

Pastry brush: Used to brush egg washes, melted butter, or glazes onto baked goods. The natural or nylon bristles are usually 1"–2" wide.

Measuring spoons and cups: A must for every baker or cook.

Rolling pin: Available in different sizes and materials. Wood is preferred for pie crusts and dough, while marble is perfect for fine pastry since it stays cool and does not soften the butter in the pastry dough.

Rubber spatula: A must kitchen tool for scraping down the sides of bowls or folding in egg whites. Available in different sizes.

Scale: A good scale is important in baking. It should have $1/4$-ounce increments.

Sifter: A metal or plastic canister, fitted with mesh screens and a handle, which rotates when turned. Used to sift and aerate dry ingredients, such as flour, cocoa, or confectioners' sugar.

Whisk:

Balloon whisk: More round and thinner to incorporate air.

Flat whisk: Whisking sauces and gravies and removing lumps.

Sauce whisk: Whisking ingredients without air. Stiff wires.

Basic Cooking Tools

Brushes:

Soft bristle: For brushing foods with butter, glazes, and marinades.

Medium bristle: Cleaning and brushing dirt off vegetables.

Can opener: No electric please. A high-quality manual can opener will do the job.

Cheesecloth: A lightweight, natural cotton cloth, available in coarse or fine weaves, primarily used for straining and filtering stocks or sauces. It is most commonly used for a bouquet garni, where a bundle of herbs is tied in cheesecloth and added to a cooking liquid to infuse the flavor.

Colander: A metal or plastic bowl-like container perforated with small holes to drain foods when washed or cooked.

Cutting board: Should have a solid, heavy, wooden cutting board at least 12" x 18". While using, place a damp cloth under the board to avoid slipping. Clean daily with a mild solution of bleach and water, especially when cutting chicken.

Grater: A metal or plastic washboardlike device containing various sized sharp holes to grate, rasp, or shred foods for preparation. Perfect for rinds or shredding potatoes for rösti.

Knives: The best are carbon-stainless steel knives, preferably from a German or Swiss manufacturer. Chef specialty stores, mail order, or restaurant supply stores open to the public are your best bet. The most important types to have in your kitchen are the following:

Boning knife: A very narrow, curved-edged blade, 6"–8" long, for cutting easily around the bones of raw meats and fish.

Bread knife: A straight, serrated blade, 8"–12" long, for cutting through crusty breads or firm vegetables.

Carving knife: A long, thin, sharp, even blade for slicing or shaving roasted meats or smoked fish.

Chef's knife: A wide, tapered blade, 8"–12" long, for chopping, slicing, dicing, and mincing.

Paring knife: A small, tapered blade, 3"–4" long, for paring, carving, and peeling fruits and vegetables.

Ladle: Stainless steel or heat-resistant, small plastic bowl with a long handle to scoop up liquids or stews. Also perfect for skimming stocks and saucing foods.

Measuring spoons and cups: Have both sets — a must for every cook.

Meat mallet: Also called a pounder or meat tenderizer. Used for flattening and tenderizing boneless meats, ideal for schnitzels. The flat side of the hammer is for smoothing or flattening. The rough side with blunt teeth is for breaking the fibers in the meat to tenderize.

Potato masher: A perforated or bent-wire grid, attached to a sturdy handle. Perfect for making mashed potatoes when pressed down repeatedly into the cooked potatoes.

Slotted spoon: A large metal spoon with oval holes, designed to remove solid foods from liquids.

String: Also called butcher twine, it is a soft pliable linen string used for tying roasts or trussing poultry.

Thermometer: A good instant-read thermometer is mandatory. Look for the ones with the thin probe, which is very accurate and leaves only a small hole in the meat when penetrated. Avoid digital thermometers, they break down easily.

Tongs: These clawlike tools are perfect for grasping hot foods without piercing them and are usually 10"–12" long. Also great as a serving tool on buffets or for salads.

Zester: A small, short-handled metal blade with 4–6 sharp-edged holes, designed to remove strips of fruit peel.

Blender

As part of the complete kitchen, a good, solid, quality blender is a great tool for pureeing sauces, soups, and even making pesto.

Standing blender: Electric motors encased in plastic or metal spin the propeller-type blade in the wide-mouth canister holding 5-8 cups.

Immersion blender: These handheld blenders are also an inexpensive tool to puree sauces and soups or for foaming liquids. With its extended blade, it can fit into any pot. Compared to a standing blender, it incorporates more air, making it better for frothy or foamy concoctions.

Mixer

A good mixer from a reputable company, such as Kitchen Aid, (preferably a standing mixer) comes with many attachments:

Dough hook: For kneading bread.

Meat grinder: For grinding meat for ground meat or sausage.

Paddle: For mixing batters and creaming butter and sugar.

Wire whisk: For whipping cream and beating egg whites.

Pots & Pans

Broiler pan: A standard size 9" x 12" rectangular tray, sized to fit under the oven's broiler, including a slotted tray to direct drippings to the bottom of the pan.

Casserole: A deep baking dish with a tight-fitting lid.

Dutch oven: A large round or oval pot or kettle. Usually made of enameled cast iron with a tight-fitting lid. Ideal for braising or stewing.

Roasting pan with rack: A heavy, large rectangular pan with handles, often fitted with a slightly raised rack to elevate the meat while roasting to prevent cooking in the drippings and to improve heat circulation.

Saucepan: A round, long-handled pan, with straight or sloping sides, available in 1-pint-5-quart sizes and made from various materials. Stainless steel is highly recommended by most chefs. Being versatile, it is perfect for sauces, boiling, soups, and even braising.

Sauté pan: This straight-sided frying pan has a high, angled handle and high, curved sides, making it perfect for flipping food over high heat. Sizes range from 6"–14 $^1/_4$". It is great for browning or searing food quickly. Recommended materials are stainless steel or aluminum.

Skillet: Also known as a frying pan and often confused with a sauté pan. A skillet has gently sloping sides, perfect for foods that have to be stirred or turned out of the pan. Sizes range from 9"-14". Recommended materials are cast iron, aluminum, or non-stick.

Stockpot: A high, narrow, two-handled heavy pot, ranging from 8-12 quarts. Perfect for making stocks or multipurpose boiling of vegetables and pasta.

Strainer: Designed to separate foods, drain, or puree. Comes in various types:

    Chinois: To clarify stocks or puree foods.

    Colander: A large bowl-like container perforated with small holes to drain foods when washed or cooked.

    Course-wire mesh strainers: To blanch foods.

    Fine-wire mesh strainers: To strain delicate consommés and sauces, removing unwanted particles.

Grills

TYPE	FUEL	BENEFIT	DOWNFALL
Charcoal Grill	Charcoal	Flavor	Difficult to control
Gas Grill	Propane, gas	Clean, adjustable	Poor flavor
Electric Grill	Electric	Indoor use	No flavor, poor heat
Hibachi Grill	Charcoal, electric	Portable	Small servings per grilling
Range-Top Grill (grill-like grate to place atop indoor stove)	Electric, gas	Simple application	Requires power exhaust if used indoors

Grilling Lingo

Direct heat: Quickly grilling thin cuts of meat over medium-to- high coals or gas flames.

Indirect heat: Slowly grilling or flavoring large cuts of meat over a low flame or away from smoldering charcoal — a technique used especially in southern-style BBQ (slowly grilled and smoked). Adding wood chips to the coals will intensify the flavor by creating smoke. Use fruitwoods, such as apple or cherry wood.

Common Measurements & Equivalents

1 teaspoon	=	60 drops or $1/6$ fluid ounce
3 teaspoons	=	1 tablespoon or $1/2$ fluid ounce
$1/2$ tablespoon	=	$1 1/2$ teaspoons
1 tablespoon	=	3 teaspoons or $1/2$ fluid ounce
2 tablespoons	=	$1/8$ cup or 1 fluid ounce
3 tablespoons	=	$1 1/2$ fluid ounces or 1 jigger
4 tablespoons	=	$1/4$ cup or 2 fluid ounces
8 tablespoons	=	$1/2$ cup or 4 fluid ounces
16 tablespoons	=	1 cup, 8 fluid ounces, or $1/2$ pint
$1/8$ cup	=	2 tablespoons or 1 fluid ounce
$1/4$ cup	=	4 tablespoons or 2 fluid ounces
$1/3$ cup	=	5 tablespoons plus 1 teaspoon or $2 2/3$ fluid ounces
$3/8$ cup	=	$1/4$ cup plus 2 tablespoons or 3 fluid ounces
$1/2$ cup	=	8 tablespoons or 4 fluid ounces
$2/3$ cup	=	10 tablespoons plus 2 teaspoons or $5 1/3$ fluid ounces
$5/8$ cup	=	$1/2$ cup plus 2 tablespoons or 5 fluid ounces
$3/4$ cup	=	12 tablespoons or 6 fluid ounces
$7/8$ cup	=	$3/4$ cup plus 2 tablespoons or 7 fluid ounces
1 cup	=	16 tablespoons, $1/2$ pint, or 8 fluid ounces
2 cups	=	1 pint or 16 fluid ounces
1 pint	=	2 cups or 16 fluid ounces
1 quart	=	4 cups, 2 pints, or 32 fluid ounces
1 gallon	=	16 cups, 8 pints, 4 quarts, or 128 fluid ounces

FOOD SOURCES – WHERE TO FIND IT

The enthusiasm to take on a favorite recipe can be dampened when recipes feature hard-to-find ingredients. Luckily, thanks to the food network and America's rediscovery of regional food, artisan farm markets, web sites, and gourmet stores are offering hard-to-find products. We hope the following sources that we have used ourselves are helpful in your culinary endeavor.

We have listed Adirondack, as well as national purveyors. For very specific and more Adirondack-related food sources and purveyors, check *The Adirondack Book* by Elizabeth Folwell, published by Berkshire House Publishers, Inc.

Barbecue

Tail O' The Pup
Route 86 Ray Brook, NY 12977
518-891-5092

Cookware

Bridge Kitchenware
214 E. 52nd St.
New York, NY 10022
212-688-4220; 800-274-3435
www.bridgekitchenware.com

Chef's Catalog
3215 Commercial Ave.
Northbrook, IL 60062
972-401-6300; 800-825-8255
www.chefscatalog.com

Farmers' Markets

Adirondack Farmers' Market Cooperative
P.O. Box 136
Chazy, NY 12921
518-298-3755
(organizes farmers' markets throughout the region)

Cornell Cooperative Extension
67 Sisco St.
Westport, NY 12993
518-962-6810
(promoter/organization of marketing food products from Champlain Valley and Adirondack producers)

Green Market
Union Square
E. 117th St. & Broadway
New York, NY 10027
Year-round: Mon., Wed., Fri., Sat.
Contact: Joel Patraker
212-477-3220

Lake Placid-Essex County Visitors Bureau
Bridge Rd.
Crown Point, NY 12928
518-597-4646
(listings of farm stands throughout the region)

Foie Gras

D'Artagnan
280 Wilson Ave.
Newark, NJ 07105
973-344-0565; 800-DARTAGN

Hudson Valley Foie Gras
80 Brooks Rd.
Ferndale, NY 12374
914-292-2500; 877-BUY-FOIE
www.foiegras.net

Sonoma Foie Gras
P.O. Box 2007
Sonoma, CA 95476
707-928-1224; 800-427-4559
www.sonomafoiegras.com

Game/Rare (hard-to-find) Meats

Polarica
105 Quint St.
San Francisco, CA 94124
415-647-1300; 800-426-3872
www.polarica.com

General Food Web Sites

www.adirondackcuisine.com
www.digitalchef.com
www.epicurious.com
www.foodtv.com
www.gourmetspot.com
www.starchefs.com

Ham

Calhoun's Ham House
211 South East St.
Culpepper, VA 22701
540-825-8319; 877-825-8319
www.calhounhams.com

Oscar's Adirondack Mountain Smokehouse
22 Raymond Ln.
Warrensburg, NY 12885
800-627-3431
(catalog upon request)

Honey

By LuLu Gourmet Products
888-693-5800
E-mail: customerservice@restaurantlulu.com
(white truffle honey)

Maple Syrup

Alstead Farms
Alstead Hill Rd.
Keene, NY 12942
518-576-4793

Frog Alley Farm
Rte. 73
Keene Valley, NY 12943
518-576-9835

Leadley's Adirondack Sugar Bush
Rte. 30
Speculator, NY 12164
518-548-7093

Toad Hill Maple Products
766 Zaltz Rd.
Athol, NY 12810
518-623-2272

Mushrooms

Fresh & Wild
P.O. Box 2981
Vancouver, WA 98668
360-737-3652; 800-222-5578

Mr. Mushroom
www.mushroom.com
(on-line catalog of specialty mushrooms)

New York State Wines

web sites:
www.corningsteuben.com
www.fingerlakes.net
www.hudsonriver.com

Northeastern Local Cheese

web sites:
www.cowgirlcreamery.com
www.thefoodstores.com

Grafton Village Cheese Co.
Four Star Vermont Cheddar Cheese
802-843-2221
E-mail: cheese@sover.net

Old Chatham Sheepherding Co.
155 Shaker Museum Rd.
Old Chatham, NY 12136
www.blacksheepcheese.com
(producer of Hudson Valley Camembert)

Olive Oil

Mas Portell
www.casaponsusa.com
(extra-virgin olive oil with natural flavors)

Smoked Fish/Caviar

Petrossian
182 W. 58th St.
New York, NY 10019
212-245-0303; 800-337-0007
www.petrossian.com

Seafood.com
430 Market Rd.
Lexington, MA 02421
781-861-1760
www.seafood.com

Smoked Meats/Fish/Cheese

Nodines Smoke House
Torrington, CT 06790
800-222-2059

Oscar's Adirondack Mountain Smokehouse
22 Raymond Ln.
Warrensburg, NY 12885
800-627-3431

Specialty Groceries

Balducci's
424 Sixth Ave.
New York, NY 10011
212-260-0400
800-225-3822; 800-221-7714
www.balduccis.com

Dean & Deluca
360 Broadway
New York, NY 10012
212-431-1691; 800-221-7714
www.deandeluca.com

Gourmet Market
800-913-9247
www.gourmetmarket.com
(on-line source for hard-to-find groceries)

King Arthur Flour Bakers Catalogue
P.O. Box 876
Norwich, VT 05055
800-827-6836

Specialty Wild Foods
800-333-0193
(pine-scented jelly)

Sutton Gourmet Market Place/Hay Day
www.suttongourmet.com

Zingerman's
422 Detroit St.
Ann Arbor, MI 48104
734-769-1625; 888-636-8162
www.zingermans.com

Specialty Produce

The Chef's Garden
9009 Huron Avery Rd.
Huron, OH 44839
419-433-4947; 800-289-4644

Freida's Rare & Exotic Foods
P.O. Box 58488
Los Angeles, CA 90058
714-826-6100; 800-241-1721
www.freidas.com

Indian Rock Produce
P.O. Box 317
530 California Rd.
Quakertown, PA 18951
215-536-9600; 800-882-0512

Spices

Penzey's Spices
W 19362 Apollo Dr.
Muskego, WI 53150
414-679-7207

Truffles/Truffle Products

Gourmand
2869 Towerview Rd.
Herndon, VA 20271
703-708-0000; 800-627-7272
www.gourmand.com

Urbani
29-24 40th St.
Long Island City, NY 11101
800-281-2330

OTHER ADIRONDACK RESOURCES & ORGANIZATIONS

Adirondack Books

North Country Books
315-735-4877
(Adirondack titles)

Culinary School

Paul Smith College
Paul Smiths, NY 12970
518-327-6227
www.paulsmiths.edu

Furnishings

The Ray Brook Frog
Route 86
Ray Brook, NY 12977
518-891-333

General Information

www.adirondack.com
(recreational, lodging, business, related links)

www.adirondack.net
(recreational listings)

www.adirondacks.com
(extensive site covering every aspect of Adirondack Park)

www.adirondacks.org
(Adirondack Regional Tourism Council)

Hunting/Fishing

Dept. of Environmental Conservation
50 Wolf Rd.
Albany, NY 12223
www.dec.state.ny.us/huntfish.com

Lodging

Adirondack Bed & Breakfast Association
www.adirondackbb.com

Adirondack by Owner
www.adirondackbyowner.com [See general info]
(vacation rentals/real estate)

Adirondack Inns
www.adirondackinns.com

Museums

Adirondack History Center
Court St., Rte. 9
Elizabethtown, NY 12932
518-873-6466

Adirondack Museum
Blue Mountain Lake, NY 12812
518-352-7311
www.adkmuseum.org

1812 Homestead
Rte. 22
Willsboro, NY 12996
518-963-4071

Travel

Adirondack Regional Information
518-846-8016; 800-487-6867
www.adk.com

Saratoga Regional Information
518-434-1217; 800-732-8259
www.capital-saratoga.com

INDEX

ABOUT THE AUTHORS

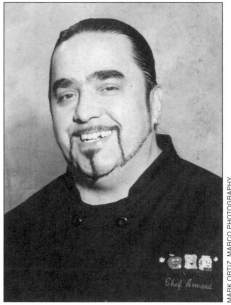

ARMAND C. VANDERSTIGCHEL, trained as a classic cooking school apprentice in Europe, has worked various chef positions for conglomerates, such as Hilton, Radisson International, Marriott, and Novotel. On a smaller scale, he wore the toque in various country clubs and landmark hotels. After being Corporate Chef for the Lessings Corporation on Long Island, Armand rejoined old restaurant friends as Executive Chef of the prestigious Miller Place Inn on Long Island, New York.

Besides being the author of *Chicken Wings Across America,* co-author of *The Adirondack Cookbook* and *Adirondack Cuisine,* and culinary editor for *Dish D'Jour* magazine, Armand teaches classes in international cuisine in adult education courses on Long Island. As co-host of "The Radio Gourmet" on WGBB 1240am and the "Long Island Gourmet TV Show," he emphasizes the importance of using fresh foods in cooking, be it for taste or for health. He is a great promoter and fan of regional cuisine in America and can be seen at bookstores, festivals, libraries, and on national TV shows, performing live cooking demonstrations with his mobile kitchen.

He is active in the community as a Career Day chef at schools, fund-raising activist, and a promoter for organizations such as the American Heart Association, the American Kidney Foundation. Using his ethnic, European background to enhance the New Regional American Cuisine, he creates his signature dishes by merging both cultures.

As a full-time resident of Long Island and a part-time resident of the Adirondacks, he has received recognition on Long Island as "Chef of the Year" by the Suffolk Community College's Chef Hall of Fame Committee, and he is a returning favorite on various TV networks in the Albany, New York, area. His hobbies include advanced photography, fishing, and hiking.

ROBERT E. BIRKEL, JR., a former Navy aerial photographer in Vietnam, has been active in the food industry as manager, purchaser, and consultant for Howard Johnson Airport Hotels, Ground Round, and Canterbury Ales Restaurants.

He is involved in such community organizations as the American Legion, the Lion's Club, and the Masonic Lodge, and is a former member of the Big Brother/Big Sister Organization, known throughout the United States.

Robert is now a New York State peace officer and dabbles part-time in various forms of photography. He is also co-host with Chef Armand of "The Radio Gourmet" on WGBB 1240am and the "Long Island Gourmet TV Show." He is a big fan of the Adirondacks and Saratoga Springs, New York.

For more information on the authors, see their web site: www.adirondackcuisine.com.